I0012801

Hands-On Salesforce Einstein Studio and GPT Intelligence

Transform your CRM with AI for enhanced productivity with value-driven implementation

Joseph Kubon

Luke Pond

Andy Forbes

Melissa Shepard

Philip Safir

Hands-On Salesforce Einstein Studio and GPT Intelligence

Group Product Manager: Aaron Tanna
Publishing Product Manager: Kushal Dave
Book Project Manager: Prajakta Naik
Senior Editor: Nisha Cleetus
Technical Editor: Vidhisha Patidar
Copy Editor: Safis Editing
Proofreader: Nisha Cleetus
Indexer: Subalakshmi Govindhan
Production Designer: Gokul Raj S.T

First published: September 2024

Production reference: 1300824

Published by Packt Publishing Ltd.
Grosvenor House
11 St Paul's Square
Birmingham
B3 1RB, UK

ISBN 978-1-83620-377-3

www.packtpub.com

From the immortal words of Bruce Springsteen, "You'll need a good companion now, for this part of the ride." To the three people who are my whole world... Lisa, Paige Ellen, and Alex, you inspire me to face the world with passion and wake up each day loved and spoiled. Remember "Faith will be rewarded." All my love, all my life.

#LivingProof

– Joseph Kubon

To Elizabeth and Naomi, with my gratitude for all the inspiration and joy you bring me every day.

– Luke Pond

À John McCarthy, Marvin Minsky, Nathaniel Rochester et Claude Shannon—votre vision et votre initiative lors du Dartmouth Summer Research Project en 1956 ont préparé le terrain pour le domaine de l'intelligence artificielle. Vous avez fait œuvre de pionniers et avez inspiré d'innombrables innovations, notamment les technologies qui propulsent aujourd'hui Salesforce Einstein Copilot. Je vous suis reconnaissant pour le chemin que vous avez tracé, ouvrant la voie à un avenir où l'IA continue de transformer notre façon de connecter, de créer et de réussir.

– Andy Forbes

I would like to dedicate this book to everyone who has inspired and supported me on my Trailblazer Journey, from Admin to CTA to MVP, especially the late Gemma Blezard, who was a mentor, a friend, and so much more along the way.

– Melissa Shepard

We would like to thank the team at Packt for their sponsorship, guidance, and expertise throughout the creation of this book.

Thank you to our technical reviewers whose expertise and feedback helped us iterate towards a quality final product.

To the team of Creators and Product Owners at Salesforce, thank you for developing an innovative platform that empowers businesses and for embracing the promise and potential of generative AI.

To our readers, we thank you for sharing a common interest in this topic and hope that this book serves you well in your Salesforce journey.

- Joseph, Luke, Andy, Melissa, and Philip

Foreword

Hello! My name is Christopher Long, and I've been working in the web technology space for the last 25 years. I started learning to code when I was ten years old. Today, learning to code at ten might be considered a late start, but in the Eighties, it made me feel like a trailblazer. My grandfather, a code breaker for the U.S. government and a true technophile, taught me how to play Zork on his cassette-based Commodore 64 and how to connect to the internet to check the local bank's message board for the day's weather forecast. From that moment, I never looked back. Currently, I work at Salesforce in Partner Alliances, where it's my great joy to enable our Salesforce Partners to maximize their use of our products.

Salesforce has been incorporating AI into its platform for many years, and now, with the arrival of Einstein Copilot, we're poised to take things to the next level. With this book, Joseph and Andy have created an invaluable resource, guiding readers through the diverse features of Einstein Copilot and illustrating how it can transform opportunities within Sales Cloud, Service Cloud, and Marketing Cloud. Drawing on their extensive experience, they offer practical insights that make this book a crucial asset for anyone looking to maximize the value of their Salesforce investment. I'm fortunate to have met and spent time with both of them.

In March 2024, at TrailblazerDX in San Francisco, I was sitting with my coworker Arvind in the back of the main hall, watching as brave souls stepped up to the microphone one after another to share their thoughts with Salesforce leadership. It's a memory that will always stick with me. "Salesforce True to the Core" is a forum where Salesforce executives and product managers engage directly with the user community in an open Q&A format. After four or five questions, someone wearing very stylish glasses walked up to the mic. It was Joseph, and that day he was a true champion for Salesforce Partners. He politely pointed out that while Einstein had arrived, Salesforce Partners were struggling to get hands-on experience with it. Needless to say, Einstein was soon in the hands of Salesforce Partners.

Andy and I met at the Salesforce office in Atlanta, Georgia, during an "AI+Data+CRM" camp for Salesforce Partners. He introduced himself in the lobby, and I could immediately tell by his long ponytail and even longer trench coat that he was no novice to consulting. Throughout the two-day camp, Andy quickly proved himself to be a legitimate expert. The goal of the camp was to build a solution using Data Cloud and Einstein Copilot, and Andy was way ahead of the curve. Yes, everyone was working from the same workbooks that I had provided, but Andy was fully engaged and actively contributing to the conversation. He offered intelligent, cohesive thoughts grounded in experience and was excited to be there, building with new tools. In addition to his technical prowess, it became evident that he has an eye for detail. Remember the workbooks I mentioned? Andy was the only person who really took note of how they were written. He made several comments about them to the group. It's not every day you meet someone with a true appreciation for instructional, technical documentation.

What a combo! A true and valued Salesforce community advocate, and one of the most detail-oriented, seasoned Salesforce consultants in the game. I can't think of a better duo to introduce you to the current state of the Salesforce platform, starring Einstein Copilot.

The strength of this book lies not only in its coverage of Einstein Copilot's features but also in the clarity and precision with which these concepts are explained. Each chapter is written to ensure that you can easily grasp the complexities of AI-driven automation, from setting up and customizing the Copilot to leveraging it for specific business needs. Joseph and Andy's expertise shines through as they methodically explore how Einstein Copilot can be applied across different domains, providing actionable strategies to enhance productivity, streamline workflows, and drive better customer outcomes. The inclusion of real-world examples and detailed walkthroughs further enhances the practical utility of this guide, making it a must-read for professionals at all levels.

As you dive into the pages of this book, you'll not only gain a thorough understanding of how Salesforce Einstein Copilot works but also find a roadmap for applying these advanced tools to the unique challenges and opportunities your business faces. Joseph and Andy have done an excellent job breaking down complex technologies into accessible, actionable knowledge. Whether you're a seasoned Salesforce user or new to the platform, this book will equip you with the insights needed to leverage AI in the flow of work for truly transformative results.

Christopher Long

Director, AI+Data+CRM Partner Enablement Success

Contributors

About the authors

Joseph Kubon, Salesforce MVP is an experienced Technical Architect for global enterprise-level Salesforce implementations, with 40+ Salesforce certifications, and an inventor (holding several patents), he navigates the realms of TTH and manufacturing industries with a results-driven approach. Skilled in Business Processes and Architecture Values, he carries a toolkit replete with Salesforce configuration and customization expertise for groundbreaking development. Joseph's deep methodical skills shine as he navigates data and analytics, business intelligence, and design best practices. Guided by the wisdom that 'just because it can be built doesn't mean it should be', Joseph embraces the multiplicity of solutions to tomorrow's challenges measuring success with his "Time to Value" principles driving his customers to realize Strategic ROI with innovative solutions.

Luke Pond is a Senior Technical Director with thirty years of experience in software development and consulting. In the realm of Salesforce Commerce and Marketing, he holds 14 certifications and enjoys playing the role of technical lead on complex cross-cloud projects, where he translates business and integration requirements into detailed development specifications. With a long-term background in designing both transactional and analytical databases and a strong interest in Data Science, he has a keen understanding of how to use the capabilities of Salesforce Data Cloud and Model Builder to generate business insights and value in a world of data surplus.

Andy Forbes has an extensive career in technology, spanning over four decades, and is now channeling his IT experience towards investigating the impact of artificial intelligence, especially Generative AI, on Salesforce project delivery. His expertise in CRM and project management is complemented by his ITIL and Salesforce certifications. Having spent a decade at a Global Systems Integrator and driven by his entrepreneurial mindset, Andy has successfully led numerous Salesforce projects for Fortune 500 clients. His commitment to innovation and excellence is evident in his approach to enhancing IT service delivery and usage with the help of AI.

Melissa Shepard, Salesforce CTA is a distinguished Salesforce Certified Technical Architect (CTA) and Advisory Consulting Partner with over 20 years of experience in Information Technology and Software Development, focusing on Salesforce CRM for the past 18 years. She has a rich background in System Architecture, System Analysis, and Application Development, working with companies ranging from startups to global corporations across various commercial industries and professional services. An advocate for the Salesforce community, Melissa is also a MuleSoft Ambassador, Well-Architected Ambassador, and a prominent figure in several mentorship and nonprofit initiatives. As the Founder of ScaleUp Archs and Architect Ohana Slack, she is committed to empowering and upskilling Salesforce architects, guiding them towards achieving their CTA certification.

Philip Safir is a visionary digital strategist and technology executive renowned for driving profitable growth and enterprise transformation through technology and operational excellence. He leads at the forefront of applied Generative AI in customer experience and business operations, including in his role as Vice President of Strategy and Operations with a renowned Salesforce consulting partner. Philip's career spans Fortune 500, start-up, and international companies across various industries, including a commitment to community non-profits.

About the technical reviewer

Nadina D. Lisbon, M.S., Salesforce CTA is a dedicated CRM Enterprise Architect with over 10 years of experience in the Salesforce ecosystem. She is also a Salesforce Certified Technical Architect, holds a Master's degree in Computational Science, and actively contributes to the Salesforce community. A #DF23 Golden Hoodie Recipient, Nadina is also an active member of the Salesforce community. She holds several roles, including Salesforce MVP, MuleSoft Ambassador, and Credential Ambassador. Nadina also mentors through programs like SXSW and Ladies Be Architects. Additionally, she is a Salesforce Well-Architected Ambassador, Rad Coach, Salesforce User Group Leader, and serves on the Advisory Board of ScaleUp Archs.

Table of Contents

3

Utilizing Prompt Builder   49

4

Working with Copilot Builder   67

5

How Data Cloud Works with Einstein Studio   85

6

Exploring Functionalities of Model Builder   119

7

Leveraging Copilot Actions with Flows and More   145

11

Working with Einstein Copilot and Commerce Cloud   259

12

What's Next with Einstein Copilot   279

Preface

The recent intersection of artificial intelligence with the Salesforce platform opens new avenues for innovation and efficiency. This book is a testament to this exciting era, focusing on the integration of Einstein Studio tools (Copilot, Prompt Builder, Model Builder, and more) with Salesforce development—a synergy that is evolving on a daily basis. We are tasked with driving value with innovative approaches for customer relationship management features in profound ways.

This work is a collaborative effort among four co-authors, each contributing their distinct expertise and writing style. Due to our varied backgrounds, you may notice differences in language, formatting, and the level of detail in each chapter. These variations reflect our individual approaches and are part of the collaborative nature of this project. We have aimed to integrate these diverse perspectives into a coherent and informative guide. While each chapter may differ slightly in style, our collective goal remains to provide you with a useful and comprehensive resource. We appreciate your understanding as you encounter these variations and hope that the book serves as a valuable tool in your studies and professional endeavors.

Thank you for choosing our book, and we hope you find it informative and helpful.

Who this book is for

This book is designed for Salesforce professionals, including administrators, developers, consultants, business analysts, and product owners, who seek to leverage AI to optimize business processes, enhance customer experiences, and drive growth. For each of these roles, understanding the drivers that influence the implementation of AI with these tools will bring value to enormous capabilities on the platform with Einstein.

This book offers a practical guide to implementing Einstein Copilot in Salesforce. You will learn to set up, configure, and integrate AI features to enhance business processes. You'll also learn to optimize your Salesforce Demo ORG effectively with step-by-step instructions and real-world examples.

What this book covers

This book provides a hands-on approach to implementing Einstein Copilot in Salesforce. You will learn to set up, configure, and customize Einstein Copilot features, integrate them with Salesforce components, and leverage AI-driven insights to enhance business processes. Step-by-step guides and practical examples ensure a seamless, effective learning experience.

Chapter 1, Introduction to Salesforce Einstein Copilot, explores the foundational concepts and transformative potential of Salesforce Einstein Copilot, setting the stage for its role in driving innovation and efficiency in Salesforce projects.

Chapter 2, Setting Up Einstein Studio, provides a step-by-step guide to integrating and configuring Einstein Copilot within the Salesforce ecosystem, ensuring your environment is ready for advanced AI-driven functionalities.

Chapter 3, Utilizing Prompt Builder, delves into creating and managing prompts to enhance user interactions and automate responses within Salesforce.

Chapter 4, Working with Copilot Builder, offers an in-depth exploration of the Copilot Builder tool, guiding users through creating, configuring, and deploying AI-driven copilots tailored to specific business needs.

Chapter 5, How Data Cloud Works with Einstein Studio, explains the integration of Data Cloud and Einstein Studio, showing how to centralize data, train AI models, and drive intelligent interactions.

Chapter 6, Exploring Functionalities of Model Builder, covers how to create, train, and deploy custom AI models using Salesforce Model Builder to enhance CRM capabilities.

Chapter 7, Leveraging Copilot Actions with Flows and More, teaches how to harness Copilot Actions to automate tasks, enhance user interactions, and streamline workflows within Salesforce.

Chapter 8, Synergy between Einstein Copilot and Sales Cloud, explores how integrating Einstein Copilot with Sales Cloud can revolutionize sales processes through AI-driven insights and automation.

Chapter 9, Integrating Einstein Copilot and Service Cloud, shows how Einstein Copilot can enhance customer support by automating case management, providing real-time recommendations, and improving service efficiency.

Chapter 10, Integrating Einstein Copilot and Marketing Cloud, highlights how AI-driven insights can optimize marketing strategies, improve campaign performance, and enhance customer engagement.

Chapter 11, Working with Einstein Copilot and Commerce Cloud, demonstrates how to use Einstein Copilot in Commerce Cloud to personalize shopping experiences, automate customer interactions, and optimize e-commerce operations.

Chapter 12, What's Next with Einstein Copilot, discusses future trends and possibilities for Einstein Copilot as it continues to evolve within Salesforce's expanding AI ecosystem.

To get the most out of this book

While the authors tried to make this book usable to the broadest possible audience, it does presume a basic understanding of Salesforce configuration and administration. The use case chapters presume some fundamental understanding of the primary features of those clouds being discussed.

Software covered in the book	Operating system / Other requirements
Web Browser	Windows, macOS, or Linux
Salesforce	For Salesforce, the latest stable version of Chrome is recommended.

This book has been created by authors, technical experts, and a professional publishing team. We use many tools, including cutting-edge AI such as ChatGPT, to create the best possible material for our readers to help them on their IT journey.

> Disclaimer:
>
> While traditionally Salesforce does 3 releases per year (Spring, Summer, and Winter) for the platform, the Einstein AI and Data Cloud features and tools have experienced an accelerated monthly release schedule. If you find that images or steps differ when using this book at a later time, please note that they were accurate at the time of publication.

> Note:
>
> The power of Salesforce flow is undeniable. At present, the Copilot Actions can leverage particular types of flows. At the time of this writing, Einstein for Flow was just released in Beta two weeks ago and is not covered in depth in this edition of the book. For the latest information please refer to Salesforce Help & Trailhead. We'll aim to include this in more detail in the next edition.

Learning alongside the contents of this book

We created a companion Trailmix on Trailhead by Salesforce to complement the learning from this book. It is not exhaustive of all the learning resources available, as they do continue to evolve, but a decent sampling of projects and modules that are essential to learning Einstein tools. It includes Trails that will enable you to get learning playgrounds enabled with Einstein features (`https://trailhead.salesforce.com/users/sforcerocker/trailmixes/einstein-studio`).

Trailmix by Joseph Kubon
Hands-On Implementing Salesforce Einstein Studio & GPT Intelligence
Trailmix to go hand-in-hand with the learnings from the book.

Accessing the Salesforce Einstein Studio

How do learners gain access to resources from Salesforce for the Copilot, Prompt Builder, and other Einstein AI features?

1. Open Trailmix (Requires Trailhead account.)
2. Open the **Get Started with Einstein Copilot** Trail, first item.
3. Open the **Quick Start: Einstein Copilot** project.
4. Open the **Connect Your Flows to Einstein Copilot** lesson.
5. Follow the steps to sign up for a Trial Org with Einstein Generative AI.
6. Check the box for email confirmation.
7. Press **Create Playground** for a 14-day Org. as shown:

This Badge Requires a New Custom Einstein AI Playground

You'll have limited time to complete this badge and any other badge requiring a Einstein AI Playground. If you run out of time, you'll lose access to this Playground and may need to start over.

Create Playground

☑ I can receive a password reset email at joseph.kubon@gmail.com

ⓘ Need to change your email address? Go to Email Preferences

Company Profile:
Land of Hope & Dreams Manufacturing

We created for ourselves an imaginary manufacturing company to use throughout the book as often as possible to provide a consistent understanding around the connected parts of Einstein Studio, Copilot and Prompt builder and the practical use cases to apply the concepts and enhance the value of the book.

Overview

LH&D Manufacturing is a leading manufacturer specializing in high-quality industrial equipment and machinery. Founded in September 1949 and headquartered in Freehold, New Jersey, LH&D Manufacturing has established a global presence with operations in multiple countries. Known for its commitment to innovation and customer satisfaction, LH&D Manufacturing serves a diverse range of industries, including automotive, aerospace, construction, and energy.

Mission Statement

"Delivering superior manufacturing solutions that drive industrial innovation and efficiency."

Core Values

- Quality: Committed to producing high-quality products that meet rigorous industry standards.

- Customer Focus: Prioritizing customer needs and building lasting relationships through exceptional service.

- Innovation: Continuously improving products and processes through cutting-edge technology.

- Integrity: Upholding the highest standards of ethics and transparency in all business practices.

- Sustainability: Implementing sustainable practices to minimize environmental impact.

Products & Services

- Industrial Equipment:

  - Precision Machinery: High-performance machines used in manufacturing processes.

  - Automation Solutions: Advanced robotics and automation systems for increased efficiency.

  - Tooling Systems: Durable and precise tools and dies for various manufacturing applications.

- Customer Support and Services:

  - Sales and Service Cloud: Utilizing Salesforce Sales and Service Cloud to manage customer relationships and support.

  - Self-Service Portal: A comprehensive portal with features such as a help bot, Knowledge Base, live chat with agents, case creation, and an integrated webstore for online sales.

  - Onsite Service and Maintenance: Providing onsite service and maintenance in local areas through authorized resellers and certified maintenance technicians in local companies, ensuring optimal performance and longevity of assets sold to customers.

Key Metrics

- Revenue: $500 million annually.

- Employees: 1,500 globally.

- Customers: Over 500 clients worldwide, based on the East Coast and Midwest of the USA, with recent expansion into the Pacific Coast.

Strategic Goals

- Market Expansion: Increase market share by expanding into emerging markets and industries.

- Product Innovation: Invest in research and development to introduce new and improved industrial equipment.

- Customer Satisfaction: Enhance customer support services and maintain a high customer satisfaction rate.

- Sustainability: Implement sustainable practices across operations and product development.

Recent Achievements

- Award-Winning Products: Recognized for innovation in industrial equipment design and manufacturing.

- Successful Implementations: Delivered successful automation solutions for major clients in the automotive and aerospace industries.

- Global Recognition: Named one of the top 50 manufacturing companies to work for due to employee satisfaction and company culture.

Use of Salesforce & Einstein Copilot

LH&D Manufacturing leverages Salesforce Sales and Service Cloud as the backbone of its CRM strategy, integrating various Salesforce products to streamline operations and enhance customer engagement. The company utilizes its self-service portal to provide customers with easy access to support and sales resources, including a help bot, Knowledge Base, live chat, case creation, and a webstore for purchasing products.

- Managing Customers and Accounts:

  - Customer Data Management: Salesforce CRM allows LH&D Manufacturing to maintain comprehensive records of all customer interactions, including contact information, purchase history, and communication logs. This central repository ensures that all customer-facing teams have access to up-to-date information.

  - Account Management: By organizing customer data into accounts, LH&D Manufacturing can track the performance of individual clients, manage contracts, and identify opportunities for upselling and cross-selling.

- Opportunities and Sales Pipeline:

  - Opportunity Management: Salesforce Sales Cloud enables the company to manage its sales pipeline effectively by tracking opportunities from initial contact to closing. Sales representatives can update opportunity stages, forecast revenue, and prioritize high-value deals.

  - Sales Pipeline Visibility: Dashboards and reports provide real-time visibility into the sales pipeline, helping sales managers to monitor performance, identify bottlenecks, and make informed decisions to accelerate the sales cycle.

- Customer Support and Service:

  - Case Management: Salesforce Service Cloud streamlines customer support by allowing service agents to create, manage, and resolve cases efficiently. The system prioritizes cases based on urgency and complexity, ensuring timely responses to customer issues.

  - Self-Service Portal: The self-service portal empowers customers to find answers independently through the Knowledge Base, initiate live chats with support agents, and create service cases when needed. This reduces the burden on support staff and enhances customer satisfaction.

- Einstein Copilot Integration:

  - AI-Driven Insights: With the introduction of Einstein Copilot, LH&D Manufacturing leverages AI to gain deeper insights into customer behavior, sales trends, and service performance. Einstein Copilot provides predictive analytics and recommendations, enabling the company to make data-driven decisions.

- Automation: Einstein Copilot automates routine tasks such as data entry, follow-up emails, and case assignments, freeing employees to focus on more strategic activities. This enhances productivity and ensures a more efficient workflow.

- Personalization: By analyzing customer data, Einstein Copilot helps personalize interactions, offering tailored recommendations and solutions based on individual customer needs and preferences.

Conventions used

Bold: Indicates a new term, an important word, or words that you see onscreen. For instance, words in menus or dialog boxes appear in **bold**. Here is an example: "Use the **Data Stream** interface in Data Cloud to process and import the uploaded files to a DLO."

> Tips or important notes
> Appear like this.

Get in touch

Feedback from our readers is always welcome.

General feedback: If you have questions about any aspect of this book, email us at `customercare@packtpub.com` and mention the book title in the subject of your message.

Errata: Although we have taken every care to ensure the accuracy of our content, mistakes do happen. If you have found a mistake in this book, we would be grateful if you would report this to us. Please visit `www.packtpub.com/support/errata` and fill in the form.

Piracy: If you come across any illegal copies of our works in any form on the internet, we would be grateful if you would provide us with the location address or website name. Please contact us at `copyright@packt.com` with a link to the material.

If you are interested in becoming an author: If there is a topic that you have expertise in and you are interested in either writing or contributing to a book, please visit `authors.packtpub.com`.

Connect with the authors

The authors are active on most professional social channels in the Salesforce ecosystem, including LinkedIn, the Trailblazer Community, and X (formerly Twitter). They welcome the opportunity to engage with you directly about this book.

Joseph and Melissa frequently participate in events like Dreamforce, TrailblazerDX, and community Dreamin' conferences , where they discuss a range of technical topics and best practices. If you'd like them to present this topic to your Trailblazer Community Group, please feel free to reach out.

Share Your Thoughts

Once you've read *Hands-On Salesforce Einstein Studio and GPT Intelligence,* we'd love to hear your thoughts! Scan the QR code below to go straight to the Amazon review page for this book and share your feedback.

https://packt.link/r/1836203772

Your review is important to us and the tech community and will help us make sure we're delivering excellent quality content.

Download a free PDF copy of this book

Thanks for purchasing this book!

Do you like to read on the go but are unable to carry your print books everywhere?

Is your eBook purchase not compatible with the device of your choice?

Don't worry, now with every Packt book you get a DRM-free PDF version of that book at no cost.

Read anywhere, any place, on any device. Search, copy, and paste code from your favorite technical books directly into your application.

The perks don't stop there, you can get exclusive access to discounts, newsletters, and great free content in your inbox daily

Follow these simple steps to get the benefits:

1. Scan the QR code or visit the link below

https://packt.link/free-ebook/978-1-83620-377-3

2. Submit your proof of purchase
3. That's it! We'll send your free PDF and other benefits to your email directly

Part 1:
Navigating the Tool:
The How of Einstein Studio

This part provides a foundational understanding of Salesforce Einstein Copilot, guiding you through its core functionalities and how to effectively integrate it within the Salesforce ecosystem. Beginning with an introduction to Einstein Copilot, the part delves into setting up and customizing the tool to suit organizational needs, ensuring that readers are well-equipped to leverage its AI-driven capabilities.

Chapters 2 and *3* focus on the practical aspects of getting started, including setting up the environment, configuring user permissions, and utilizing tools like Prompt Builder. These steps are crucial for ensuring that the platform is tailored to specific business requirements and that users can efficiently navigate and optimize the tool's features.

As you progress, *Chapters 4* through *6* explore more advanced functionalities such as Copilot Builder and Model Builder, offering deep dives into the customization and deployment of AI models. This progression ensures that users not only understand the basics but also gain the skills needed to create sophisticated, AI-enhanced solutions that integrate seamlessly with Salesforce components.

Finally, *Chapter 7* ties everything together by demonstrating how Copilot Actions can be leveraged to automate tasks and enhance workflows. This part of the book emphasizes practical application, ensuring that you can apply what you've learned to create powerful, AI-driven solutions that drive real business outcomes. By the end of *Part 1*, you will have a comprehensive understanding of how to navigate and utilize Einstein Studio effectively within their Salesforce environments.

This part has the following chapters:

1

Introduction to Salesforce Einstein Copilot

Welcome to *Hands-On Salesforce Einstein Studio and GPT Intelligence*. This book is the go-to resource for understanding and using Einstein Copilot in Salesforce. Whether a Salesforce user, developer, architect, administrator, or business analyst, this guide will provide you with practical examples and best practices to make the most of this exciting AI tool.

This book is meant to be a reference guide, so we recommend jumping to the chapter that addresses your current need, rather than reading from the beginning.

In this chapter, we will cover the following:

- What is Einstein Copilot?
- What makes Einstein Copilot special?
- How Einstein Copilot enhances Salesforce

What is Einstein Copilot?

Salesforce Einstein Copilot represents a revolutionary step in the evolution of **Customer Relationship Management (CRM)** through **Artificial Intelligence (AI)**. Einstein Copilot is designed to augment the capabilities of multiple Salesforce clouds by embedding advanced AI technologies directly into users' workflows. This tool is specifically tailored to enhance the productivity and effectiveness of sales representatives, marketers, and customer service personnel by automating routine tasks and providing insightful data-driven recommendations.

The core of Einstein Copilot is its deep embedding within the Salesforce platform, particularly within the Salesforce Clouds – Sales Cloud, Service Cloud, Marketing Cloud, and Commerce Cloud. This allows it to pull and analyze data across these diverse environments to provide unified insights and recommendations.

In Sales Cloud, Einstein Copilot enhances the sales process by providing sales representatives with actionable insights and recommendations, based on the analysis of previous sales data and customer interactions. For example, it can suggest the most opportune time to contact a prospect, based on historical engagement data, or predict which deals are most likely to close. This integration not only speeds up the sales process but also increases its efficiency by prioritizing actions that are more likely to succeed.

Within Service Cloud, Einstein Copilot automates many routine tasks, such as ticket classification and routing, based on the nature of customer queries and past resolution data. It can also suggest solutions to customer service agents in real time, based on similar past incidents, thus improving the speed and accuracy of customer service.

In Marketing Cloud, Einstein Copilot helps marketers design and implement more effective campaigns by analyzing customer behavior and predicting trends. It can automatically segment audiences based on their engagement levels and preferences, allowing for highly targeted and personalized marketing communications.

For Commerce Cloud, Einstein Copilot optimizes e-commerce operations by providing insights into customer buying patterns and preferences. It can recommend changes to product placement, promotions, and pricing strategies based on predictive analytics, thus enhancing the shopping experience and increasing sales.

Einstein Copilot significantly enhances user experience across Salesforce applications by providing a unified, intuitive interface where users can access AI-driven insights. This integration ensures that regardless of the Salesforce product being used, the interface and functionality remain consistent, reducing learning curves and increasing productivity.

One of the standout features of Einstein Copilot is its ability to use Data Cloud to connect and synthesize data across various Salesforce platforms and third-party applications. This is crucial for businesses that use multiple Salesforce products or integrate their Salesforce data with other systems, such as ERP or external databases.

With the increasing importance of mobile platforms, Einstein Copilot is fully integrated into the Salesforce mobile app, allowing users to access AI-driven insights on the go. This mobile integration ensures that sales representatives and service agents can remain productive and informed, no matter where they are.

Einstein Copilot processes data in real time, providing users with up-to-the-minute insights. This capability is critical in environments where conditions change rapidly, such as in sales or customer service scenarios.

Einstein Copilot with Salesforce also emphasizes security and compliance with international data protection regulations. Salesforce ensures that all data handled by Einstein Copilot is processed securely, maintaining the integrity and confidentiality of sensitive information.

Einstein Copilot not only enhances the functionality and efficiency of Salesforce applications but also transforms how businesses interact with their customers, manage their operations, and make strategic decisions. The seamless integration of Einstein Copilot across the Salesforce platform exemplifies how AI can be leveraged to create a more connected, insightful, and responsive business environment.

Salesforce Einstein Copilot is a groundbreaking advancement in CRM, leveraging AI to enhance multiple Salesforce clouds by integrating advanced AI technologies directly into user workflows. It boosts the productivity of sales, marketing, and customer service teams by automating routine tasks and providing data-driven recommendations. Embedded deeply within Sales Cloud, Service Cloud, Marketing Cloud, and Commerce Cloud, it unifies insights and streamlines processes across these platforms. By using Data Cloud to connect data from various sources and integrating seamlessly with the Salesforce mobile app, Einstein Copilot offers real-time insights, ensures security and compliance, and transforms business operations and customer interactions. This sets the stage for a review of what makes Einstein Copilot special and unique in the AI and CRM landscape.

What makes Einstein Copilot special?

Salesforce Einstein Copilot stands out from other AI tools on the market through a series of distinct features, tailored to enhance the Salesforce ecosystem, making it an indispensable asset across various business operations.

At the heart of Einstein Copilot's uniqueness is its seamless integration with Salesforce Clouds. Unlike standalone AI tools that can require complex integrations, Einstein Copilot is natively embedded within Salesforce, giving it direct access to a wide array of data across Sales Cloud, Service Cloud, Marketing Cloud, and beyond. This integration allows it to provide comprehensive, synthesized insights across a customer's entire journey, ensuring that recommendations are both holistic and actionable.

Einstein Copilot excels in predictive analytics and real-time decision-making. By analyzing past and present data, it can forecast future customer behaviors, sales trends, and service needs, allowing businesses to proactively prepare and respond. Its ability to process data in real time ensures that these insights are always up to date, providing timely guidance that is critical in fast-paced business environments.

The platform also leverages advanced **Natural Language Processing** (**NLP**) to facilitate interactions that require no technical expertise, enabling a broader range of users to benefit from sophisticated AI analytics. Beyond generic models, Einstein Copilot offers the capability to develop custom AI models tailored to specific business needs, enhancing the personalization of insights and recommendations.

Automation is another cornerstone of Einstein Copilot's functionality, with the tool automating tasks across various functions such as lead scoring, email marketing, case routing, and customer segmentation. This automation extends across multiple CRM functions, streamlining operations and enhancing efficiency without increasing the workload on human teams.

Designed with the end user in mind, Einstein Copilot features user-friendly interfaces that improve usability and foster higher adoption rates across organizations. Its scalable AI solutions are designed to grow with an organization, ensuring that businesses of all sizes can leverage its capabilities without performance degradation.

Einstein Copilot is also adaptable, learning continuously from new data and interactions to refine its algorithms and outputs. This ensures that the tool remains effective even as business conditions and data inputs evolve. Security is paramount within the Salesforce ecosystem, and Einstein Copilot upholds these high standards by ensuring that all the data it handles is secured against unauthorized access and breaches.

Einstein Copilot doesn't just react to data but also provides insights and alerts to help organizations anticipate and tackle emerging challenges and opportunities. This proactive capability helps organizations maintain a competitive edge.

Salesforce's commitment to ethical AI practices is evident in how Einstein Copilot was developed. The emphasis on fairness, transparency, and accountability in its algorithms ensures that businesses can trust the tool to not only be effective but also to align with broader ethical standards.

Through these features, Einstein Copilot distinguishes itself as not only a tool but also as a transformative force within CRM, driving smarter decisions, optimizing operations, and enhancing customer experiences with unparalleled efficacy.

Natural Language Processing

Einstein Copilot, an advanced component of Salesforce's AI suite, leverages NLP to transform how users interact with the CRM system, making these interactions more intuitive and efficient. The use of NLP is a critical aspect of Einstein Copilot, as it enables the system to understand, interpret, and respond to human language in a way that feels natural and easy to use.

NLP allows Einstein Copilot to process and make sense of a user query in natural language, whether it's typed text or spoken words. This technology underpins the AI's ability to comprehend queries and commands as they are naturally expressed, eliminating the need for users to learn specific command languages or navigate complex menus.

Once Einstein Copilot understands the query, it processes the relevant data to provide an answer. NLP plays a role here as well, allowing the system to generate responses in a language that users can easily understand. This capability ensures that the communication between the user and Einstein Copilot is as smooth and natural as a conversation with a human colleague.

By integrating NLP, Einstein Copilot greatly enhances the user interface of Salesforce's CRM platform. Users can simply type or speak their questions and commands without needing to navigate through multiple screens or make sense of report data. This ease of use dramatically reduces the learning curve for new users and enhances productivity for all users.

NLP enables Einstein Copilot to handle more complex queries that involve multiple variables and conditions. For example, a user might ask, "*Show me the pipeline of deals closing next month with a* *value over $50,000.*" Here, Einstein Copilot uses NLP to parse the query, understand the conditions (next month and over $50,000), and retrieve the appropriate data from the CRM.

NLP allows Einstein Copilot to understand the context of queries, which is crucial for providing accurate responses. For instance, if a user asks a follow-up question without specifying all the details, the system can infer the missing information from the previous interaction. This context-awareness mimics human conversation, making the AI interaction more fluid and natural.

Einstein Copilot's NLP is designed to handle errors and ambiguities in user input gracefully. If the system does not understand a query, it can ask clarifying questions or suggest alternative phrasings, much like a human would. This interactive feedback loop helps to minimize frustrations and ensures that users can correct and refine their queries to get the desired results.

NLP within Einstein Copilot can be customized and specialized according to industry-specific terminology and workflows. This customization ensures that the system can understand and respond accurately to terms and phrases that are unique to a particular business or sector, enhancing the relevance and accuracy of its responses.

Through these capabilities, NLP within Einstein Copilot not only enhances the functionality of Salesforce's CRM system but also revolutionizes the way users interact with it, making it a more intuitive, responsive, and effective tool for managing customer relationships.

Machine learning

Machine Learning (**ML**) is at the core of Einstein Copilot's capabilities, enabling it to analyze vast amounts of data, identify patterns, and improve its responses and recommendations. This advanced technology allows Salesforce to offer a CRM tool that not only manages data but also actively learns from it, making smarter predictions that can enhance business decisions across various domains.

Einstein Copilot utilizes ML to delve deep into the historical data stored within the Salesforce ecosystem. By analyzing past interactions, sales outcomes, customer feedback, and other relevant metrics, the system can identify trends and patterns that might not be obvious, even to experienced analysts. This capability is particularly useful in sales and marketing, where understanding subtle customer behavior patterns can significantly impact the effectiveness of strategies.

ML allows Einstein Copilot to refine its understanding based on new data. As users interact with the system and as new customer data is collected, the ML models update and improve. This ongoing learning process ensures that the system's recommendations stay relevant and accurate over time, adapting to changing market conditions and evolving customer preferences.

A significant benefit of ML in Einstein Copilot is its ability to enhance personalization. By analyzing individual customer data, the system can tailor interactions and recommendations to meet specific customer preferences and needs.

Einstein Copilot also utilizes ML to optimize workflows and automate routine tasks. For instance, it can automatically categorize and route customer service inquiries based on their content and urgency, prioritize sales leads based on their likelihood of closure, or schedule marketing emails at the most effective times.

ML enables Einstein Copilot to provide actionable insights into business operations. It can identify inefficiencies in processes, suggest areas where costs can be reduced, and recommend strategies to increase operational efficiency. These insights are derived from comprehensive data analysis that would be impractical for human analysts to perform at the same scale.

In addition to these internal capabilities, Einstein Copilot's ML algorithms can interface with external data sources to enhance their predictive accuracy. For example, integrating external market trends, economic indicators, and competitive analysis into the predictive models can provide a more comprehensive view of the business landscape, further enhancing the strategic recommendations provided by Einstein Copilot.

The adaptability of ML within Einstein Copilot is also noteworthy. The system can be configured to suit different industries and business sizes, ensuring that its capabilities are accessible to all Salesforce users, from small businesses to large enterprises. This flexibility makes it a valuable tool regardless of the specific challenges or opportunities a business may face.

Finally, Einstein Copilot commits to ethical AI practices in its use of ML, ensuring that all data is handled with respect to privacy and without bias. This commitment is crucial for maintaining trust and compliance, particularly in sensitive industries where data accuracy and ethics are paramount.

Through these diverse applications, ML within Einstein Copilot fundamentally enhances how businesses interact with and leverage their CRM systems, driving not just operational efficiency but also strategic foresight and customer-centric personalization. Salesforce Einstein Copilot stands out from other AI tools due to its seamless integration within the Salesforce ecosystem, providing direct access to a vast array of capabilities and data across various Salesforce clouds. This integration enables comprehensive and synthesized insights that are holistic and actionable. Einstein Copilot excels in real-time decision-making and NLP, making sophisticated AI accessible to all users. It automates tasks across different functions, enhancing efficiency and productivity, with user-friendly interfaces designed for scalability and adaptability. Security, ethical AI practices, and proactive capabilities further distinguish Einstein Copilot as a transformative force in CRM. The next section will detail how Einstein Copilot enhances Sales Cloud, Service Cloud, Marketing Cloud, and Commerce Cloud, showcasing its practical benefits in these key areas.

How Einstein Copilot enhances Salesforce

Sales Cloud, Service Cloud, Marketing Cloud, and Commerce Cloud – each cloud offers unique advantages when integrated with Einstein Copilot, from boosting sales productivity and enhancing customer service to optimizing marketing campaigns and improving online shopping experiences.

Einstein Copilot can drive efficiency, personalization, and growth in each of these key clouds, helping organizations leverage AI to its fullest potential.

Sales Cloud

Einstein Copilot significantly enhances the capabilities of Salesforce's Sales Cloud by streamlining processes such as lead scoring and sales predictions. These functionalities directly impact sales efficiency by enabling sales teams to focus on the most promising leads and anticipate sales trends more accurately.

One of the primary benefits of Einstein Copilot in Sales Cloud is its advanced lead-scoring capabilities. Traditionally, lead scoring could be a somewhat subjective process, influenced by a salesperson's intuition or inconsistent criteria. Einstein Copilot automates and refines this process by using ML to analyze historical data on successful conversions and identify the characteristics of high-quality leads. This data-driven approach ensures that leads are scored based on objective criteria, significantly increasing the accuracy of lead prioritization.

Einstein Copilot also enhances sales predictions by analyzing current sales data and historical trends to suggest sales activities. This capability allows sales teams to anticipate market changes, adjust their strategies accordingly, and better align their resources with predicted sales volumes.

With Einstein Copilot, sales representatives can optimize their follow-up strategies. By analyzing the outcomes of previous interactions, Einstein Copilot can recommend the best methods for following up leads. This tailored approach not only improves the chances of converting leads but also enhances the overall efficiency of the sales process.

Einstein Copilot automates routine tasks such as data entry and report generation. This automation frees up sales representatives to focus more on engaging with clients and closing deals, rather than spending time on administrative tasks. The reduction in manual workloads leads to a more productive sales force and faster sales cycles.

As businesses grow, their sales strategies and operations must scale accordingly. Einstein Copilot supports this scalability by adapting to increasing volumes of data and more complex sales processes. Its ML algorithms continuously learn and improve, ensuring that the system remains effective no matter the scale of operations.

These enhancements show how Einstein Copilot not only improves the efficiency of individual sales activities but also transforms the broader sales strategy within Salesforce's Sales Cloud. By leveraging AI to streamline operations, automate tasks, and provide actionable insights, Einstein Copilot helps businesses optimize their sales processes and achieve better sales outcomes.

Service Cloud

Einstein Copilot significantly enhances the capabilities of Salesforce's Service Cloud by leveraging AI to improve customer service operations. It facilitates faster resolution times and provides personalized service recommendations, which are crucial for increasing customer satisfaction and loyalty.

Einstein Copilot accelerates issue resolution by automating the initial stages of the customer service process. Using AI to interpret incoming service requests, the system can categorize and route the requests to the appropriate team or individual. This automated sorting eliminates delays that typically occur when tickets are manually processed and ensures that customers receive timely responses.

For common issues or questions, Einstein Copilot can generate automated responses based on a knowledge base of previously resolved cases and standardized information. This not only speeds up the resolution of frequently asked questions but also frees up customer service representatives to focus on more complex inquiries that require human intervention.

By analyzing a customer's history and previous interactions, Einstein Copilot can provide personalized service recommendations to support agents. For example, if a customer has repeatedly faced a specific issue, Einstein Copilot can suggest a permanent solution or an upgrade that might prevent the problem from recurring. These tailored recommendations enhance the customer experience by showing that the company understands and anticipates their needs.

Einstein Copilot increases agent productivity by providing them with all the necessary information about a case as soon as it's routed to them. This includes customer history, past issues, and any relevant documentation. With this information at their fingertips, agents can resolve cases more quickly and effectively without needing to toggle between systems or manually search for information.

Using NLP, Einstein Copilot can analyze customer sentiment during interactions, providing agents with insights into a customer's mood and satisfaction levels. This capability allows agents to adjust their approach in real time, enhancing communication effectiveness and customer satisfaction.

Einstein Copilot facilitates a continuous improvement cycle by regularly analyzing service interactions and outcomes. This analysis helps identify areas where processes can be refined or where additional training might be needed. By continuously learning from interactions, Einstein Copilot helps organizations adapt their service strategies to meet evolving customer expectations.

In today's digital age, customers reach out through various channels – email, social media, phone, and so on. Einstein Copilot manages this multichannel communication seamlessly, ensuring consistent service across all platforms. By integrating data from different channels, it provides a comprehensive view of each customer's journey, enabling more effective and personalized interactions.

By enhancing customer satisfaction through faster resolutions, personalized service, and proactive support, Einstein Copilot directly contributes to higher customer retention rates. Satisfied customers are less likely to switch to competitors and more likely to recommend the company to others.

Through these diverse capabilities, Einstein Copilot transforms the operational efficiency and strategic effectiveness of customer service teams using Salesforce's Service Cloud. By integrating AI-driven insights and automations, it not only improves the customer experience but also empowers agents and managers to excel in their roles.

Marketing Cloud

Einstein Copilot, integrated with Salesforce's Marketing Cloud, significantly enhances the marketing process by refining customer segmentation and personalizing marketing campaigns. This powerful tool utilizes advanced AI capabilities to analyze customer data, predict behaviors, and deliver highly targeted content, revolutionizing the way businesses engage with their audiences. Einstein Copilot applies sophisticated ML algorithms to analyze vast amounts of customer data, collected through various interactions across channels. It identifies patterns and trends in this data, which allows you to create highly detailed and accurate customer segments. This refined segmentation enables marketers to understand their audience's preferences and behaviors at a granular level, facilitating more effective targeting.

Unlike static segmentation methods that categorize customers into fixed groups, Einstein Copilot enables dynamic segmentation. This means customer segments can continuously evolve based on new data, ensuring that marketing efforts are always aligned with current customer behaviors and preferences. This adaptability is crucial in responding to market changes and maintaining the relevance of marketing messages.

With detailed insights into customer segments, Einstein Copilot helps marketers personalize their campaigns to an unprecedented degree. Each customer or segment receives tailored messages based on their specific interests, behaviors, and predicted needs. This personalization not only enhances customer engagement but also significantly improves conversion rates as messages resonate more deeply with recipients.

Einstein Copilot helps automate various aspects of campaign management, from the scheduling of emails to dynamic content personalization in real time. This automation streamlines the marketing process, reduces the likelihood of human error, and ensures that campaigns are executed efficiently and effectively.

Einstein Copilot ensures that personalized marketing campaigns are consistent across all channels, whether it's email, social media, web, or mobile. This omnichannel approach is essential for delivering a cohesive customer experience, reinforcing brand messages, and increasing the overall impact of marketing efforts.

By analyzing customer interactions, Einstein Copilot can adjust the content of ongoing campaigns to optimize performance. If certain content or offers are not performing as expected, the system can dynamically change them, enhancing the relevance and effectiveness of the campaign as it unfolds.

Einstein Copilot maps and analyzes complex customer journeys, identifying key touchpoints where personalized interventions can significantly enhance the customer experience. By understanding these journeys, marketers can design campaigns that engage customers at the right time, with the right message, boosting both satisfaction and loyalty.

Einstein Copilot can detect specific behaviors that trigger the need for targeted marketing actions. For instance, if a customer abandons a shopping cart, the system can trigger a personalized email, reminding the customer of their cart and possibly offering a discount to encourage completion of the purchase.

Einstein Copilot provides deep insights into campaign performance and customer reactions. These insights help marketers understand what works and what doesn't, allowing for continuous improvement in campaign strategies and tactics.

Einstein Copilot's capabilities scale with a business, accommodating increasing volumes of data and more complex marketing needs without losing performance. This scalability ensures that businesses of all sizes can benefit from AI-driven marketing, regardless of their customer base size.

By automating routine tasks and optimizing campaign strategies, Einstein Copilot helps reduce marketing costs. The increased efficiency and effectiveness of campaigns also mean that the return on investment is maximized, contributing to overall business profitability.

Through these capabilities, Einstein Copilot transforms how businesses use Salesforce's Marketing Cloud to engage with their customers. By refining customer segmentation and personalizing marketing campaigns, it ensures that marketing efforts are not only more efficient but also more effective, leading to increased customer engagement and business growth.

Commerce Cloud

Einstein Copilot integrates seamlessly with Salesforce's Commerce Cloud, leveraging its sophisticated AI capabilities to optimize inventory management and personalize shopping experiences. This advanced tool transforms the e-commerce sector by providing businesses with actionable insights and automations, enhancing both operational efficiency and customer satisfaction.

Einstein Copilot plays a crucial role in inventory management within Commerce Cloud. By analyzing historical sales data, seasonal trends, and current market conditions, it predicts inventory requirements with high accuracy. This predictive capability ensures that businesses maintain optimal stock levels – enough to meet customer demand but not so much that it leads to overstocking and increased holding costs.

Einstein Copilot continuously monitors sales activity and updates its forecasts in real time. If sudden changes in demand are detected, perhaps due to a viral product trend or a change in consumer preferences, Einstein Copilot quickly adjusts the recommended inventory levels. This dynamic response prevents potential stock-outs or excess inventory, both of which can be costly to businesses.

Einstein Copilot enhances the shopper's experience by personalizing the e-commerce interface. Based on individual customer data such as past purchases, browsing history, and search patterns, it tailors product recommendations to match each customer's preferences. This personalization makes the shopping experience more engaging and can significantly increase conversion rates.

Einstein Copilot improves product discovery on e-commerce sites by optimizing search results and product placements. It uses customer interaction data to understand what shoppers are most likely to buy and modifies search algorithms to highlight products that meet these preferences, thus enhancing user experience and boosting sales.

In addition to personalizing individual shopping experiences, Einstein Copilot uses customer segmentation to enhance marketing efforts. By identifying distinct customer groups based on shopping patterns and preferences, it enables businesses to run targeted marketing campaigns that are more likely to resonate with each segment.

With the increasing prevalence of mobile commerce, Einstein Copilot optimizes the shopping experience on mobile devices. It ensures that mobile interfaces are user-friendly and that personalized recommendations are effectively displayed, catering to the growing number of customers who shop on their smartphones and tablets.

Einstein Copilot identifies potential cross-selling and upselling opportunities by analyzing customer preferences and purchasing behaviors. It suggests relevant products to customers at the point of sale, increasing the average order value and enhancing revenue per customer.

By analyzing comprehensive customer data, Einstein Copilot predicts customer lifetime value. This insight allows businesses to tailor their engagement strategies to foster and maintain relationships with high-value customers, optimizing marketing and sales efforts for long-term profitability.

Through these diverse functionalities, Einstein Copilot transforms how businesses use Commerce Cloud, optimizing inventory management and personalizing the shopping experience to meet the high expectations of today's consumers. Salesforce Einstein Copilot enhances Sales Cloud, Service Cloud, Marketing Cloud, and Commerce Cloud by leveraging AI to boost productivity, personalization, and operational efficiency. In Sales Cloud, Copilot streamlines lead scoring and sales predictions, improving sales strategies and outcomes. Service Cloud benefits from automated issue resolution and personalized service recommendations, enhancing customer satisfaction and agent productivity. Marketing Cloud sees improved customer segmentation and campaign personalization, leading to more effective marketing efforts. Commerce Cloud is optimized through accurate inventory management and personalized shopping experiences, boosting customer satisfaction and sales. These enhancements showcase how Einstein Copilot transforms various Salesforce Clouds, setting the stage for a deeper understanding of its unique benefits throughout this book.

Summary

This initial look at Salesforce Einstein Copilot has demonstrated how advanced AI is revolutionizing CRM capabilities. We reviewed the core functionalities of Einstein Copilot, emphasizing its integration within the Salesforce ecosystem to enhance Sales Cloud, Service Cloud, Marketing Cloud, and Commerce Cloud. This has provided an initial look at the transformative impact of Einstein Copilot on productivity, personalization, and efficiency in these Salesforce Clouds.

The next chapter on Setting Up Einstein Studio for development is an exciting and practical guide for developers and technical teams eager to harness the full potential of AI within their Salesforce environments. As we dive into the technical prerequisites and step-by-step processes to integrate Einstein Copilot, you will gain invaluable insights into customizing and optimizing this powerful tool to meet your specific business needs. From initial setup and configuration to detailed customization techniques, this chapter will equip you with the knowledge to transform your CRM system into a highly efficient, AI-driven powerhouse.

2

Setting Up Einstein Studio

The rapid evolution of **artificial intelligence** (**AI**) has profoundly impacted various industries, reshaping how businesses operate and interact with their customers. In **customer relationship management** (**CRM**), tools such as Salesforce's Einstein Copilot represent a significant leap forward, offering unparalleled capabilities to enhance efficiency, drive innovation, and deliver superior customer experiences. Einstein Copilot, powered by sophisticated AI algorithms, provides actionable insights and automation that empower organizations to make data-driven decisions and optimize their operations. This introductory chapter sets the stage for integrating Einstein Copilot within your Salesforce ecosystem, ensuring that you are well-equipped to harness the full potential of this transformative tool.

In this chapter, you will cover the foundational steps required to integrate and configure Einstein Copilot. From preparing your Salesforce environment to ensuring data security and compliance, each section is designed to provide you with the knowledge and skills needed to set up Einstein Copilot effectively. You will learn how to secure the appropriate licenses, configure user permissions, and enable various Einstein features, all while customizing the tool to meet your organization's unique needs. This chapter also addresses common setup issues and offers troubleshooting tips to ensure a smooth and seamless integration process.

Understanding the difficulties of integrating Einstein Copilot is crucial for maximizing its benefits. By following the step-by-step instructions and best practices outlined in this chapter, you will be able to tailor Einstein Copilot so that it aligns with your business objectives, thereby enhancing productivity and driving better outcomes. The importance of mastering these foundational skills cannot be overstated as they form the foundation upon which advanced AI-driven functionalities can be built. Whether you're a Salesforce administrator, developer, or business analyst, the knowledge you'll gain from this chapter will be instrumental in unlocking the full potential of Einstein Copilot.

One of the key aspects of Einstein Copilot is its ability to provide intelligent insights and automation, which can significantly reduce manual efforts and streamline workflows. By leveraging AI, Einstein Copilot helps you identify trends, predict outcomes, and make informed decisions, thereby enhancing operational efficiency. The integration process covered in this chapter will equip you with the skills to configure and customize these AI capabilities, ensuring that they're aligned with your organizational goals and deliver maximum value. Furthermore, understanding how to secure and manage data within the Salesforce environment is essential for maintaining trust and compliance, especially in an era where data privacy regulations are becoming increasingly stringent.

The value of learning these key skills extends beyond the immediate setup and configuration of Einstein Copilot. As AI continues to evolve and become more integrated into business processes, having a solid foundation in AI tools such as Einstein Copilot will position you as a forward-thinking professional capable of driving innovation and transformation within your organization. The ability to effectively implement and utilize AI-powered tools will not only enhance your career prospects but also contribute to the overall success and competitiveness of your organization.

In conclusion, this introductory chapter serves as a critical starting point for anyone looking to leverage Einstein Copilot into their Salesforce environment. By mastering the skills and concepts outlined, by the end of this chapter, you will be well-prepared to harness the power of AI to drive better business outcomes. The journey to integrating and optimizing Einstein Copilot is one of continuous learning and adaptation, and this chapter provides the essential building blocks to set you on the path to success. Embrace the opportunity to learn and innovate and let Einstein Copilot transform the way you manage customer relationships and achieve your business goals.

Preparing your Salesforce environment for Einstein Copilot

Preparing your Salesforce environment for Einstein Copilot is the first crucial piece toward leveraging AI to enhance your organization's efficiency and innovation. This preparation involves ensuring your Salesforce instance is up to date, verifying system requirements, and making necessary configurations. By setting a solid foundation, you pave the way for a smooth and effective integration of Einstein Copilot.

In today's competitive business landscape, leveraging AI to drive operational efficiency and innovation is not just a luxury but a necessity. Einstein Copilot, with its robust AI capabilities, promises to transform how businesses interact with their customers and manage their internal processes. However, the success of this transformation heavily relies on how well-prepared your Salesforce environment is. Proper preparation ensures that you can maximize the benefits of Einstein Copilot without facing unnecessary disruptions or technical issues.

Ensuring that your Salesforce instance is up to date is fundamental. Regular updates from Salesforce include crucial security patches, performance improvements, and new features that are designed to keep your CRM system at the forefront. Running the latest version of Salesforce not only enhances compatibility with Einstein Copilot but also ensures that you're benefiting from the latest advancements in CRM technology.

Verifying system requirements is another critical aspect of preparation. This involves assessing your current hardware and software infrastructure to ensure it can handle the additional load and complexity introduced by AI-driven functionalities. Performance optimization, regular maintenance, and database indexing are practices that will keep your system running smoothly, even as it processes large volumes of data and complex AI algorithms.

Lastly, user readiness is a vital component of preparation. It is not enough to have a technically sound system; the users who interact with Einstein Copilot must be well-trained and comfortable with the new tools and features. Effective user training programs, clear communication, and hands-on workshops can significantly boost user adoption and satisfaction, ensuring that your investment in AI yields tangible results.

Key goals and outcomes

In this section, you will do the following:

- Understand the prerequisites needed for integrating Einstein Copilot
- Learn about the hardware and software requirements necessary for optimal performance

Gain insights into the essential initial setup configurations to enable Einstein's features

Integrating Einstein Copilot is not merely a technical upgrade but a strategic initiative that can redefine how your organization operates. Understanding the prerequisites for this integration is essential for planning and resource allocation. Here, you will learn about the critical updates and configurations that your Salesforce instance requires, all of which will set the stage for a successful AI deployment.

The hardware and software requirements for Einstein Copilot ensure that your system can handle the increased computational demands of AI processing. This knowledge will enable you to make informed decisions about infrastructure investments and performance optimization strategies. By verifying these requirements, you can prevent potential bottlenecks and ensure a seamless integration process.

Essential initial setup configurations are the foundation upon which Einstein Copilot will operate. These configurations include setting up user permissions, enabling key features, and ensuring data integrity. Understanding these setups will equip you with the skills needed to customize Einstein Copilot to meet your organization's unique needs, maximizing its effectiveness and value.

Ensuring your Salesforce instance is up to date

To start, it is essential to confirm that your Salesforce instance is up to date. Running the latest version ensures compatibility with Einstein Copilot and access to the newest features and improvements. You must do the following:

1. **Check for updates**:

    I.   Navigate to **Setup** in Salesforce.

    II. In the **Quick Find** box, type `Release Updates` and select it.

    III. Review the available updates and apply them if necessary.

    Example: Ensure your Salesforce instance is running the latest version to support the newest Einstein Copilot features.

2. **Verify version compatibility:**

    I.   Refer to the Salesforce Release Notes and Einstein Copilot specifications.

    II.   Confirm that your current Salesforce version is compatible with Einstein Copilot.

Example: Using a compatible version ensures all Einstein Copilot functionalities are available and working correctly.

Keeping your Salesforce instance up to date not only provides access to the latest features but also enhances system security and performance.

System requirements verification

Ensuring that your system meets the necessary hardware and software requirements is vital for the optimal performance of Einstein Copilot. This step involves verifying that your servers and network infrastructure are adequate and that your software environment is compatible. Let's take a look:

- **Hardware and software requirements:**

  - Ensure your servers and network infrastructure meet the minimum requirements
  - Check compatibility with operating systems and browsers

  Example: Adequate server capacity and network bandwidth will handle the increased data processing from AI functionalities.

- **Performance optimization:**

  - Conduct regular maintenance and database indexing
  - Allocate resources appropriately to ensure smooth operation

  Example: Optimized performance leads to faster data processing and improved user experience.

By verifying and optimizing system requirements, you can avoid performance bottlenecks and ensure your environment can handle the demands of AI processing.

Environment readiness

Preparing your Salesforce environment involves more than just updating software and verifying system requirements. It also includes using a sandbox environment for testing and ensuring your data is ready for AI integration. Let's take a closer look:

- **Sandbox environment:**

  Use a Salesforce sandbox to test Einstein Copilot features before deploying them to production. To do this, follow these steps:

  I.   Navigate to **Setup | Sandboxes**.

II.   Create a new sandbox or refresh an existing one.

III.   Test Einstein features in the sandbox environment.

Example: Identifying and resolving issues in the sandbox environment prevents disruptions in the live environment.

- **Data readiness**:

  - Ensure your data is clean, accurate, and properly formatted

  - Use Salesforce data cleansing tools and best practices

  Example: Clean data improves the accuracy and reliability of AI-driven insights from Einstein Copilot.

A well-prepared environment minimizes risks and ensures a smoother transition when integrating new features.

User readiness

Finally, preparing your users for the new tools and features is crucial for successful adoption. Training and educating your users on Einstein Copilot will help them understand and utilize the new capabilities effectively. Let's take a closer look:

- **Training and education**:

  - Prepare training materials such as tutorials, guides, and FAQs

  - Conduct workshops, webinars, and hands-on training sessions

  Example: Educating users on Einstein Copilot features increases adoption and effective usage.

Ensuring your users are well-prepared and confident in using the new tools will lead to higher adoption rates and more effective utilization of Einstein Copilot.

Challenges solved and value provided

In this section, we'll take a closer look at the challenges that can be solved and the value that's provided by using Einstein Copilot.

Challenges solved

Preparing your Salesforce organization for the use of Einstein features resolves familiar challenges for most users:

- **Compatibility issues**: Ensuring the Salesforce environment is up to date prevents feature incompatibility
- **Performance bottlenecks**: Verifying system requirements and optimizing performance ensures smooth operation
- **Data inaccuracy**: Preparing data and using a sandbox environment helps identify and resolve issues before they impact the live environment
- **User adoption**: Training and education overcome resistance to recent technology

In the journey to integrate AI into your CRM, several challenges may arise. Compatibility issues are common, especially if your Salesforce instance isn't running the latest version. By ensuring your system is up to date, you eliminate the risk of running into feature incompatibility, which could hinder the deployment of Einstein Copilot. This proactive step also brings along the benefits of enhanced security and performance.

Performance bottlenecks can significantly impede the effectiveness of AI-driven tools. By thoroughly verifying system requirements and optimizing your infrastructure, you can ensure that your environment can handle the increased demands of AI processing. This step is crucial for maintaining a smooth and responsive system that delivers real-time insights and automation.

Data accuracy is paramount for AI models to function correctly. Preparing your data by cleansing and formatting it appropriately ensures that the insights generated by Einstein Copilot are reliable and actionable. Using a sandbox environment for testing allows you to identify and resolve data-related issues without impacting your live operations, ensuring a smooth transition to the new system.

User adoption is often a significant hurdle when implementing innovative technology. Resistance to change can be mitigated through comprehensive training and education programs that equip users with the knowledge and confidence to use Einstein Copilot effectively. These programs not only facilitate a smoother transition but also enhance overall productivity by ensuring that users can leverage the full capabilities of the tool.

Value provided

The value of a well-prepared Salesforce environment for integrating Einstein Copilot cannot be overstated:

- **Seamless integration**: Proper preparation leads to a smooth and efficient integration of Einstein Copilot
- **Improved performance**: Optimized system performance results in faster data processing and more reliable AI insights

- **Accurate data**: Clean and well-structured data enhances the effectiveness of AI algorithms
- **Higher adoption rates**: Educated users are more likely to embrace and utilize new features effectively

Seamless integration ensures that your AI tools function correctly from day one, minimizing disruptions and maximizing the return on investment. Optimized system performance translates to faster data processing and more accurate AI-driven insights, which are critical for making informed business decisions.

Accurate and well-structured data is the backbone of effective AI. By ensuring your data is clean and correctly formatted, you enhance the reliability of the insights generated by Einstein Copilot. This accuracy allows your organization to trust and act on the recommendations provided by the AI, driving better outcomes across various business processes.

Higher adoption rates are a direct result of thorough training and preparation. When users are educated and confident in using new tools, they are more likely to fully utilize the features and capabilities of Einstein Copilot. This increased adoption leads to greater overall productivity and more significant benefits from your AI investment.

Licensing and user permissions for Einstein Copilot

Securing the appropriate licenses and configuring user permissions are crucial steps in setting up Einstein Copilot. This section will guide you through obtaining the necessary licenses and managing permissions to ensure seamless functionality and access control.

Licensing and user permissions are foundational aspects of integrating Einstein Copilot into your Salesforce environment. Without the proper licenses, you cannot access the full range of features offered by Einstein Copilot. Additionally, correctly configured user permissions ensure that the right individuals have the appropriate access to these powerful tools, maintaining security and operational efficiency.

The process of obtaining licenses involves identifying the specific needs of your organization and purchasing the appropriate licensing package from Salesforce. This step requires careful consideration of your current and future requirements to ensure that you select the most cost-effective and comprehensive option. Working closely with your Salesforce account executive can provide valuable insights and potential discounts, optimizing your investment.

Configuring user permissions is equally important. Custom permission sets tailored to distinct roles within your organization provide flexibility and control over who can access specific features. This granular control helps maintain data security while ensuring that users have the necessary permissions to perform their tasks efficiently. Establishing clear role hierarchies further organizes data access and sharing rules, reflecting your organizational structure and enhancing operational efficiency.

Key goals and outcomes

In this section, you will learn about the following aspects:

- How to identify and obtain the appropriate licenses for Einstein Copilot
- The steps to configure user permissions to ensure proper access and functionality

Understanding the licensing requirements for Einstein Copilot is critical for ensuring that you have access to all the features necessary for your business operations. This knowledge allows you to make informed decisions about which licenses to purchase and how to allocate them within your organization. By securing the correct licenses, you avoid potential disruptions and ensure that your team can fully leverage the capabilities of Einstein Copilot.

Configuring user permissions is a multi-step process that involves creating custom permission sets, assigning them to users, and defining role hierarchies. These steps ensure that users have the appropriate access based on their roles and responsibilities, maintaining both security and functionality. By mastering these configurations, you can create a secure and efficient operational environment that supports your AI-driven initiatives.

Obtaining the appropriate licenses

- **Identify license requirements**:

  - Determine the specific Einstein Copilot features your organization needs and identify the corresponding licenses
  - Review Salesforce's official documentation and licensing guides to understand the different licensing tiers and their features

  Example: Identifying the right licenses ensures that your organization has access to all necessary Einstein Copilot functionalities.

- **Purchase licenses**:

  - Contact your Salesforce account executive to discuss and purchase the required licenses
  - Evaluate any available discounts or bundled packages that may benefit your organization

  Example: Securing the right licenses at a favorable cost can optimize your budget and resource allocation.

- **Assign licenses**:

  - Once purchased, assign the licenses to the appropriate users through Salesforce **Setup**. To do so, go to **Setup | Company Settings | Licenses to manage and assign licenses**.

  Example: Proper license assignment ensures that all the necessary users have access to Einstein Copilot features.

Configuring user permissions

- **Create permission sets**:

  - Create custom permission sets tailored to the needs of different user roles who will interact with Einstein Copilot

  - **Navigation**: Go to **Setup | Permission Sets** and click **New** to create a new permission set

  Example: Custom permission sets provide flexibility and control over feature access.

- **Assign permissions**:

  - Assign the created permission sets to users or profiles based on their roles and responsibilities

  - **Navigation**: Go to **Setup | Users | Permission Set Assignments** to assign the necessary permissions

  Example: Assigning permissions correctly ensures users have the appropriate level of access needed for their tasks.

- **Define role hierarchies**:

  - Establish a clear role hierarchy to ensure proper data access and sharing rules are in place

  - **Navigation**: Go to **Setup | Role Hierarchies** and configure the roles to reflect your organizational structure

  Example: A well-defined role hierarchy ensures secure and organized data access.

Managing access control

- **Field-level security**:

  - Implement field-level security to control access to sensitive data fields.

  - **Navigation**: Go to **Setup | Object Manager** > [select `Object`] | **Fields & Relationships** | [select `Field`] | set `Field-Level Security`

  Example: Field-level security helps protect sensitive information by restricting access based on user roles.

- **Record-level security**:

  - Utilize sharing rules and manual sharing to manage record-level access

  - **Navigation**: Go to **Setup | Sharing Settings** and configure sharing rules as needed

  Example: Record-level security ensures that users can only access records relevant to their role.

- **Monitor user access**:

  - Regularly review user access and permissions to ensure they align with current organizational needs and security policies

  - **Tools**: Use Salesforce's security health check and audit trail features to monitor and review access permissions

  Example: Regular monitoring helps maintain security and compliance with organizational policies.

Challenges solved and value provided

Challenges solved

Here are the key benefits of taking time to ensure security is well established:

- **Access management**: Effectively managed licenses and permissions ensure users have the necessary access without compromising security

- **Compliance**: Ensuring compliance with organizational policies and regulatory requirements through structured permissions and regular reviews

- **Role-based access**: Implementing role hierarchies and field-level security to control data access efficiently

Effective access management is essential for maintaining the security and integrity of your Salesforce environment. By responsibly managing licenses and permissions, you ensure that users have access to the tools they need while protecting sensitive data from unauthorized access. This balance between accessibility and security is crucial for efficient and secure operations.

Compliance with organizational policies and regulatory requirements is a significant challenge for many businesses. By structuring permissions and conducting regular reviews, you can ensure that your data practices align with legal and organizational standards. This proactive approach helps prevent compliance issues and builds trust with customers and stakeholders.

Role-based access control allows you to efficiently manage data access based on user roles. Implementing clear role hierarchies and field-level security ensures that users can only access the information necessary for their tasks, reducing the risk of data breaches and enhancing operational efficiency.

Value provided

The effort of going through an effective security setup in your organization brings about the following benefits:

- **Enhanced security**: Protect sensitive data with well-defined permissions and regular monitoring

- **Operational efficiency**: Streamlined licensing and permissions processes reduce administrative overhead

- **Regulatory compliance**: Maintain compliance with industry regulations through robust access control measures

Enhanced security is one of the primary benefits of properly configured licenses and user permissions. By defining clear access controls and monitoring user activity, you can protect sensitive data from unauthorized access and potential breaches. This security not only protects your organization but also builds trust with customers and partners.

Operational efficiency is another significant benefit. Streamlined processes for managing licenses and permissions reduce the administrative burden on IT and operations teams, allowing them to focus on more strategic tasks. This efficiency translates to cost savings and better resource allocation, enhancing overall productivity.

Maintaining regulatory compliance is essential in today's business environment. Robust access control measures ensure that your data practices align with industry regulations, avoiding legal penalties and reputational damage. By staying compliant, you protect your organization and build a solid foundation for sustainable growth.

Enabling Einstein's features and configurations

Enabling and configuring Einstein's features within Salesforce is a critical step in leveraging the full potential of Einstein Copilot. This section provides a detailed guide on the initial setup, activation, and configuration of key functionalities.

The power of Einstein Copilot lies in its advanced AI capabilities, which can significantly enhance your CRM processes. However, to unlock these capabilities, you need to enable and configure the relevant Einstein features within your Salesforce environment. This process involves a series of steps that ensure the features are activated correctly and tailored to meet your organization's specific needs.

The Einstein Setup Assistant is an invaluable tool that guides you through enabling various Einstein features. This assistant simplifies the setup process, providing a step-by-step walkthrough that helps you activate key components such as Einstein Activity Capture, Lead Scoring, and Opportunity Insights. Each of these features offers unique benefits that can transform how you manage customer interactions and sales processes.

Configuring these features involves customizing user settings, dashboards, and AI models so that they align with your business objectives. Personalizing these configurations ensures that the insights and automation provided by Einstein Copilot are relevant and actionable for your team. Initial testing in a sandbox environment allows you to identify and resolve any issues before you deploy the features to your live environment, ensuring a smooth transition.

Key goals and outcomes

In this section, you will learn about the following:

- The step-by-step process to enable and configure Einstein features within Salesforce

How to customize these features to meet your organization's specific needs

Mastering the step-by-step process to enable and configure Einstein's features is crucial for maximizing the value of Einstein Copilot. This knowledge allows you to activate the relevant features efficiently and ensures that they are set up correctly from the start. By following these steps, you can avoid common pitfalls and ensure a seamless integration process.

Customizing Einstein's features to meet your organization's specific needs is essential for deriving maximum value from the tool. This customization includes adjusting user settings, creating tailored dashboards, and configuring AI models so that they align with your business goals. By personalizing these configurations, you can ensure that the insights and automation provided by Einstein Copilot are highly relevant and actionable for your team.

Accessing the Einstein Setup Assistant

Follow these steps:

- **Navigate to the Einstein Setup Assistant**:

    I.   Navigate to **Setup in Salesforce**.

    II.   Enter `Einstein` in the **Quick Find** box and select **Einstein Setup Assistant**.

    III. Toggle the `Off/On` button and then follow the guided setup prompts to enable individual Einstein features.

    Example: The assistant will provide a step-by-step walkthrough for activating the necessary components, such as Einstein Activity Capture and Einstein Lead Scoring:

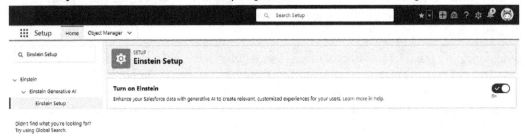

Figure 2.1 -Einstein Setup in your organization

Enabling key Einstein features

At the time of writing, there are 20+ different Einstein features between Service (Einstein Case Classification, Einstein Reply Recommendations) and Sales (Activity Capture, Lead Scoring) and more if your company uses Commerce Cloud, Marketing Cloud, and other tools, such as Slack. The primary focus of this book is to address Einstein Copilot and the use of tools such as Copilot, Prompt Builder, Copilot Actions, Data Cloud, and Model Builder while providing you with real use cases. We'll walk through a couple of the wizards for implementing these "out of the box" Einstein components, but you should refer to Salesforce Help and tutorials in the wizards for the latest up-to-date information about each of them.

> **Note**
> While you'll have the opportunity to learn about them on Trailhead, gaining access to the feature in your organization may require additional licensing from Salesforce.

Readiness assessors

Searching for `Einstein Accessor` in the **Setup** menu provides you access to Salesforce's automated organization readiness report, specific to the data in your organization. You need to look at this in production as data volumes, accuracy, and completeness impact the effectiveness of the results for your organization:

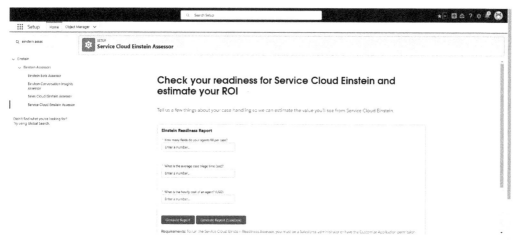

Figure 2.2 – The Service Cloud Einstein Assessor screen. Others will vary

Service Cloud

- ### Einstein Classification

  Purpose: Automate the categorization of incoming cases using AI to streamline case management and ensure that cases are routed to the appropriate teams based on content and context

  Follow these steps to set it up:

  I.   Navigate to **Setup | Einstein Classification**.

  II.   Turn on **Apps**.

  III. Toggle **Get Started with Case Classification**.

  IV.   Enable the feature and follow the setup wizard.

  V.   Customize classification settings, including field mappings and criteria.

  VI.   Allow time for the AI to analyze past cases and train the model (this may take several hours).

  VII. Monitor and adjust classification thresholds as necessary.

  Example: Automatically classifying and routing cases ensures that customer issues are handled efficiently, reducing response times and improving customer satisfaction:

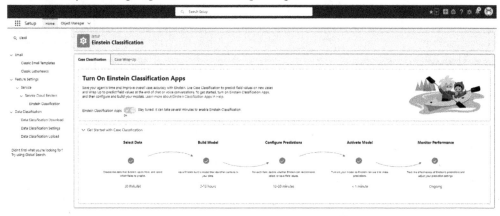

Figure 2.3 – Setting up Screen Flow to enable Einstein Classification

- ### Einstein Reply Recommendations

  Purpose: Use AI to suggest the most appropriate replies to cases or customer inquiries, enabling faster and more consistent communication.

  Follow these steps to set it up:

  I.   Navigate to **Setup | Einstein Reply Recommendations**.

  II.   Enable the feature and follow the configuration process.

III.   Set up **Grounding**.

IV.   Customize the reply templates and configure the AI to learn from historical responses.

V.   Set up the system to display reply recommendations directly in the case feed.

VI.   Review and adjust the AI's learning criteria as needed.

Example: AI-driven reply suggestions help support agents respond to customer inquiries quickly and consistently, improving response times and maintaining high-quality communication:

Figure 2.4 – Einstein Reply Recommendations

Sales Cloud

- **Einstein Activity Capture**

  Purpose: Automatically capture email and event data from your users' Microsoft or Google accounts and relate them to Salesforce records.

- Follow these steps to set it up:

  I.   Navigate to **Setup | Einstein Activity Capture**.

  II.   Click **Settings**, then **Get Started**, and follow the prompts to connect your email accounts:

  You will have different options for User Level or Workspace Marketplace, depending on whether you pick Google, Microsoft Office 365, or Microsoft Exchange

  III.   Configure data sharing settings and select users who will have their activities captured:

  ▪ In our example, consider connecting your private Google account. There are six steps in the wizard:

  I.   Name your connection.

  II.   Review **Sync Settings**.

  III.   **Advanced Settings** (filter date, private events, deleted items, and related items to Salesforce records).

  IV.   Add **Users & Profiles**.

V.   **Excluded Addresses** – pay close attention to the options for customers and internal users.

VI.   **Set Default Activity Sharing** – either **Share** or **Share with Everyone**.

Example: Automatically capturing and logging activities helps maintain accurate and up-to-date customer interaction records:

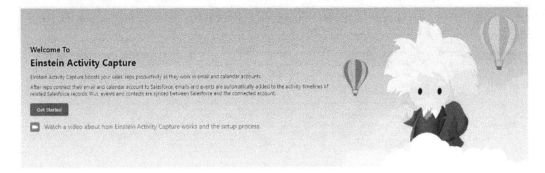

Figure 2.5 – Einstein Activity Capture

The following figure shows the screen for finishing the setup process:

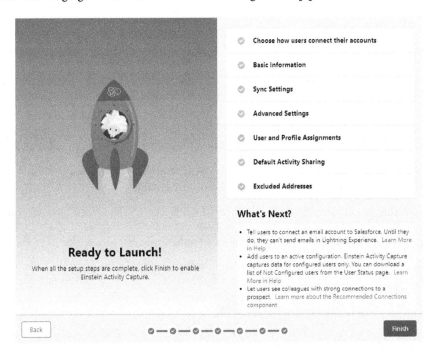

Figure 2.6 – Finishing the setup process for Einstein Activity Capture

- **Einstein Lead Scoring**

Purpose: Use AI to score leads based on their likelihood to convert.

Follow these steps to set it up:

I.   Navigate to **Setup | Einstein Lead Scoring**.

II. Click **Get Started** and enable the feature:

- Your path forward with **Default** or **Custom** can vary greatly based on decisions made in the wizard and the quality of your data

- It could take up to 48 hours (about 2 days) to analyze your leads

- Salesforce has limits around the number of segments the organization has for free; additional costs apply

- Lead scores can be shown on page layouts, list views, and CRM analytics

- Customize scoring settings and review the data model used for lead scoring

Example: AI-driven lead scoring helps prioritize high-value leads, increasing sales efficiency:

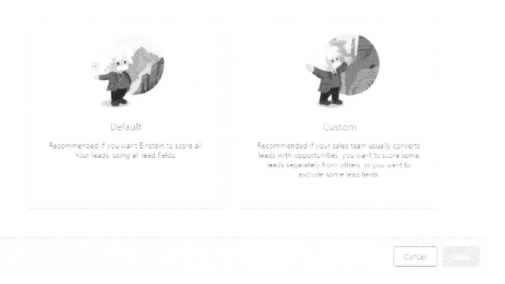

Figure 2.7 – The Einstein Lead Scoring starting screen when the feature is turned on

The Einstein lead scoring is enabled here as shown:

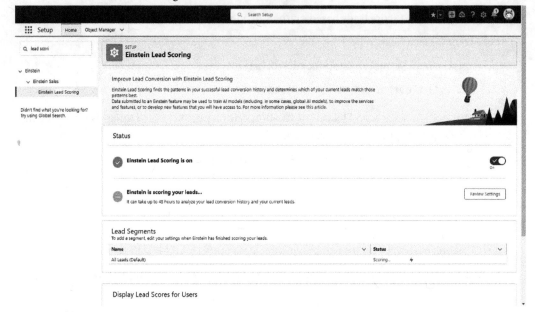

Figure 2.8 – Einstein Lead Scoring enabled

- **Einstein Opportunity Scoring**

   Purpose: Provide AI-driven insights on opportunities to help sales reps prioritize and close deals.

   Follow these steps to set it up:

   I.   Navigate to **Setup | Einstein Opportunity Scoring**.

   II.   Review **Notice of Data Usage**.

   III.   Click **Set Up**. There are differing steps based on what you select regarding the main questions within the wizard:

   - All opportunities or based on a set of conditions

   - All fields or exclude certain fields

   - Include Activity Capture

   IV.   Enable the feature and customize insight settings based on your sales process.

   V.   It could take up to 48 hours (about 2 days) to see results.

Example: Opportunity insights help sales teams focus on the most promising deals and strategies:

Figure 2.9 – Start screen for Einstein Opportunity Scoring

The Einstein opportunity scoring is enabled as shown:

Figure 2.10 – Einstein Opportunity Scoring enabled

Configuring access to Einstein features

The biggest aspect to keep apprised of in this section is that most features require specific permission and/or permission sets, as well as access to fields. Let's take a closer look:

- **User settings configuration**:

    I.   Customize user settings to tailor Einstein's features to distinct roles and preferences.

II.   **Navigation**: Go to **Setup | Users** and select the user you wish to configure settings for.

III.   Adjust notification preferences, data visibility, and other user-specific settings.

Example: Personalizing settings ensures that each user gets the most relevant and useful insights from Einstein's features.

- **Customize dashboards and reports**:

    I.   Create and customize dashboards and reports to display insights from Einstein features.

    II.   **Navigation**: Go to **Reports** or **Dashboards in Salesforce** and use the report builder to add Einstein insights components.

    Example: Customized dashboards provide actionable insights tailored to specific user roles, enhancing decision-making.

Initial feature testing

- **Test in a sandbox environment**: Conduct initial testing of Einstein's features in a sandbox environment to identify and resolve any issues before deploying to production.

    Follow these steps:

    I.   Create a new sandbox or refresh an existing one.

    II.   Test Einstein's features in the sandbox environment.

    Example: Testing in a sandbox environment helps ensure that the new features work as expected without affecting the live environment.

- **User feedback and adjustments**:

    I.   Collect feedback from users during the testing phase to identify areas for improvement.

    II.   Make necessary adjustments to settings and configurations based on user feedback.

    Example: Adjusting configurations based on user feedback helps optimize the user experience and effectiveness of Einstein's features.

Challenges solved and value provided

Here, we outline the major challenges faced and the solutions that were implemented.

Challenges Solved

- **Feature activation**: Step-by-step guidance ensures that all the necessary Einstein features are enabled and configured correctly

- **Customization needs**: Configure features and dashboards to meet specific organizational needs

- **Testing and feedback**: Initial testing and user feedback help identify and resolve issues before full deployment

Activating and configuring Einstein's features can be a complex process, but step-by-step guidance simplifies it significantly. This structured approach ensures that all the necessary components are enabled and configured correctly, minimizing the risk of errors, and ensuring a smooth setup.

Customization is a critical aspect of maximizing the benefits of Einstein Copilot. By configuring features and dashboards so that they align with your organization's specific needs, you can ensure that the insights and automation provided are relevant and actionable. This customization enhances the overall effectiveness of the tool and drives better business outcomes.

Initial testing and user feedback are invaluable for identifying and resolving issues before full deployment. Testing in a sandbox environment allows you to catch potential problems early and make necessary adjustments without them impacting your live environment. Gathering feedback from users during this phase helps you refine the configurations to better meet their needs, ensuring a successful rollout.

Value provided

- **Optimized operations**: Properly configured Einstein features enhance operational efficiency and decision-making

- **Personalized insights**: Custom dashboards and user settings provide relevant and actionable insights

- **Improved performance**: Testing and feedback ensure that features work optimally in the live environment

Optimized operations are a direct result of properly configured Einstein features. By setting up the tool correctly, you can enhance operational efficiency, streamline workflows, and improve decision-making processes. This optimization leads to better overall performance and more effective CRM strategies.

Personalized insights are one of the most significant benefits of customizing Einstein's features. Tailored dashboards and user settings ensure that the information provided is relevant to each user's role and responsibilities. This relevance enhances the value of the insights, making them more actionable and impactful.

Improved performance can be achieved through thorough testing and feedback. By identifying and resolving issues before deployment, you ensure that Einstein's features work optimally in your live environment. This approach minimizes disruptions and ensures that your team can fully leverage the capabilities of Einstein Copilot from day one.

Data security and compliance with Einstein Copilot

Ensuring data security and compliance is paramount when integrating Einstein Copilot. This section will cover best practices for safeguarding data and maintaining compliance with relevant regulations.

Data security and compliance are critical considerations when integrating any modern technology, and Einstein Copilot is no exception. Given the sensitive nature of the data that's managed within

Salesforce, it is essential to implement robust security measures and adhere to regulatory requirements to protect your organization and its customers.

Salesforce Shield is a powerful tool that provides enhanced security features, including encryption, monitoring, and auditing capabilities. By implementing Salesforce Shield, you can safeguard sensitive data, monitor user activity, and maintain detailed audit trails that help detect and prevent unauthorized access. These features are crucial for maintaining the integrity and confidentiality of your data.

Setting up data access controls, such as field-level and record-level security, ensures that sensitive information is only accessible to authorized users. This granular control helps prevent data breaches and ensures that users can only access the data necessary for their roles. Regular monitoring and auditing further enhance security by providing insights into user activity and enabling early detection of potential security issues.

Compliance with industry regulations, such as GDPR, CCPA, and HIPAA, is a legal requirement for many organizations. Understanding these regulations and implementing the necessary compliance controls within Salesforce ensures that your data practices align with legal standards. Regular compliance reviews help you maintain adherence to these regulations and adapt to any changes in the legal landscape.

Key goals and outcomes

In this section, you will learn about the following:

- Best practices for ensuring data security when using Einstein Copilot
- How to comply with industry regulations and Salesforce's security model

Ensuring data security when using Einstein Copilot involves implementing a combination of tools and best practices designed to protect sensitive information. By mastering these security measures, you can safeguard your data and maintain the trust of your customers and stakeholders. Understanding how to leverage tools such as Salesforce Shield, set up data access controls, and monitor user activity is essential for maintaining a secure environment.

Compliance with industry regulations is a complex but necessary aspect of data management. Learning how to implement compliance controls within Salesforce ensures that your data practices align with legal requirements, helping you avoid legal penalties and maintain customer trust. Regular compliance reviews and audits are critical for adapting to changes in regulations and maintaining ongoing compliance.

Ensuring data security

- **Implement Salesforce Shield**:

  Purpose: Salesforce Shield provides encryption, monitoring, and auditing tools to enhance data security.

Follow these steps:

I.   Navigate to **Setup | Salesforce Shield**.

II.   Enable **Platform Encryption**, **Event Monitoring**, and **Field Audit Trail**.

Example: Encrypting sensitive data helps protect it from unauthorized access.

- **Set up data access controls**:

  - **Field-level security**: Implement field-level security to control access to sensitive data fields:

    - Navigation: Go to **Setup | Object Manager** > [select **Object**] | **Fields & Relationships** | [select **Field**] > set **Field-Level Security**.

  - **Record-level security**: Use sharing rules and manual sharing to manage record-level access.

    - **Navigation**: Go to **Setup | Sharing Settings** and configure sharing rules as needed.

  Example: Field-level and record-level security ensure that sensitive data is only accessible to authorized users.

- **Monitoring and auditing**:

  Purpose: Regularly monitor and audit data access to detect and prevent unauthorized activities.

  Follow these steps:

  I.   Enable **Event Monitoring** and set up alerts for unusual activities.

  II.   Regularly review audit logs and access reports.

  Example: Monitoring and auditing help detect potential security breaches early.

Compliance with regulations

- **Understand regulatory requirements**: Familiarize yourself with relevant regulations, such as GDPR, CCPA, and HIPAA.

  Example: Understanding these regulations helps ensure that your data practices comply with legal requirements.

- **Implement compliance controls**

  Purpose: Set up controls within Salesforce to comply with regulatory requirements.

  Setup steps:

  I.   Use Salesforce's compliance tools to manage data privacy and protection.

  II.   Set up data retention policies and consent management.

  Example: Implementing compliance controls helps you avoid legal penalties and ensures customer trust.

- **Regular compliance reviews**

  Purpose: Conduct regular reviews to ensure ongoing compliance with regulations.

  Setup steps:

  I.   Schedule periodic audits and reviews of data security practices.

  II.   Update policies and controls as regulations change.

  Example: Regular compliance reviews help maintain adherence to legal standards and adapt to new requirements.

Challenges solved and value provided

Challenges solved

- **Data security**: Implementing encryption and access controls prevents unauthorized access to sensitive data

- **Regulatory compliance**: Setting up compliance controls and conducting regular reviews ensures adherence to legal requirements

- **Early detection**: Monitoring and auditing help detect security breaches early and mitigate potential damage

Data security challenges are prevalent in today's digital landscape. Implementing encryption and access controls is essential for preventing unauthorized access to sensitive information. These measures protect your organization from data breaches and ensure the confidentiality and integrity of your data.

Regulatory compliance is a significant challenge for many organizations. By setting up compliance controls within Salesforce and conducting regular reviews, you can ensure that your data practices align with legal requirements. This proactive approach helps you avoid legal penalties and build trust with customers and stakeholders.

Early detection of security breaches is critical for mitigating potential damage. Regularly monitoring and auditing user activity provides insights into suspicious behavior, enabling you to respond quickly and prevent further issues. These practices enhance your overall security posture and ensure that your data remains protected.

Value provided

- **Enhanced security**: Protecting sensitive data builds customer trust and prevents security breaches

- **Legal compliance**: Complying with regulations avoids legal penalties and ensures ethical data practices

- **Operational efficiency**: Regular reviews and audits maintain a high standard of data security and compliance

Enhanced security is one of the primary benefits of implementing robust data protection measures. Protecting sensitive data from unauthorized access builds customer trust and enhances your organization's reputation. This security is crucial for maintaining long-term relationships with customers and partners.

Legal compliance is essential for avoiding penalties and ensuring ethical data practices. By adhering to industry regulations, you protect your organization from legal repercussions and demonstrate a commitment to data privacy and protection. This compliance builds trust with customers and stakeholders, enhancing your overall credibility.

Operational efficiency is achieved through regular reviews and audits. These practices help maintain a high standard of data security and compliance, ensuring that your data management processes are effective and reliable. By continuously monitoring and improving your security measures, you can enhance overall efficiency and protect your organization from potential threats.

Initial customization of Einstein Copilot

Customizing Einstein Copilot to fit your organization's specific needs is essential for maximizing its effectiveness. This section covers the initial customization options and configuration settings to optimize the user experience.

Einstein Copilot offers a range of customization options that allow you to tailor its features to your organization's unique requirements. Customization is crucial for ensuring that the AI-driven insights and automation provided by Einstein Copilot are relevant and actionable for your team. By aligning the tool with your business processes, you can maximize its value and drive better outcomes.

Setting up custom fields allows you to capture data specific to your organization's needs. This customization ensures that the information that's collected is relevant and useful for your business operations. Creating custom reports and dashboards provides users with tailored insights that enhance decision-making and streamline workflows. These customizations make it easier for users to access the information they need and act on it effectively.

Personalizing user settings is another critical aspect of customization. By tailoring notification preferences, data visibility, and other user-specific settings, you can ensure that each user receives the most relevant and useful insights. This personalization enhances user satisfaction and encourages greater adoption of the tool.

Configuring AI models so that they align with your organization's data and objectives ensures that the predictions and recommendations provided by Einstein Copilot are accurate and actionable. By adjusting model parameters and training data, you can improve the performance of the AI models and ensure that they meet your specific needs.

Key goals and outcomes

In this section, you will learn about the following:

- How to customize Einstein Copilot so that it aligns with your organizational needs
- Initial configuration settings to enhance the user experience

Customizing Einstein Copilot so that it aligns with your organization's needs is essential for maximizing its effectiveness. This section will teach you how to set up custom fields, create tailored reports and dashboards, personalize user settings, and configure AI models. By mastering these customization techniques, you can ensure that the tool provides relevant and actionable insights that drive better business outcomes.

Initial configuration goals and outcomes settings are critical for enhancing the user experience. Understanding how to personalize settings and tailor features to specific user roles ensures that each user receives the most relevant information and can leverage the tool effectively. This personalization boosts user satisfaction and encourages greater adoption of the tool.

> **Note**
>
> In later chapters, we will go through detailed steps regarding the interface and call out key aspects of using Copilot, Prompt Builder, Model Builder, and Copilot Actions. In those sections, you'll see accompanying screenshots to help you learn more about the tool.

Customizing Einstein Copilot

- **Set up custom fields**

  Purpose: Add custom fields to capture data specific to your organization's needs.

  Setup steps:

  I.   Navigate to **Setup | Object Manager**.

  II.   Select the object you want to customize (for example, **Lead**, **Opportunity**, and so on).

  III. Click **Fields & Relationships | New** to create a custom field.

  Example: Adding a custom field to track product interest on the **Lead** object helps tailor marketing efforts.

- **Create custom reports and dashboards**

  Purpose: Provide users with insights tailored to their roles.

  Setup steps:

  I.   Navigate to **Reports** or **Dashboards** in Salesforce.

II.   Click **New Report** or **New Dashboard** and select the appropriate report type or dashboard components.

III.   Customize filters, groupings, and charts to display relevant data.

Example: A custom dashboard for the sales team showing pipeline stages and conversion rates helps prioritize efforts.

- **Personalize user settings**

    Purpose: To tailor Einstein Copilot features to individual user preferences.

    Setup steps:

    I.   Navigate to **Setup | Users** and select the user who you wish to configure settings for.

    II.   Adjust notification preferences, data visibility, and other user-specific settings.

    Example: Personalizing notification settings ensures users receive relevant alerts without being overwhelmed.

- **Configure AI models**

    Purpose: Customize AI models so that they better align with your organization's data and objectives.

    Setup steps:

    I.   Navigate to **Einstein Settings** in Salesforce.

    II.   Select the AI model you want to configure (for example, **Lead Scoring** or **Opportunity Insights**).

    III.   Adjust the model parameters and training data to improve accuracy.

    Example: Customizing the lead scoring model to prioritize leads from specific industries improves sales targeting.

Enhancing the user experience

- **Implement user training programs**

    Purpose: Ensure users understand how to utilize the customized features effectively.

    Setup steps:

    I.   Develop training materials such as guides, tutorials, and FAQs.

    II.   Conduct workshops, webinars, and hands-on training sessions.

    Example: Training sessions on using custom dashboards help users leverage data insights for decision-making.

- **Gather user feedback**

    Purpose: Continuously improve customization based on user feedback.

Setup steps:

I.   Implement feedback mechanisms such as surveys and suggestion boxes.

II.   Regularly review and analyze user feedback to identify areas for improvement.

Example: Adjusting custom fields and reports based on user feedback ensures the system remains relevant and useful.

- **Monitor and adjust customizations**

   Purpose: Ensure customizations continue to meet organizational needs.

   Setup steps:

   I.   Regularly review customization settings and adjust as needed.

   II.   Monitor system performance and user adoption rates to identify issues.

   Example: Adjusting AI model parameters based on performance metrics improves accuracy over time.

Challenges solved and value provided

Challenges solved

- **Relevance**: Customizing fields, reports, and AI models ensures that the system aligns with organizational needs

- **User adoption**: Personalizing settings and providing training programs enhance user adoption and effectiveness

- **Continuous improvement**: Gathering feedback and monitoring customizations ensure the system evolves with organizational needs

Relevance is a significant challenge when implementing innovative technology. By customizing fields, reports, and AI models, you can ensure that Einstein Copilot aligns with your organization's specific needs. This relevance enhances the value of the tool and ensures that the insights provided are actionable and impactful.

User adoption is often a hurdle when introducing new tools. Personalizing settings and providing comprehensive training programs help users understand and effectively utilize the new features. This approach increases user satisfaction and ensures that the tool is fully leveraged to drive better business outcomes.

Continuous improvement is essential for maintaining the effectiveness of Einstein Copilot. By gathering user feedback and monitoring customizations, you can ensure that the system evolves with your organization's changing needs. This iterative approach ensures that the tool remains relevant and valuable over time.

Value provided

- **Tailored insights**: Custom fields and reports provide relevant insights, enhancing decision-making
- **Higher adoption rates**: Personalizing settings and training programs ensure users utilize the system effectively
- **Enhanced performance**: Continuous adjustments and monitoring improve system accuracy and relevance

Tailored insights are one of the most significant benefits of customizing Einstein Copilot. Custom fields and reports provide relevant information that enhances decision-making and drives better business outcomes. This customization ensures that the tool meets your specific needs and delivers maximum value.

Higher adoption rates can be achieved through personalization and training. By tailoring settings to individual user preferences and providing comprehensive training programs, you can ensure that users utilize the system effectively. This increased adoption enhances overall productivity and maximizes the benefits of the tool.

Enhanced performance is a result of continuous adjustments and monitoring. By regularly reviewing and refining customizations, you can improve the accuracy and relevance of the AI models and insights provided by Einstein Copilot. This iterative approach ensures that the tool remains valuable and effective over time.

Troubleshooting common setup issues

While setting up Einstein Copilot, you may encounter various issues that can hinder its integration and functionality. This section covers common problems and provides solutions to help you troubleshoot effectively.

Setting up Einstein Copilot can be a complex process, and it's common to encounter issues along the way. Troubleshooting these issues effectively is crucial for ensuring smooth integration and maximizing the benefits of the tool. This section provides a comprehensive guide to identifying and resolving common setup problems, ensuring that you can quickly overcome any obstacles and maintain optimal functionality.

Common setup issues include problems with feature activation, data syncing, AI predictions, performance degradation, and user access. Each of these issues can impact the effectiveness of Einstein Copilot and hinder your ability to leverage its full potential. By understanding these common problems and knowing how to address them, you can ensure a smoother setup process and avoid disruptions to your operations.

Effective troubleshooting involves a combination of best practices, regular monitoring, and user training. By utilizing available resources, conducting regular maintenance, and gathering user feedback, you can identify and resolve issues quickly and efficiently. This proactive approach minimizes downtime and ensures that your team can fully leverage the capabilities of Einstein Copilot.

Key goals and outcomes

In this section, you will learn about the following aspects:

- Common setup issues encountered during Einstein Copilot integration
- Solutions and best practices for troubleshooting these issues

Understanding the common setup issues that are encountered during Einstein Copilot integration is essential for effective troubleshooting. By familiarizing yourself with these issues, you can quickly identify potential problems and implement solutions to resolve them. This knowledge ensures that you can maintain optimal functionality and avoid disruptions to your operations.

Solutions and best practices for troubleshooting these issues involve a combination of proactive monitoring, regular maintenance, and user training. By implementing these best practices, you can prevent issues before they occur and ensure a smoother setup process. Regular monitoring and maintenance help maintain system performance, while user training ensures that your team can utilize the new features effectively.

Common setup issues and solutions

1. **Issue**: Einstein features not appearing in **Setup**.

- **Description**: After enabling Einstein features, they do not appear in the **Setup** menu.
- **Solution**:
    - Verify that the necessary licenses are assigned to your Salesforce organization
    - Ensure that your Salesforce instance has been updated to the latest version
    - Clear your browser cache and refresh the Salesforce **Setup** page

    Example: If Einstein Lead Scoring is not appearing, check that the Lead Scoring license has been assigned and your instance is compatible.

2. **Issue**: Data not syncing with Einstein Activity Capture.

- **Description**: Emails and events are not being captured and logged in Salesforce.
- **Solution**:
    - Verify that the email accounts are correctly connected, and permissions are granted
    - Check that the data sharing settings have been configured correctly
    - Ensure there are no security systems or security settings blocking data sync

    Example: If Google Workspace emails are not synchronizing, reauthorize the Google account and check for any connectivity issues.

3. **Issue**: Inaccurate AI Predictions

    Description: AI models are providing inaccurate predictions or insights.

    - **Solution**:

        - Review the training data used for the AI models and ensure it is clean and relevant

        - Adjust the model parameters and retrain the model with updated data

        - Conduct a thorough analysis of the model's performance metrics and make necessary adjustments

    Example: If Lead Scoring predictions are inaccurate, refine the training data so that it includes more relevant lead characteristics.

4. **Issue**: Performance degradation.

    Description: Salesforce instance performance is slow after enabling Einstein features.

    - **Solution**:

        - Optimize your Salesforce instance by conducting regular maintenance and database indexing

        - Allocate sufficient resources and ensure your hardware meets the requirements

        - Monitor system performance and adjust configurations as needed

    Example: If overall system performance is affected, review resource allocation and optimize database performance.

5. **Issue**: User access problems.

    Description: Users are unable to access Einstein features despite having the necessary permissions.

    - **Solution**:

        - Verify that the correct permission sets and roles have been assigned to the users

        - Check for any conflicting permissions or restrictions

        - Ensure users have the necessary licenses assigned

    Example: If a user cannot access Einstein Opportunity Insights, verify that the correct permission set has been assigned and there are no conflicting restrictions.

Best practices for troubleshooting

- **Documentation and support**

    Purpose: Utilize available resources and documentation to aid in troubleshooting.

    Follow these steps:

    I.   Refer to Salesforce's official documentation and knowledge base for guidance.

    II.   Reach out to Salesforce support for assistance with complex issues.

Example: Use Salesforce Trailhead modules and support articles to resolve specific setup problems.

- **Regular monitoring and maintenance**

  Purpose: Proactively monitor system performance and conduct regular maintenance to prevent issues.

  Follow these steps:

      I.   Implement monitoring tools to track system performance and detect issues early.

      II.   Schedule regular maintenance and updates to keep your Salesforce instance optimized.

  Example: Use Salesforce Health Check to monitor and maintain system security and performance.

- **User training and feedback**

  Purpose: Ensure users are well-trained and can provide valuable feedback on issues encountered.

  Steps:

      I.   Conduct training sessions and provide resources to help users understand and utilize Einstein features.

      II.   Implement feedback mechanisms to gather user input on any issues or improvements needed.

  Example: Regular training and feedback sessions help identify and resolve user-specific issues quickly.

Challenges solved and value provided

Challenges solved

- **Setup issues:** Providing solutions to common setup issues ensures a smoother integration process
- **Performance problems:** Regular monitoring and maintenance prevent performance degradation and ensure system reliability
- **User adoption:** Training and feedback mechanisms address user-specific issues and improve adoption rates

Setup issues are common when integrating modern technology. By providing solutions to these common problems, you can ensure a smoother integration process and minimize disruptions. This proactive approach helps you maintain optimal functionality and maximize the benefits of Einstein Copilot.

Performance problems can significantly impact the effectiveness of AI-driven tools. Regular monitoring and maintenance prevent performance degradation and ensure system reliability. By identifying and addressing performance issues early, you can maintain a high standard of system performance and ensure that your team can fully leverage the capabilities of Einstein Copilot.

User adoption is often a challenge when introducing new tools. Training and feedback mechanisms address user-specific issues and improve adoption rates. By providing comprehensive training and gathering user feedback, you can ensure that users understand and utilize the new features effectively, enhancing overall productivity and satisfaction.

Value provided

- **Efficient integration**: Effective troubleshooting minimizes setup delays and ensures a smooth integration process

- **Optimized performance**: Regular maintenance and monitoring keep the system performing at its best

- **Enhanced user experience**: Addressing user issues promptly enhances satisfaction and adoption rates

Efficient integration is achieved through effective troubleshooting. By identifying and resolving setup issues quickly, you can minimize delays and ensure a smooth integration process. This efficiency maximizes the return on investment and ensures that your team can fully leverage the capabilities of Einstein Copilot from day one.

Optimized performance is a result of regular maintenance and monitoring. By conducting regular maintenance and proactively monitoring system performance, you can prevent performance degradation and ensure that the system operates at its best. This optimization enhances the overall effectiveness of the tool and drives better business outcomes.

Enhanced user experience is achieved by addressing user issues promptly. By providing comprehensive training and gathering user feedback, you can ensure that users understand and utilize the new features effectively. This approach enhances satisfaction and adoption rates, maximizing the benefits of Einstein Copilot for your organization.

Summary

Integrating and utilizing Salesforce's Einstein Copilot is a meaningful change for businesses looking to enhance their CRM capabilities with advanced AI. The setup process, while comprehensive, is designed to be straightforward and user-friendly, ensuring that even those with limited technical expertise can implement it effectively. Throughout this chapter, we covered the essential steps to prepare your Salesforce environment, secure the necessary licenses, configure user permissions, enable key Einstein features, and ensure data security and compliance. By following these guidelines, you can seamlessly integrate Einstein Copilot into your existing Salesforce infrastructure, leveraging its powerful AI capabilities to drive efficiency, innovation, and superior customer experiences.

The advantages of Einstein Copilot are manifold. From automating routine tasks and providing actionable insights to enhancing decision-making and improving customer engagement, this tool is designed to elevate your business operations. By customizing Einstein Copilot to fit your organization's specific needs, you can ensure that it aligns perfectly with your business processes and goals. The ability to personalize user settings, create custom reports and dashboards, and configure AI models allows you to extract maximum value from the tool, making your CRM efforts more effective and impactful.

One of the key strengths of Einstein Copilot is its ability to evolve and improve over time. Salesforce continuously updates its AI capabilities, incorporating the latest advancements in machine learning and data analytics. To stay updated with the latest features and best practices, it is crucial to leverage Salesforce's extensive resources, including the Salesforce Help and Knowledge Base. These platforms provide a wealth of information, from detailed documentation and troubleshooting guides to expert tips and user forums. Additionally, Salesforce Trailhead offers a range of interactive learning modules that can help you deepen your understanding of Einstein Copilot and stay ahead of the curve in AI-driven CRM.

In conclusion, mastering the integration and customization of Einstein Copilot is an investment in your organization's future. By harnessing the power of AI, you can transform your Salesforce environment into a dynamic, data-driven ecosystem that drives business success. The skills and knowledge you've gained from this chapter will empower you to implement Einstein Copilot with confidence, ensuring a smooth setup and optimal performance. As you continue to explore the capabilities of Einstein Copilot, remember to utilize Salesforce's resources, and stay engaged with the latest updates and training opportunities. Embrace the potential of AI to revolutionize your CRM strategy and unlock new levels of efficiency, innovation, and customer satisfaction.

In the next few chapters of this portion of this book, we will highlight the robust feature set of Prompt Builder, Model Builder, Copilot Builder, and Data Cloud. These tools represent the forefront of AI integration within Salesforce, offering unparalleled capabilities for you to customize and optimize your CRM processes. Prompt Builder allows you to create tailored AI prompts that can guide user interactions and automate complex workflows. Model Builder provides a platform to develop and refine AI models that drive predictive insights and decision-making, while Copilot Builder offers tools to design and deploy AI-driven assistants that can enhance user productivity and engagement. Finally, Data Cloud serves as the backbone, ensuring that your AI applications have access to high-quality, real-time data.

These features are invaluable for businesses aiming to stay ahead in the competitive landscape. By leveraging Prompt Builder, Model Builder, and Copilot Builder, you can create a highly responsive and intelligent CRM system that adapts to your unique business needs. Data Cloud ensures that your AI-driven tools are fed with accurate and timely data, enhancing their effectiveness. Together, these tools empower you to unlock new levels of efficiency, innovation, and customer satisfaction.

As you continue reading, you'll gain a deep understanding of how to utilize these advanced tools to their fullest potential. Each chapter will provide detailed insights and practical steps to help you implement and customize these features within your Salesforce environment. Embrace the journey ahead, as mastering these tools will significantly elevate your CRM capabilities and drive meaningful business outcomes.

3
Utilizing Prompt Builder

Salesforce Prompt Builder is a powerful tool designed to enhance user interactions and automate responses within the Salesforce platform. By creating and managing prompts, businesses can streamline workflows, improve user engagement, and deliver contextually relevant responses. This chapter provides a comprehensive guide to navigating the Prompt Builder interface, creating effective prompts, integrating them with Salesforce components, customizing and personalizing prompts, and optimizing their performance through testing and analytics.

Mastering the Prompt Builder interface is essential for efficiently creating and managing prompts. The skills you'll learn in this chapter will enable you to design and implement prompts that enhance the user experience and drive business objectives. Understanding the interface's layout and functionalities is the first step toward leveraging its full potential, followed by learning how to craft effective prompts that resonate with your audience.

Integrating prompts with various Salesforce components is crucial for creating a seamless user experience. This involves connecting prompts with objects, fields, and workflows to ensure they are contextually relevant. Customizing and personalizing prompts based on user data can significantly enhance their effectiveness. This chapter will guide you through the process of tailoring prompts to meet specific business needs and user preferences.

Testing and optimizing prompt performance is another key aspect that will be covered in this chapter. You will learn how to conduct A/B testing, utilize performance analytics, and continuously improve prompts based on insights gained from these activities. These skills are vital for ensuring that your prompts achieve their desired outcomes and contribute to overall business success.

By the end of this chapter, you will have a deep understanding of how to utilize Salesforce Prompt Builder to its fullest potential. The knowledge and skills gained will empower you to create dynamic, AI-driven prompts that enhance user interactions, streamline workflows, and drive engagement. So, let's dive into the details of each section and explore the capabilities of Salesforce Prompt Builder.

Introduction to Salesforce Prompt Builder

Salesforce Prompt Builder is a tool that's designed to create prompts that enhance user interactions and automate responses within the Salesforce platform. This section provides an overview of its functionality and key features.

Salesforce Prompt Builder allows users to design prompts that can guide interactions, provide instructions, and automate routine tasks. It includes features such as a drag-and-drop editor, real-time preview, and a library of pre-built templates. These features are designed to make the creation process intuitive and accessible, even for users who may not have extensive technical backgrounds. The ability to drag and drop components means that you can build a prompt quickly and see how it will look in real time, which significantly reduces the time required for testing and revisions.

One of the standout features of Prompt Builder is its integration capabilities. It can seamlessly connect with various Salesforce components, such as objects, fields, and flows. This ensures that the prompts you create are not only functional but also contextually relevant, providing users with the information they need when they need it. This level of integration helps in creating a more cohesive and user-friendly experience.

Key goals and outcomes

The primary goal of Salesforce Prompt Builder is to improve user engagement and streamline workflows within the Salesforce environment. By using this tool, you can create prompts that guide users through processes, provide timely information, and automate responses to common inquiries. This enhances the user experience and increases efficiency by reducing the need for manual intervention.

Another critical outcome is the ability to customize and personalize prompts. With Prompt Builder, you can tailor prompts to meet the specific needs of different user segments. This means that each user receives information that is most relevant to them, improving their overall experience and increasing the likelihood of successful interactions.

A real-world example for LH&D Manufacturing

LH&D Manufacturing uses Salesforce Prompt Builder to automate customer service responses. For instance, when a customer visits their self-service portal and begins a chat, a prompt guides them through common troubleshooting steps. This reduces the load on live agents and provides quick resolutions to common issues. The prompts are designed to be intuitive and easy to follow, which helps in resolving issues efficiently without the need for live agent intervention.

In another scenario, LH&D Manufacturing uses prompts to gather customer feedback after a service interaction. This real-time feedback collection helps the company to continuously improve its services based on customer input. The prompts are customized to ask relevant questions and collect meaningful data, which is then analyzed to identify areas for improvement.

Perform the following steps to implement this:

1. **Access Prompt Builder**: Go to **Salesforce Setup**, search for `Prompt Builder` in the **Quick Find** box, and click on it. This will take you to the main interface, where you can start creating prompts.

2. **Create a new prompt**: Click **New Prompt** to start creating a new prompt.

   - **Prompt**: `Summarize the recent cases for the customer, highlighting the case subjects and statuses.`

   - You can use the text editor to enter your prompt message. Make sure the message is clear and concise to ensure it is easily understood by users.

3. **Select a template**: Choose a template from the library that matches your use case. The templates are designed to provide a starting point so that you don't have to begin from scratch. You can customize them further to meet your specific needs.

4. **Customize the prompt**: Use the drag-and-drop editor to add components and customize the message. You can add text boxes, buttons, images, and other elements to make the prompt more engaging. Ensure that all the elements are arranged logically and are easy to navigate.

5. **Set trigger conditions**: Define when and where the prompt should appear, such as on the self-service portal when a chat begins. Triggers can be based on user actions, time-based events, or specific conditions in Salesforce. This ensures that the prompts are shown at the right time and context.

6. **Save and activate**: Save the prompt and activate it to start guiding customers through troubleshooting steps. Once activated, the prompt will appear to users based on the trigger conditions you have set. You can monitor its performance and adjust it as needed.

Challenges solved and value provided

Prompt Builder addresses the challenge of managing high volumes of customer inquiries by automating responses. It provides value by improving response times, reducing operational costs, and enhancing customer satisfaction through immediate assistance. By automating routine responses, customer service teams can focus on more complex issues that require human intervention. This not only improves efficiency but also enhances the quality of customer service.

Additionally, Prompt Builder helps in standardizing responses across the organization. This ensures that all customers receive consistent and accurate information, which helps in building trust and reliability. The ability to customize and personalize prompts further enhances their effectiveness, making them a powerful tool for improving user interactions and achieving business objectives.

Navigating the Prompt Builder interface

The Salesforce Prompt Builder interface is designed for ease of use, offering a user-friendly layout that allows for efficient creation and management of prompts.

This section covers the key components of the Prompt Builder interface, including the drag-and-drop editor, real-time preview, and template library. The interface is designed to be intuitive so that even users who are new to Salesforce can quickly get up to speed. The drag-and-drop editor allows you to add, remove, and rearrange components with ease, making it simple to create complex prompts without needing to write any code.

The real-time preview feature is particularly useful as it allows you to see how your prompt will look and function before you deploy it. This helps in identifying any issues or areas for improvement early in the design process. Finally, the template library offers a variety of pre-built prompts that you can use as a starting point, saving you time and effort:

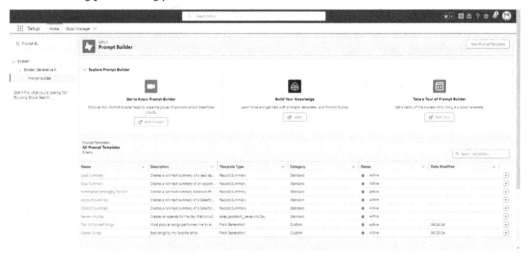

Figure 3.1 – The Prompt Builder interface

Key goals and outcomes

The primary goal of this section is to help you become proficient in navigating the Prompt Builder interface. By understanding its layout and functionalities, you can create and manage prompts more efficiently. This proficiency will enable you to quickly build and deploy prompts that meet your specific business needs.

Another key outcome is the ability to leverage the template library effectively. The templates are designed to cover a wide range of use cases so that you can find one that closely matches your needs and customize it as required. This not only speeds up the creation process but also ensures that your prompts are built on a solid foundation.

A real-world example for LH&D Manufacturing

LH&D Manufacturing's team uses the drag-and-drop editor to quickly build prompts that guide users through the equipment maintenance process. The real-time preview feature ensures that these prompts are clear and functional before deployment. By using the template library, the team can start with a basic maintenance prompt and then customize it to include specific instructions for diverse types of equipment.

In addition, the team uses the interface to update and refine existing prompts based on user feedback. For example, if customers report that a certain step in the maintenance process is unclear, the team can quickly update the prompt to provide additional clarification. This iterative approach helps in continuously improving the user experience.

Follow these steps to implement this:

1. **Open Prompt Builder**: Navigate to **Salesforce Setup** and search for `Prompt Builder`. This will open the main interface, where you can create and manage prompts.

2. **Start a new prompt**:

    • **Prompt**: `Summarize the recent cases for the customer, highlighting the case subjects and statuses.`

        • Choose the type you wish to use – **Field generation**, **Flex**, or **Record Summary**

        • Provide a name and description

        • Select the object you wish to use

Figure 3.2 – The New Prompt Template pop-up screen

- Click **New Prompt** to begin. Enter the prompt message in the text editor and format it as needed.

> **Note**
> Your picklist may be different if you have licensed addition sales_agent or service_agent Einstein features.

3. **Use the drag-and-drop editor**: Drag components such as text, images, and buttons into the editor to create the prompt. Arrange the components logically to ensure the prompt is easy to follow. You can also add interactive elements such as buttons to guide users through different steps.

4. **Template properties**: This section allows you to pick your **Model Type** and **Source**. At the time of writing, you can select from custom, Anthropic, Azure, or ChatGPT models.

5. **Preview the prompt**: Use the real-time preview feature to see how the prompt will look and function. Make sure all the elements are displayed correctly, and the prompt is easy to understand.

6. **Adjust as needed**: Make necessary adjustments based on the preview. This might include rearranging components, changing text, or adding additional elements to improve clarity.

7. **Save and deploy**: Save the prompt and deploy it to guide users through the maintenance process. Once deployed, the prompt will appear to users based on the trigger conditions you've set. You can monitor its performance and make further adjustments as needed.

The following screenshot shows the main screen and controls of the Prompt Builder interface:

Figure 3.3 – Prompt Builder

Becoming familiar with the various sections

In this section, we'll uncover the various sections of the Prompt Builder interface.

Prompt Template Workspace

This is the area in which you write your prompt. You can merge resources with the prompt to bring in fields from objects and target the **Object Field** area for the user to update:

Figure 3.4 – The Prompt Builder layout | Prompt Template Workspace

Preview

The purpose of the **Preview** section is to see how your prompt resolves with the sample record data and test the response from your model:

Figure 3.5 – The Prompt Builder layout | Preview

Challenges solved and value provided

Navigating the interface efficiently reduces the time required to create and deploy prompts. It ensures that prompts are designed and tested accurately, leading to better user experiences and more efficient workflows. The ability to quickly create and update prompts means that you can respond to user feedback and changing business needs promptly.

The drag-and-drop editor and real-time preview feature make the design process more accessible, allowing users with varying levels of technical expertise to create effective prompts. This democratization of the design process means that more team members can contribute to creating and improving prompts, leading to a more collaborative and innovative approach.

As we move through different examples throughout this book, you can refer to this section for screenshots, but essentially, the steps remain the same in the interface described previously.

Creating effective prompts

Creating effective prompts involves understanding the needs of your audience and crafting messages that resonate with them. Effective prompts are clear, concise, and actionable.

This section explains how to design prompts that enhance user interactions and achieve business objectives. The key to creating effective prompts is to focus on the user's perspective. What information do they need? What actions do you want them to take? By answering these questions, you can create prompts that are both helpful and engaging.

Effective prompts should also be concise. Users are often looking for quick answers or guidance, so it is important to keep your messages short and to the point. Avoid using jargon or overly technical language that might confuse users. Instead, use clear and straightforward language that is easy to understand.

Key goals and outcomes

This section's main goal is to help you create engaging and effective prompts. By focusing on the user's needs and keeping your messages concise, you can create prompts that guide users toward the desired actions. This not only improves the user experience but also helps in achieving your business objectives.

Another key outcome is the ability to create prompts that are tailored to different user segments. By understanding the specific needs and pain points of different user groups, you can create prompts that are more relevant and effective. This level of personalization helps in building stronger relationships with users and increases the likelihood of successful interactions.

A real-world example for LH&D Manufacturing

LH&D Manufacturing creates prompts that guide customers through the product selection process on their web store. These prompts are designed to help customers find the right product based on their specific needs. For example, a prompt might ask customers a series of questions about their requirements and then recommend products that match those criteria.

The prompts are designed to be clear and concise, making it easy for customers to understand and follow. By providing relevant information and guidance, the prompts help customers make informed decisions, which improves their overall shopping experience and increases the likelihood of a purchase.

Follow these steps to implement this:

1. **Identify your audience's needs**: Research customer needs and pain points related to product selection. This might involve conducting surveys, analyzing customer feedback, or reviewing support inquiries.

2. **Create a new prompt**:

   - **Prompt:** `Summarize the recent cases for the customer, highlighting the case subjects, statuses, and any notes related to resolutions.`

   - Start a new prompt. Enter the prompt message in the text editor and format it as needed.

3. **Write clear messages**: Draft messages that are easy to understand and address customer needs. Use simple language and avoid jargon. Make sure the messages are concise and to the point.

4. **Add actionable elements**: Include buttons or links that guide customers to take specific actions, such as viewing product details or adding items to the cart. Interactive elements can help in making the prompts more engaging and effective.

5. **Set triggers**: Define when the prompt should appear, such as when a customer visits the product category page. Triggers ensure that the prompts are shown at the right time and context, making them more relevant and useful.

6. **Save and activate**: Save the prompt and activate it on the web store. Once activated, the prompt will appear to users based on the trigger conditions you have set. You can monitor its performance and adjust it as needed.

Challenges solved and value provided

Effective prompts reduce user confusion and improve engagement by providing clear guidance. This enhances the overall user experience and drives higher conversion rates on the web store. By helping customers find the right products and guiding them through the purchase process, prompts can significantly improve sales and customer satisfaction.

Additionally, well-crafted prompts can reduce the number of support inquiries by providing users with the information they need upfront. This not only improves the user experience but also reduces the workload on support teams, allowing them to focus on more complex issues that require human intervention.

Integrating prompts with Salesforce components

Integration with Salesforce components is essential for creating a seamless user experience. Prompts can be integrated with objects, fields, and workflows to ensure they are contextually relevant.

This section covers how to integrate prompts with various Salesforce components to enhance their functionality and relevance. By integrating prompts with Salesforce objects and workflows, you can ensure that the prompts are shown at the right time and place, providing users with the information they need when they need it.

Integration also allows you to create more dynamic and interactive prompts. For example, a prompt can be triggered based on changes to a specific field or object, ensuring that the prompt is always relevant and up to date. This level of integration helps in creating a more personalized and engaging user experience.

Key goals and outcomes

The primary goal of this section is to help you understand how to integrate prompts with Salesforce components. By doing so, you can create prompts that are more relevant and useful, enhancing the overall user experience. Integration also allows you to automate certain tasks, reducing the need for manual intervention and improving efficiency.

Another key outcome is the ability to create prompts that are dynamic and responsive. By integrating prompts with Salesforce objects and workflows, you can ensure that they are always up-to-date and relevant. This helps in providing users with timely and accurate information, which improves their overall experience.

A real-world example for LH&D Manufacturing

In another scenario, prompts are used to notify sales representatives of important updates or actions they need to take. For example, a prompt might appear when a new lead is assigned, providing the representative with information about the lead and suggesting the next steps. This helps in ensuring that important tasks are not overlooked and that representatives have the information they need to follow up effectively.

LH&D Manufacturing integrates prompts with their customer service workflows. For example, prompts appear when a service agent opens a case, providing relevant troubleshooting steps based on the case details. This helps in guiding the agent through the resolution process, reducing the time required to resolve issues and improving customer satisfaction.

Follow these steps to implement this:

1. **Open Prompt Builder**: Access Prompt Builder from **Salesforce Setup**. This will open the main interface, where you can create and manage prompts.

2. **Create a new prompt**:

   - **Prompt**: `Summarize the recent cases for the customer, highlighting the case subjects, statuses, priority, and urgency levels.`

   - Click **New Prompt** to start creating a new prompt. Enter the prompt message in the text editor and format it as needed.

3. **Link to objects**: Select the relevant Salesforce objects (for example, cases) where the prompt should appear. This ensures that the prompt is contextually relevant and appears at the right time.

4. **Define field triggers**: Set triggers based on specific field values (for example, case status) to display the prompt. Triggers ensure that the prompt is shown when it is most relevant and useful.

5. **Customize content**: Add troubleshooting steps or relevant information to the prompt. Make sure the content is clear and concise, giving users the information they need to act.

6. **Save and activate**: Save the prompt and activate it within the customer service workflow. Once activated, the prompt will appear to users based on the trigger conditions you have set. You can monitor its performance and adjust it as needed.

Challenges solved and value provided

Integrating prompts with Salesforce components ensures they are relevant and useful, enhancing the user experience. It also automates responses based on specific triggers, improving efficiency. By providing users with timely and accurate information, prompts can help in resolving issues more quickly and effectively.

Additionally, integration helps in creating a more cohesive and streamlined user experience. By ensuring that prompts are shown at the right time and place, you can provide users with the information they need when they need it, improving their overall experience and satisfaction.

Customizing and personalizing prompts

Customization and personalization are key to making prompts more effective and engaging.

This section explains how to customize prompts to match brand and audience preferences and personalize them based on user data. Customization involves adjusting the layout, colors, fonts, and images to match your brand's identity. Personalization involves using user data to tailor prompts to the specific needs and preferences of individual users.

By customizing and personalizing prompts, you can create a more engaging and relevant user experience. Customization helps in creating a consistent brand identity, while personalization ensures that each user receives information that is most relevant to them. This not only improves the user experience but also increases the likelihood of successful interactions.

Key goals and outcomes

The primary goal of this section is to help you customize and personalize prompts to make them more effective and engaging. By doing so, you can create prompts that are both visually appealing and relevant to the user. This enhances the overall user experience and increases the likelihood of successful interactions.

Another key outcome is the ability to create prompts that are tailored to different user segments. By understanding the specific needs and preferences of different user groups, you can create prompts that are more relevant and effective. This level of personalization helps in building stronger relationships with users and increases their satisfaction.

A real-world example for LH&D Manufacturing

In another scenario, prompts are personalized based on the customer's location. For example, a prompt might provide information about local service centers or upcoming events in the customer's area. This level of personalization helps in creating a more relevant and engaging user experience.

LH&D Manufacturing customizes prompts to match their brand colors and logo. They personalize prompts by including the customer's name and previous purchase history to provide tailored recommendations. For example, a prompt might recommend products based on the customer's previous purchases or browsing history.

Follow these steps to implement this:

1. **Open Prompt Builder**: Access Prompt Builder in **Salesforce Setup**. This will open the main interface where you can create and manage prompts.

2. **Create a new prompt**:

   - **Prompt**: `Summarize the recent cases for the customer related to LH&D's products, highlighting frequently asked questions and providing links to the FAQ section on the website.`

   - Start a new prompt. Enter the prompt message in the text editor and format it as needed.

3. **Customize the layout**: Adjust the layout, colors, fonts, and images so that they match the company's branding. Make sure the prompt is visually appealing and consistent with your brand's identity.

4. **Use personalization tokens**: Insert personalization tokens (for example, customer name and previous purchase history) into the prompt. Personalization tokens allow you to tailor the prompt to the specific needs and preferences of individual users.

5. **Set personalization rules**: Define rules for when and how personalization should be applied. This might involve using user data to determine which prompts are shown to different user segments.

6. **Preview and adjust**: Use the real-time preview feature to ensure the prompt looks personalized. Make any necessary adjustments to improve the appearance and relevance of the prompt.

7. **Save and activate**: Save the customized prompt and activate it. Once activated, the prompt will appear to users based on the personalization rules you have set. You can monitor its performance and adjust it as needed.

Challenges solved and value provided

Customization enhances brand consistency, while personalization makes prompts more relevant and engaging for users. This leads to better user experiences and higher engagement rates. By tailoring prompts to the specific needs and preferences of individual users, you can create a more relevant and personalized experience, which increases the likelihood of successful interactions.

Additionally, customization and personalization help in building stronger relationships with users. By providing users with information that is most relevant to them, you can increase their satisfaction and loyalty. This not only improves the user experience but also helps in achieving your business objectives.

Testing and optimizing prompt performance

Testing and optimization are crucial for ensuring that your prompts are effective and achieving their desired outcomes.

This section covers how to test and optimize prompts to maximize their performance and impact. Testing involves creating different versions of a prompt and comparing their performance, while optimization involves using the insights gained from testing to improve the prompts.

By testing and optimizing prompts, you can ensure that they are performing at their best and achieving the desired outcomes. This not only improves the user experience but also helps in achieving your business objectives. Testing and optimization are ongoing processes, so it is important to continuously monitor and refine your prompts to ensure they remain effective.

Key goals and outcomes

The primary goal of this section is to help you test and optimize prompts to ensure they are effective and achieve the desired outcomes. By conducting A/B testing and utilizing performance analytics, you can identify the best-performing prompts and adjust to improve their performance.

Another key outcome is the ability to continuously improve prompts based on insights gained from testing and analytics. This iterative approach helps in refining prompts to better meet the needs of users and achieve business objectives. By continuously monitoring and refining prompts, you can ensure they remain effective and relevant.

A real-world example for LH&D Manufacturing

In another scenario, the team uses performance analytics to track the effectiveness of customer service prompts. By monitoring metrics such as response times and customer satisfaction, the team can identify areas for improvement and adjust to enhance the effectiveness of the prompts.

LH&D Manufacturing conducts A/B testing on different versions of a sales prompt to determine which one drives higher conversion rates. They use Salesforce analytics tools to track performance metrics and optimize the prompts accordingly. For example, one version of the prompt might emphasize product features, while another version might emphasize customer reviews. By comparing the performance of each version, the team can identify which approach is more effective and adjust accordingly.

Follow these steps to implement this:

1. **Create multiple versions**: In Prompt Builder, create different versions of the same prompt for testing. This might involve changing the wording, layout, or call-to-action to see which version performs better.

2. **Set up A/B testing**: Use Salesforce A/B testing features to split your audience and test each version. This involves dividing your audience into two groups and showing each group a different version of the prompt.

3. **Track performance metrics**: Monitor metrics such as click-through rates, conversion rates, and user engagement using Salesforce analytics tools. This will help you identify which version of the prompt is performing better.

4. **Analyze the results**: Compare the performance of each version to identify the best-performing prompt. Look for patterns and insights that can help you understand why one version is more effective than the other.

5. **Optimize your prompts**: Adjust your prompts based on the insights gained from testing to improve prompt performance. This might involve combining elements from the best-performing versions or making other changes to enhance the effectiveness of the prompt.

6. **Implement the best version**: Deploy the best-performing prompt to all users. Once implemented, continue to monitor its performance, and adjust it as needed to ensure it remains effective.

Challenges solved and value provided

Testing and optimization ensure that prompts are performing at their best, leading to improved user engagement and higher conversion rates. By identifying the best-performing prompts and adjusting to improve their performance, you can ensure that your prompts are effective and achieve the desired outcomes.

Additionally, testing and optimization help in continuously refining prompts to better meet the needs of users. By continuously monitoring and refining prompts, you can ensure they remain relevant and effective, improving the overall user experience and helping you achieve your business objectives.

Advanced techniques for prompt management

Advanced prompt management techniques involve using Salesforce Prompt Builder's more sophisticated features to create dynamic and interactive prompts.

This section explores advanced techniques for managing prompts, including conditional logic, interactive elements, and integration with external systems. By using these advanced features, you can create more dynamic and engaging prompts that provide a better user experience.

Conditional logic allows you to create prompts that change based on user behavior or other conditions. For example, a prompt might provide different information to inexperienced users compared to returning users. Interactive elements, such as buttons and forms, can make prompts more engaging and help guide users through complex processes. Integration with external systems allows you to create prompts that provide real-time information and interact with other systems, such as inventory management or customer support tools.

Key goals and outcomes

The primary goal of this section is to help you use advanced techniques to create more dynamic and engaging prompts. By using conditional logic, interactive elements, and integration with external systems, you can create prompts that provide a better user experience and achieve your business objectives.

Another key outcome is the ability to create prompts that are more responsive to user behavior and other conditions. By using conditional logic and other advanced features, you can ensure that your prompts are always relevant and useful, improving the overall user experience.

A real-world example for LH&D Manufacturing

In another scenario, the company integrates prompts with its inventory management system to provide real-time stock updates. For example, a prompt might notify customers when a product is back in stock or provide alternative product recommendations if a desired product is out of stock. This level of integration helps in providing a more dynamic and responsive user experience.

LH&D Manufacturing uses conditional logic to display different prompts based on customer behavior on their web store. For example, new customers might see a prompt that provides an overview of the company and its products, while returning customers might see a prompt that highlights new products or exclusive offers.

Follow these steps to implement this:

1. **Open Prompt Builder**: Navigate to Prompt Builder in **Salesforce Setup**. This will open the main interface where you can create and manage prompts.

2. **Create a new prompt**:

    - **Prompt**: `Summarize the recent cases for the customer, highlighting the case subjects, statuses, priority, urgency levels, and any related notes or actions.`

    - Start a new prompt. Enter the prompt message in the text editor and format it as needed.

3. **Apply conditional logic**: Use conditional logic to define rules based on user behavior (for example, display different prompts for new versus returning customers). This might involve creating different versions of the prompt for different user segments and setting conditions for when each version is shown.

4. **Add interactive elements**: Include buttons, forms, and multimedia to enhance user engagement. Interactive elements can help guide users through complex processes and make the prompts more engaging.

5. **Integrate with external systems**: Use APIs to connect prompts with external systems (for example, inventory management) for real-time data. This might involve creating prompts that provide real-time stock updates or interact with other systems to provide more dynamic and relevant information.

6. **Test and refine**: Test the prompts to ensure they work as intended and make any necessary adjustments. This might involve conducting A/B testing or using other methods to evaluate the performance of the prompts and make improvements.

7. **Save and deploy**: Save the prompt and deploy it on the web store. Once deployed, the prompt will appear to users based on the trigger conditions and conditional logic you have set. You can monitor its performance and adjust as needed to ensure it remains effective.

Challenges solved and value provided

Advanced techniques make prompts more dynamic and engaging, providing a better user experience. By using conditional logic, interactive elements, and integration with external systems, you can create prompts that are more responsive to user behavior and other conditions, improving their relevance and effectiveness.

Additionally, advanced techniques help in creating more sophisticated prompts that can handle complex processes and provide real-time information. This level of sophistication helps in improving the overall user experience and achieving your business objectives. By providing users with dynamic and engaging prompts, you can increase their satisfaction and loyalty, helping to build stronger relationships with your customers.

Summary

By mastering Salesforce Prompt Builder, businesses can create powerful AI-driven prompts that enhance user interactions, streamline workflows, and drive engagement. This chapter has provided a comprehensive guide to navigating the interface, creating effective prompts, integrating them with Salesforce components, customizing and personalizing prompts, and optimizing their performance through testing and analytics. With these skills, you can harness the full potential of Salesforce Prompt Builder to transform your customer interactions and business processes.

The skills you learned in this chapter are invaluable for Salesforce administrators and developers. Understanding how to navigate the Prompt Builder interface allows for efficient prompt creation and management. Creating effective prompts that are clear, concise, and actionable enhances user interactions and drives business objectives. Integrating prompts with various Salesforce components ensures a seamless user experience, while customization and personalization make prompts more relevant and engaging.

Testing and optimizing prompt performance is crucial for ensuring that prompts achieve their desired outcomes. Conducting A/B testing and utilizing performance analytics provide insights that help in continuously improving prompts. Advanced techniques such as using conditional logic and integrating with external systems add more sophistication and functionality to prompts.

In conclusion, mastering Salesforce Prompt Builder empowers you to create dynamic, AI-driven prompts that enhance user interactions and drive engagement. The knowledge and skills you've gained from this chapter will enable you to leverage Salesforce Prompt Builder to its fullest potential, transforming your customer interactions and business processes. By continuously refining and optimizing your prompts, you can achieve better user experiences and drive higher business outcomes.

In the next chapter, we will explore the capabilities of Copilot Builder. This tool allows you to design and deploy AI-driven assistants that can enhance user productivity and engagement. Copilot Builder provides a platform for developing custom AI models and integrating them with Salesforce components to create intelligent, contextually relevant assistants.

Understanding the use of Copilot Builder will enable you to further optimize your Salesforce environment by automating complex workflows and providing personalized assistance to users. Stay tuned to learn how to harness the power of Copilot Builder and take your Salesforce implementation to the next level.

4
Working with Copilot Builder

Salesforce Copilot Builder is an advanced tool that's designed to harness the power of **artificial intelligence** (**AI**) to create intelligent assistants, or copilots, that enhance user interactions and streamline workflows within the Salesforce ecosystem. As businesses strive to improve efficiency and provide superior customer experiences, the integration of AI-driven copilots has become increasingly crucial. This chapter delves into the functionalities and practical applications of Copilot Builder, guiding you through the process of creating, configuring, and deploying AI copilots tailored to your specific needs.

Mastering the Copilot Builder tool provides several key skills essential for Salesforce administrators and developers. These include navigating the Copilot Builder interface, creating and configuring copilots, integrating them with various Salesforce components, customizing their actions and responses, and testing and refining their performance. Additionally, you will learn how to utilize analytics to measure copilot effectiveness and troubleshoot common issues, ensuring that their copilots deliver optimal performance and value.

Understanding the Copilot Builder interface is the first step in leveraging this powerful tool. By familiarizing yourself with its layout and functionalities, you can create and manage AI-driven copilots efficiently. The interface provides intuitive navigation and robust features that streamline the development process, allowing you to focus on designing copilots that meet your business objectives. This foundational knowledge sets the stage for more advanced configurations and integrations.

Creating and configuring copilots is at the heart of Copilot Builder's capabilities. This involves designing copilots that address specific business needs, such as automating routine tasks, providing real-time insights, or enhancing customer interactions. The flexibility of Copilot Builder allows for a high degree of customization, enabling you to tailor each copilot to your organization's unique requirements. By deploying well-configured copilots, you can drive efficiently, reduce manual workloads, and improve overall productivity.

Integrating copilots with Salesforce components ensures that they function seamlessly within your existing workflows. This involves connecting copilots with objects, fields, and workflows in Salesforce, ensuring cohesive functionality and a unified user experience. Customizing copilot actions and responses further enhances their relevance and performance, allowing you to create intelligent assistants that not only perform tasks but also adapt to user preferences and business processes.

Testing and refining copilot performance is crucial for ensuring their effectiveness. By following best practices for testing, you can identify and resolve issues early, optimizing copilot performance and accuracy. Utilizing analytics allows you to measure copilot effectiveness, providing insights into their impact and identifying areas for improvement. Troubleshooting common issues ensures that your copilots maintain optimal functionality, delivering consistent value to your organization.

In summary, mastering Salesforce Copilot Builder will equip you with the skills to design, configure, and deploy intelligent assistants that enhance user interactions and streamline workflows. This chapter provides a comprehensive guide to leveraging Copilot Builder's powerful capabilities, ensuring that you can drive innovation and efficiency in your Salesforce implementations.

Introduction to Salesforce Copilot Builder

Salesforce Copilot Builder is an innovative tool that's designed to enable the creation of AI-driven copilots that enhance user interactions and streamline business processes within the Salesforce ecosystem. This tool offers a range of functionalities that allow users to design, configure, and deploy intelligent assistants tailored to specific business needs. Understanding the capabilities and applications of Copilot Builder is essential for maximizing its potential and driving efficiency in your Salesforce environment.

The Copilot Builder interface is user-friendly and intuitive, making it accessible even to those with limited technical expertise. It provides a robust set of features that support the entire copilot development life cycle, from initial design to deployment and ongoing optimization. By leveraging these features, you can create intelligent assistants that perform a wide variety of tasks, from automating routine processes to providing real-time insights and enhancing customer interactions.

The key to successfully utilizing Copilot Builder lies in understanding its interface and capabilities. This foundational knowledge enables you to navigate the tool efficiently, harness its full potential, and create copilots that deliver significant value to your organization. As you progress through this chapter, you will gain a deep understanding of Copilot Builder's functionalities and learn how to apply them to meet your specific business objectives.

Key goals and outcomes

The primary goal of this section is to provide an in-depth understanding of Copilot Builder and its capabilities. By the end of this section, you will be able to do the following:

- **Understand the core features and capabilities of Copilot Builder**: You'll gain insights into the various functionalities that make Copilot Builder a powerful tool for enhancing user interactions and automating tasks

- **Recognize the benefits of using AI-driven copilots**: You'll learn how these intelligent assistants can streamline workflows, improve efficiency, and provide actionable insights

- **Identify potential applications within your organization**: You'll explore various use cases where Copilot Builder can be implemented to address specific business needs and challenges

By achieving these goals, you will be well-prepared to leverage Copilot Builder to its full potential. This knowledge will enable you to design and deploy intelligent assistants that address specific business needs, improve operational efficiency, and enhance the overall user experience.

A quick tour of the Copilot Builder interface

It's very important to understand the Salesforce instructions for enabling access to the features of Einstein Copilot. If the permission sets aren't set up properly, your view may look different than the screenshots provided in this book.

Main layout

From within the main layout, users can explore the Prompt Library actions included in the Einstein Copilot area of their Salesforce environment.

Figure 4.1 – Einstein Studio | The Copilot Builder main page

View Action

The **View Action** section is where the user modifies and tests the copilot configuration and actions, from walking the user through the logic from the initial user prompt to selecting actions and output:

Figure 4.2 – Einstein Studio | Copilot's View Action section

Follow these steps to implement it:

1. **Access Copilot Builder**:

    I.   Navigate to **Salesforce Setup**.

    II.   In the **Quick Find** box, type `Copilot Builder` and select it.

    III. Familiarize yourself with the interface and available features.

2. **Edit Einstein Copilot**:

    I.   Click on **Einstein Copilot**, right-click the dropdown arrow, and choose **Open in Builder** to start the creation process in Copilot Builder.

    II.   Follow the guided prompts to define the copilot's purpose and initial settings.

3. **Customize Copilot's features**:

    I.   Use the various customization options to tailor the copilot's actions and responses to your specific needs.

    II.   Test the copilot in a sandbox environment to ensure it functions as intended.

A real-world example for LH&D Manufacturing

LH&D Manufacturing, a global manufacturing company based in Freehold, New Jersey, faced challenges in managing customer interactions and streamlining their internal processes. By integrating Copilot Builder, they were able to create intelligent assistants that automated routine tasks, provided real-time insights, and improved customer engagement. For example, they developed a copilot that assisted their sales team by automating the lead qualification process, allowing sales representatives to focus on high-value opportunities. This copilot not only increased the efficiency of their sales operations but also improved the accuracy of their lead scoring, resulting in a 20% increase in conversion rates.

Challenges solved

Here's an overview of the challenges that they solved with this feature:

- **Managing customer interactions**: Automating routine tasks and providing real-time insights improved the efficiency and effectiveness of customer interactions

- **Streamlining processes**: Integrating AI-driven copilots streamlined internal processes, thus reducing manual workloads and increasing productivity

- **Improving accuracy**: AI copilots enhanced the accuracy of lead scoring and other critical tasks, driving better business outcomes

Value provided

This feature provided the following value:

- **Enhanced efficiency**: Automating routine tasks and providing real-time insights increased operational efficiency

- **Improved customer engagement**: Intelligent assistants enhanced customer interactions, leading to higher satisfaction and loyalty

- **Better decision-making**: AI-driven insights improved the accuracy and effectiveness of decision-making processes

Navigating the Copilot Builder interface

The Copilot Builder interface is designed to be intuitive and user-friendly, providing a robust set of features that support the creation, configuration, and deployment of AI-driven copilots. Understanding the layout and functionalities of the interface is crucial for efficiently navigating the tool and leveraging its capabilities to create intelligent assistants that meet your business needs.

The interface is divided into several key sections, each dedicated to distinct aspects of copilot development. These sections include the dashboard, where you can manage your copilots; Design Studio, where you can create and configure copilots; Integration Hub, where you can connect copilots with Salesforce components; and Analytics Center, where you can monitor and optimize copilot performance. Familiarizing yourself with these sections and their functionalities will enable you to navigate Copilot Builder with ease and efficiency.

Key goals and outcomes

This section's main goal is to provide a full understanding of the Copilot Builder interface. By the end of this section, you will be able to do the following:

- **Navigate the Copilot Builder interface efficiently**: Learn the layout and key components of the interface to streamline the copilot creation process

- **Utilize key features and tools within the interface**: Understand how to access and use the various tools and features available in Copilot Builder

- **Optimize your workflow within Copilot Builder**: Develop strategies to efficiently create and manage copilots, maximizing productivity

- Efficiently manage the creation, configuration, and deployment of copilots

- Utilize Analytics Center to monitor and optimize copilot performance

By achieving these goals, you will be well-equipped to leverage the full potential of the Copilot Builder interface. This knowledge will enable you to efficiently navigate the tool, streamline the development process, and create intelligent assistants that deliver significant value to your organization.

Follow these steps to implement this:

1. **Explore the interface**:

    I.   Open Copilot Builder from **Salesforce Setup**.

    II.   Familiarize yourself with the layout, including the main dashboard, menu options, and settings.

2. **Access key features**:

    I.   Utilize the menu so that you can access unique features such as creating new copilots, managing existing ones, and viewing analytics.

    II.   Explore the customization options available for tailoring copilot actions and responses.

3. **Optimize the workflow**:

    I.   Use shortcuts and best practices to navigate the interface efficiently.

    II.   Implement strategies to streamline the copilot creation and management process.

A real-world example for LH&D Manufacturing

At LH&D Manufacturing, the Copilot Builder interface played a crucial role in the development and deployment of AI-driven assistants. The sales team used the dashboard to manage their copilots, ensuring that each assistant was properly configured and deployed. Design Studio allowed them to customize copilot actions and responses, tailoring the assistants to meet their specific needs. Integration Hub facilitated seamless connections between the copilots and Salesforce components, ensuring cohesive functionality. Finally, Analytics Center provided valuable insights into copilot performance, enabling the team to make data-driven adjustments that enhanced efficiency and effectiveness.

Challenges solved

Here's an overview of the challenges that were solved with this feature:

- **Complex navigation**: The intuitive interface simplified navigation, reducing the learning curve for inexperienced users

- **Disjointed processes**: Integration Hub ensured cohesive functionality by connecting copilots with Salesforce components

- **Performance monitoring**: Analytics Center provided real-time insights into copilot performance, enabling proactive adjustments

Value provided

This feature provided the following value:

- **Streamlined development**: The user-friendly interface streamlined the copilot development process, reducing time and effort

- **Enhanced functionality**: Seamless integration with Salesforce components ensured cohesive and effective copilot functionality

- **Data-driven optimization**: Real-time performance insights enabled data-driven adjustments that improved copilot effectiveness

Creating and configuring AI-driven copilots

Creating and configuring AI-driven copilots is at the core of Copilot Builder's capabilities. This process involves designing intelligent assistants that address specific business needs, such as automating routine tasks, providing real-time insights, or enhancing customer interactions. The flexibility of Copilot Builder allows for a high degree of customization, enabling you to tailor each copilot to your organization's unique requirements.

The creation process begins with defining the copilot's objectives and scope. Once the objectives are clear, you can use Design Studio to create the copilot's structure, configure its actions and responses, and integrate it with relevant Salesforce components. This structured approach ensures that each copilot is purpose-built to address specific business challenges and deliver maximum value.

Key goals and outcomes

This section's main goal is to provide a detailed guide to creating and configuring AI-driven copilots. By the end of this section, you will be able to do the following:

- **Define the purpose and scope of your copilot**: Clearly outline what tasks your copilot will perform and how it will benefit your organization

- **Set up and configure copilot functionalities**: Learn how to customize the copilot's actions and responses to align with your business processes

- **Ensure the copilot meets your business needs**: Tailor the copilot to address specific challenges and opportunities within your organization

- Use Design Studio to create and configure copilots

- Customize copilot actions and responses to meet specific business needs

- Integrate copilots with relevant Salesforce components for cohesive functionality

By achieving these goals, you will be equipped to design and deploy intelligent assistants that enhance efficiency, improve customer interactions, and drive better business outcomes.

Following these steps to implement this:

1. **Define your copilot's purpose**:

    I.   Identify the specific tasks and goals for your copilot.

    II.   Outline the key functionalities it should have to achieve these goals.

2. **Set up functionalities**:

    I.   Use the Copilot Builder interface to configure the copilot's actions and responses.

    II.   Customize your settings to ensure the copilot operates effectively within your business context.

3. **Testing and validation**:

    I.   Test the copilot in a controlled environment to validate its performance.

    II.   Make necessary adjustments based on feedback and performance metrics.

A real-world example for LH&D Manufacturing

LH&D Manufacturing used Copilot Builder to create a series of intelligent assistants tailored to their business needs. For instance, they developed a copilot that automated the lead qualification process, significantly reducing the manual workload of their sales team. By configuring the copilot to analyze lead data and provide real-time scoring, LH&D Manufacturing improved the accuracy of their lead assessments and increased conversion rates. The copilot was seamlessly integrated with Salesforce components, ensuring cohesive functionality and a streamlined workflow.

Challenges solved

Here's an overview of the challenges that were solved with this feature:

- **Manual workloads**: Automating routine tasks reduced the manual workload of the sales team
- **Inaccurate lead scoring**: Configuring copilots to analyze data and provide real-time scoring improved lead assessment accuracy
- **Disjointed workflows**: Integrating copilots with Salesforce components ensured cohesive functionality and streamlined workflows

Value provided

This feature provided the following value:

- **Increased efficiency**: Automating routine tasks increased operational efficiency
- **Improved accuracy**: Real-time data analysis and scoring improved the accuracy of lead assessments
- **Enhanced functionality**: Seamless integration with Salesforce components ensured cohesive and effective workflows

Integrating copilots with Salesforce components

Integrating copilots with Salesforce components is essential for ensuring cohesive functionality and a seamless user experience. This integration allows copilots to interact with various objects, fields, and workflows within Salesforce, enhancing their ability to perform tasks and provide insights. By connecting copilots with the relevant components, you can create intelligent assistants that operate seamlessly within your existing Salesforce environment.

Integration Hub within Copilot Builder facilitates this process, providing tools and functionalities that simplify the integration of copilots with Salesforce components. Understanding how to use these tools effectively is crucial for creating copilots that deliver maximum value and functionality. This section will guide you through the integration process, ensuring that your copilots are well-integrated and capable of enhancing your business processes.

Key goals and outcomes

This section's main goal is to provide a comprehensive guide to integrating copilots with Salesforce components. By the end of this section, you will be able to do the following:

- **Understand how copilots interact with Salesforce components**: Learn the integration points and how to leverage them for cohesive functionality to connect copilots with Salesforce objects, fields, and workflows

- **Implement seamless integration with objects, fields, and workflows**: Ensure that your copilots can access and utilize relevant Salesforce data and processes

- **Enhance overall system efficiency**: Optimize the interaction between copilots and Salesforce components to streamline workflows and improve performance

- Ensure cohesive functionality and seamless user experiences

- Leverage integrated copilots to enhance business processes and improve operational efficiency

By achieving these goals, you will be able to create intelligent assistants that operate seamlessly within your Salesforce environment, enhancing their ability to perform tasks and providing valuable insights.

Follow these steps to implement this:

1. **Identify integration points**:

   - Determine which Salesforce components your copilot needs to interact with.

   - Identify the relevant objects, fields, and workflows for integration.

2. **Configure your integration settings**:

   - Use the Copilot Builder interface to set up integration points.

   - Ensure that the copilot can access and manipulate the necessary data.

3. **Test the integration**:

   - Test the integrated copilot in a sandbox environment to ensure it interacts correctly with Salesforce components.

   - Adjust it based on the test results to optimize performance.

A real-world example for LH&D Manufacturing

At LH&D Manufacturing, integrating copilots with Salesforce components was a critical step in optimizing their workflows. They used Integration Hub to connect their sales copilot with key objects and fields, ensuring that it could access and analyze relevant data. This integration allowed the copilot to provide real-time insights and automate routine tasks, significantly enhancing the efficiency of the sales team. By integrating the copilot with Salesforce workflows, LH&D Manufacturing ensured that the assistant could operate seamlessly within their existing processes, delivering cohesive functionality and a streamlined user experience.

Challenges solved

Here's an overview of the challenges that were solved with this feature:

- **Disjointed data access**: Integrating copilots with Salesforce components ensured that they could access and analyze relevant data

- **Inefficient workflows**: Seamless integration with Salesforce workflows enhanced the efficiency of business processes

- **Inconsistent functionality**: Ensuring cohesive functionality improved the overall effectiveness of the copilots

Value provided

This feature provided the following value:

- **Enhanced data access**: Integrated copilots could access and analyze relevant data, providing valuable insights

- **Streamlined workflows**: Seamless integration enhanced the efficiency of business processes

- **Consistent functionality**: Ensuring cohesive functionality improved the overall effectiveness and reliability of the copilots

Customizing Copilot actions and responses

Customizing copilot actions and responses is essential for ensuring that your intelligent assistants deliver relevant and effective support. Copilot Builder provides a range of customization options that allow you to tailor copilot actions and responses to meet your specific business needs. This customization enhances the relevance and performance of the copilots, ensuring that they provide maximum value to your organization.

Customization involves defining the actions that copilots should perform, such as automating tasks, providing real-time insights, or interacting with users. Additionally, you can customize the responses that copilots provide, ensuring that they are accurate, helpful, and aligned with your business processes. By leveraging the customization options available in Copilot Builder, you can create intelligent assistants that are highly effective and tailored to your organization's needs.

Key goals and outcomes

This section's main goal is to provide a detailed guide to customizing copilot actions and responses. By the end of this section, you will be able to do the following:

- **Customize copilot actions so that they align with business processes**: Tailor the tasks and actions performed by your copilots to fit your specific workflows

- **Enhance the relevance and effectiveness of copilot responses**: Ensure that the responses provided by your copilots are accurate, helpful, and contextually appropriate

- **Improve user satisfaction and engagement**: Personalize copilot interactions to enhance the user experience and drive higher satisfaction levels

- Define and configure copilot actions to automate tasks and provide insights

- Customize copilot responses to ensure accuracy and relevance

- Leverage customization options to enhance the performance and effectiveness of your copilots

By achieving these goals, you will be able to create intelligent assistants that are highly effective and tailored to your specific business needs, enhancing operational efficiency and user satisfaction.

Follow these steps to implement this:

1. **Define custom actions**:

   - Identify the specific actions your copilot needs to perform.

   - Use the Copilot Builder interface to configure these actions.

2. **Customize responses**:

   - Tailor the copilot's responses to ensure they are relevant and helpful.

   - Utilize available customization options to refine the response content and format.

3. **Test and refine**:

   - Test the customized actions and responses in a controlled environment.

   - Gather feedback and make necessary adjustments to improve performance.

A real-world example for LH&D Manufacturing

LH&D Manufacturing customized their sales copilot to perform a range of actions, such as automating the lead qualification process and providing real-time insights into sales performance. They also customized the copilot's responses to ensure that they were accurate, helpful, and aligned with the company's sales processes. By tailoring the copilot's actions and responses, LH&D Manufacturing created an intelligent assistant that significantly enhanced the efficiency and effectiveness of their sales team.

Challenges solved

Here's an overview of the challenges that were solved with this feature:

- **Generic actions**: Customizing copilot actions ensured that they were relevant and aligned with business needs
- **Inaccurate responses**: Tailoring copilot responses improved their accuracy and helpfulness
- **Ineffective support**: Customized copilots provided effective support, enhancing user satisfaction

Value provided

This feature provided the following value:

- **Relevant actions**: Customized actions ensured that copilots performed tasks that were relevant and valuable
- **Accurate responses**: Tailored responses improved the accuracy and helpfulness of copilot interactions
- **Enhanced support**: Customized copilots provided effective support, enhancing operational efficiency and user satisfaction

Testing and refining copilot performance

Testing and refining copilot performance is crucial for ensuring their effectiveness and reliability. Copilot Builder provides tools and best practices for testing copilots, optimizing their performance, and ensuring their accuracy. By following these best practices, you can identify and resolve issues early, enhancing the overall performance and effectiveness of your copilots.

Testing involves evaluating copilot performance in a controlled environment, such as a sandbox, to identify any issues or areas for improvement. Refining copilot performance involves adjusting based on test results and user feedback, ensuring that the copilots deliver optimal performance and value. By leveraging the tools and best practices provided by Copilot Builder, you can create intelligent assistants that are highly effective and reliable.

Key goals and outcomes

This section's main goal is to provide a guide to testing and refining copilot performance. By the end of this section, you will be able to do the following:

- **Implement best practices for testing copilot performance**: Learn how to conduct thorough testing to identify and address performance issues
- **Optimize copilot functionalities for improved outcomes**: Understand how to refine copilot actions and responses to enhance their effectiveness

- **Ensure copilot accuracy and reliability**: Maintain lofty standards of performance and reliability through continuous testing and refinement
- Conduct thorough testing of copilots in a controlled environment
- Identify and resolve performance issues early
- Refine copilot performance based on test results and user feedback
- Ensure that copilots deliver optimal performance and value

By achieving these goals, you will be able to create intelligent assistants that are highly effective and reliable, enhancing operational efficiency and user satisfaction.

Follow these steps to implement this:

1. **Initial testing**:

   - Conduct initial tests in a sandbox environment to identify any performance issues.
   - Use test scenarios that reflect real-world usage to ensure accuracy.

2. **Performance optimization**:

   - Analyze test results to identify areas for improvement.
   - Optimize copilot actions and responses based on test findings.

3. **Ongoing refinement**:

   - Implement a continuous improvement process to regularly test and refine copilot performance.
   - Gather user feedback and use analytics to guide refinements.

A real-world example for LH&D Manufacturing

At LH&D Manufacturing, the sales team conducted thorough testing of their sales copilot in a sandbox environment to identify any performance issues. They used the insights gained from testing to refine the copilot's actions and responses, ensuring that it delivered optimal performance. By incorporating user feedback into the refinement process, LH&D Manufacturing created a copilot that was highly effective and aligned with their business processes, resulting in improved sales performance and user satisfaction.

Challenges solved

Here's an overview of the challenges that were solved with this feature:

- **Performance issues**: Thorough testing identified and resolved performance issues early
- **Ineffective actions**: Refining copilot actions based on test results ensured that they were effective and aligned with business needs

- **User dissatisfaction**: Incorporating user feedback into the refinement process enhanced user satisfaction

Value provided

This feature provided the following value:

- **Optimal performance**: Thorough testing and refinement ensured that copilots delivered optimal performance

- **Effective actions**: Refining copilot actions based on test results ensured their effectiveness and relevance

- **Enhanced satisfaction**: Incorporating user feedback into the refinement process enhanced user satisfaction and engagement

Utilizing analytics and troubleshooting copilot issues

Utilizing analytics and troubleshooting copilot issues are essential for maintaining optimal functionality and effectiveness. Copilot Builder provides robust analytics tools that allow you to measure copilot performance and identify areas for improvement. Additionally, the tool offers best practices for troubleshooting common issues, ensuring that your copilots maintain optimal functionality.

Analytics provide valuable insights into copilot performance, allowing you to measure their effectiveness and make data-driven adjustments. By leveraging these insights, you can identify areas for improvement and optimize copilot performance. Troubleshooting involves identifying and resolving issues that may impact copilot functionality, ensuring that your copilots deliver consistent value and performance.

Key goals and outcomes

This section's main goal is to provide a comprehensive guide to using analytics and troubleshooting copilot issues. By the end of this section, you will be able to do the following:

- **Leverage analytics to track copilot performance**: Use data to measure the effectiveness of your copilots and identify areas for improvement

- **Troubleshoot common copilot issues**: Address and resolve issues quickly to maintain optimal functionality

- **Maintain lofty standards of performance and reliability**: Ensure that your copilots consistently deliver accurate and effective results

By achieving these goals, you will be able to create intelligent assistants that are highly effective and reliable, enhancing operational efficiency and user satisfaction.

Follow these steps to implement this:

1. **Set up analytics:**

    -   Configure analytics tools within Copilot Builder to track key performance metrics.
    -   Identify the metrics that are most relevant to your copilot's performance.

2. **Analyze performance data:**

    -   Regularly review analytics data to assess copilot effectiveness.
    -   Use insights from the data to identify areas for improvement.

3. **Troubleshoot issues:**

    -   Identify common issues that may arise during copilot operation.
    -   Use troubleshooting guides and best practices to resolve these issues quickly.

A real-world example for LH&D Manufacturing

LH&D Manufacturing used the analytics tools provided by Copilot Builder to measure the performance of their sales copilot. They identified areas for improvement and made data-driven adjustments that enhanced the copilot's effectiveness. Additionally, they utilized best practices for troubleshooting common issues, ensuring that the copilot maintained optimal functionality and delivered consistent value. This proactive approach resulted in improved sales performance and user satisfaction.

Challenges solved

Here's an overview of the challenges that were solved with this feature:

-   **Performance measurement**: Utilizing analytics tools provided valuable insights into copilot performance
-   **Identifying improvement areas**: Data-driven adjustments enhanced the effectiveness of copilots
-   **Maintaining functionality**: Troubleshooting best practices ensured that copilots maintained optimal functionality

Value provided

This feature provided the following value:

-   **Enhanced performance**: Utilizing analytics tools and making data-driven adjustments enhanced copilot performance

- **Data-driven optimization**: Identifying and addressing areas for improvement optimized copilot effectiveness

- **Consistent value**: Troubleshooting best practices ensured that copilots delivered consistent value and performance

Summary

Integrating and utilizing Salesforce's Copilot Builder is a transformative step for businesses looking to enhance their CRM capabilities with advanced AI. The comprehensive setup process is designed to be user-friendly, ensuring that even those with limited technical expertise can effectively implement it. Throughout this chapter, we've covered the essential steps to navigate the Copilot Builder interface, create and configure AI-driven copilots, integrate them with Salesforce components, customize their actions and responses, and test and refine their performance. By following these guidelines, you can seamlessly integrate Copilot Builder into your existing Salesforce infrastructure, leveraging its powerful AI capabilities to drive efficiency, innovation, and superior customer experiences.

The advantages of Copilot Builder are manifold. From automating routine tasks and providing actionable insights to enhancing decision-making and improving customer engagement, this tool is designed to elevate your business operations. By customizing copilots to fit your organization's specific needs, you can ensure that they align perfectly with your business processes and goals. The ability to personalize user settings, create custom reports and dashboards, and configure AI models allows you to extract maximum value from the tool, making your CRM efforts more effective and impactful.

One of the key strengths of Copilot Builder is its ability to evolve and improve over time. Salesforce continuously updates its AI capabilities, incorporating the latest advancements in machine learning and data analytics. To stay updated with the latest features and best practices, it is crucial to leverage Salesforce's extensive resources, including the Salesforce Help and Knowledge Base. These platforms provide a wealth of information, from detailed documentation and troubleshooting guides to expert tips and user forums. Additionally, Salesforce Trailhead offers a range of interactive learning modules that can help you deepen your understanding of Copilot Builder and stay ahead of the curve in AI-driven CRM.

In conclusion, mastering the integration and customization of Copilot Builder is an investment in your organization's future. By harnessing the power of AI, you can transform your Salesforce environment into a dynamic, data-driven ecosystem that drives business success. The skills and knowledge you've gained from this chapter will empower you to implement Copilot Builder with confidence, ensuring a smooth setup and optimal performance. As you continue to explore the capabilities of Copilot Builder, remember to utilize Salesforce's resources, and stay engaged with the latest updates and training opportunities. Embrace the potential of AI to revolutionize your CRM strategy and unlock new levels of efficiency, innovation, and customer satisfaction.

In the next chapters of this portion of this book, we're going to highlight the robust feature set of Data Cloud with Einstein Copilot. These tools represent the forefront of AI integration within Salesforce, offering unparalleled capabilities to customize and optimize your CRM processes. Data Cloud serves as the backbone, ensuring that your AI applications have access to high-quality, real-time data.

These features are invaluable for businesses aiming to stay ahead in the competitive landscape. By leveraging Data Cloud, you can create a highly responsive and intelligent CRM system that adapts to your unique business needs. Data Cloud ensures that your AI-driven tools are fed with accurate and timely data, enhancing their effectiveness. Together, these tools empower you to unlock new levels of efficiency, innovation, and customer satisfaction.

As you continue reading, you will gain a deep understanding of how to utilize these advanced tools to their fullest potential. Each chapter will provide detailed insights and practical steps to help you implement and customize these features within your Salesforce environment. Embrace the journey ahead, as mastering these tools will significantly elevate your CRM capabilities and drive meaningful business outcomes.

5
How Data Cloud Works with Einstein Studio

The evolution of Salesforce Data Cloud has proceeded at a breathtaking pace over the last 5 years. The product has gone through multiple rebrands and name changes as Salesforce continues to build out the capabilities of this new architectural layer that is now intimately tied together with the core **customer relationship management** (**CRM**) capabilities of Salesforce. It's easier than ever before to experiment with Data Cloud: it is automatically available for setup within any 30-day trial license of Salesforce Enterprise Edition, and Salesforce partners can request a demo org from Partner Learning Camp. Any of these free trials can be used for the hands-on activities detailed in the Trailhead courses that support Data Cloud learning and certification. Also, in any Enterprise-level production environment, Data Cloud can be set up for free with a limited number of usage credits available for experimentation purposes.

Data Cloud has assumed this central importance to the Salesforce product strategy because the AI feature set offered by Einstein Studio could potentially require access to data from any corner of the enterprise, going far beyond the familiar Sales and Service apps and objects and into the realm of data warehouses, ERP systems, and third-party vendor solutions for loyalty, marketing, analytics, and more. As a fundamental part of the broader Salesforce Customer 360 initiative, Data Cloud aims to unify customer data from disparate sources, metaphorically providing the key that unlocks trapped data, to provide a comprehensive, real-time view of each customer. This unified data approach not only enhances customer interactions but also lays a robust foundation for advanced AI applications within Einstein Studio.

Data Cloud distinguishes itself within the highly competitive environment for cloud data warehouse or customer data platform solutions in the marketplace by staying focused on supporting and automating data-driven solutions for business optimization. In many cases, the preferred approach is a no-code solution that can be confidently created and maintained by a Salesforce admin, rather than a data scientist or data engineer. Originally, the primary value proposition for Data Cloud was about enabling advanced customer data management for personalized marketing, but with the advent of Einstein Studio, Data Cloud now offers a suite of tools designed to leverage AI for a greatly extended number of business use cases. By taking advantage of Data Cloud's support for scalable storage and processing data from across the enterprise, Einstein Studio enables the creation and deployment of AI models that drive intelligent interactions and personalized experiences across all the Salesforce clouds, including Sales, Service, Marketing, and Commerce.

In this chapter, we'll explore how Data Cloud centralizes and harmonizes data from diverse sources, providing a data integration environment in which you can train and deploy AI models within Einstein Studio. This integration process involves data ingestion, cleansing, transformation, and harmonization to ensure that the data that's fed into AI models is accurate, relevant, and actionable.

Furthermore, we'll discuss the potential impact of using this system of reference on your business processes. By harnessing the power of AI, organizations can drive significant efficiency gains and foster innovation. For instance, in Sales Cloud, AI models can predict customer behavior, identify high-value leads, and optimize sales strategies. In Service Cloud, AI can enhance customer support by automating case management and providing predictive insights. In Marketing Cloud, AI-driven personalization can boost campaign effectiveness, while in Commerce Cloud, AI can optimize inventory management and personalize shopping experiences.

The integration of Data Cloud with Einstein Studio exemplifies how Salesforce is empowering businesses to become more data-driven and AI-enabled. By providing a robust infrastructure for data management and advanced AI tools, Salesforce ensures that businesses can unlock the full potential of their data, driving smarter decisions and superior customer experiences.

This chapter will equip you with the knowledge and tools necessary to harness the full potential of Salesforce's AI capabilities, driving both innovation and efficiency in your organization. By understanding and effectively utilizing Data Cloud and Einstein Studio, you can transform your business processes and achieve a competitive edge in today's data-driven landscape.

Overview of Salesforce Data Cloud

Salesforce Data Cloud is designed to centralize and harmonize data from various sources, providing a system of reference for the implementation of specific use cases when a return on investment can be reasonably projected. For larger organizations with an operational Enterprise data warehouse, Data Cloud isn't a replacement for this activity – instead, it enhances and activates the data already being gathered there. This powerful tool is part of the Salesforce Customer 360 platform and is essential for creating a unified, comprehensive view of customer information, as well as enabling employees to make use of it within the flow of their work. In this section, we will explore how Data Cloud works, the types of data it can manage, and how it integrates with other Salesforce components, highlighting its features and benefits.

Example use cases

Here are some examples of business requirements that might indicate choosing Data Cloud as the enabling technology for data activation:

- Combine customer profile data from multiple backend systems, and generate a unified profile that achieves a single view of the customer.

- Combine customer activities and engagement points stored in different backend systems and link the activities to the unified customer record. As an example, consider a simple-sounding requirement to understand the profitability of each customer by subtracting returns from their order totals. The sales order totals can be easily accessed from the e-commerce system, but the return totals must be retrieved from a backend ERP system.

- Create a segment for personalized marketing offers consisting of customers who have viewed many pages on your website within the last month, and who have been consistently engaging with your marketing emails, but who have not yet made any purchases.

Core features and functionalities

Let's take a quick tour of the most important areas in Data Cloud that most implementations will need to use for the key activity of harmonizing data from the enterprise.

Data ingestion

It's exciting when you've gained consensus on a data-activated use case that can offer your company a key strategic advantage. Most businesses immediately face a reality check when they realize the data they want to use is trapped within multiple IT backend systems and not easily accessible. This is how you know you've found a good use case for Data Cloud. Once you've identified the systems of record that provide the data you want to activate, you'll want to bring the relevant records from the source system into Data Cloud.

You can make use of Data Cloud's ability to ingest data from many different sources. This includes CRM systems, ERP systems, third-party applications, external databases, and even social media platforms. When a specific connector isn't available for your source system, file-based and API integrations are also available to implement and operationalize an ongoing data synchronization activity. The result of data ingestion, regardless of which connection method is selected, is the creation of a **data lake object** (**DLO**), where the data from the remote system can be accessed and viewed within the Data Cloud environment. By centralizing this diverse data within Data Cloud, you can ensure that all the information necessary to activate your use case is accessible from one place, eliminating the silos that often fragment organizational data.

If the source data coming in needs to be cleaned up before it will be ready for further use, it's possible to use Data Cloud tools for data transformation, running in batch or real-time mode. This provides operational support for the removal of any inaccuracies, duplicates, or inconsistencies. You can also reshape the data if necessary, altering the rows and columns to get each table ready for mapping.

Data harmonization

Once you've ingested your data and verified its data quality, you can use a mapping tool in Data Cloud to harmonize it with the Customer 360 Data Model, resulting in the creation of one or more **data model objects (DMOs)**. This concept is what achieves the promise of unifying data from different source systems. The Customer 360 Data Model provides a standardized schema for storing and linking data of all types, across a very wide variety of business domains. The harmonization process means that a complex business object such as a sales order is always referenced the same way, using the same naming conventions and structure, even if two or three different systems from different vendors all contributed records to the total collection. Harmonization ensures that the data is clean, consistent, and ready for analysis and AI modeling. It also simplifies all subsequent analytical steps because all the idiosyncrasies of the DLO disappear after it's mapped to the DMO. The employees, reports, and software can just use the DMOs directly and don't have to know any of the details about the system from which the records originated.

Note that Data Cloud supports real-time data stream processing, which is essential for business scenarios that require up-to-the-minute insights. This capability allows for dynamic customer interactions and responsive business strategies, ensuring that decisions are based on the latest information available. Real-time processing is particularly beneficial in environments where customer behavior and market conditions can change rapidly.

Scalability

Scalability is a core feature of Data Cloud. It is designed to handle large volumes of data efficiently, making it suitable for demanding workloads from enterprises of all sizes. Built on a new generation of distributed data management technology, it simply outperforms the traditional Salesforce CRM storage layer for analytical tasks so that fewer constraints and rate limits stand in the way of success. Whether you're dealing with millions of customer records, billions of sensor measurements, or integrating data from hundreds of different sources, Data Cloud can scale to meet the demands of growing businesses.

Data activation

Data Cloud provides many tools for operating on the harmonized DMOs. Identity resolution processes can link records together based on rulesets that determine a match. The Calculated Insights feature helps to develop and operationalize analytical queries to provide summary metrics and calculations across more detailed records. Segment Builder is a user interface that provides a no-code experience for exploring and defining filters to group customer records together according to the criteria of your choice. The Activations user interface allows these segments and insights to be automatically delivered to many different kinds of target systems. Finally, the harmonized data is made available for analysis, reporting, and AI modeling. Users can access this data through Salesforce's suite of analytical tools, or it can be fed into AI models within Einstein Studio to generate further actionable insights.

Privacy and compliance

As a core component of the Salesforce platform, Data Cloud must adhere to data privacy and compliance requirements that originate from the regulatory environment within some of the world's largest companies, where strict data governance policies are commonplace. There are robust features to support role-based permissions, selective visibility of data housed within the system, and privacy regulations such as GDPR and CCPA. You can trust that the platform includes the tools, secure data handling practices, and audit capabilities to ensure that data management practices meet the highest standards.

Types of data managed by Data Cloud

The wide range of different business domains that have been carefully designed and woven into the Customer 360 Data Model makes it clear that Data Cloud is not limited to managing only customer data. These different data subject areas provide the blueprint for using Data Cloud to design a system that can manage a wide variety of data types, making it a versatile tool for organizations. And just to be clear, the Customer 360 Data Model is like traditional Salesforce objects in that it provides a standard starting point that can be customized with additional fields and objects that are unique to each business. However, making use of the standard Data Model to the greatest extent possible is highly recommended as it lowers risk and increases the velocity of an implementation. The following are some of the key data types:

- **Customer data**: This includes information about who a customer is, including personal identification, demographics, and customer preferences. By centralizing this data, businesses can create detailed customer profiles that drive personalized interactions and marketing efforts. Data Cloud does not attempt to provide a single "Golden Record" for customers, but instead offers a structure where information from different sources is integrated and can be flexibly referenced as needed.

- **Transactional data**: Transactional data encompasses sales transactions, service requests, invoices and payments, and any other business interactions. This data is crucial for understanding customer purchasing behavior and identifying trends.

- **Behavioral data**: Behavioral data includes information on how customers interact with the company's digital properties, such as website visits, app usage, marketing channel engagement, and social media interactions. This data helps in understanding customer preferences and behavior patterns.

- **Operational data**: Operational data involves information related to business processes, such as supply chain data, inventory levels, and production data. This data is essential for optimizing business operations and improving efficiency.

- **Third-party data**: Data Cloud can also integrate third-party data sources, such as market research data, industry reports, and external customer data. This enriches the organization's data pool and provides a broader context for analysis.

Integration with other Salesforce components

Data Cloud's out-of-the-box connectors include sophisticated support for filtering and retrieving data from most common Salesforce products. All the complexity of API-based data retrieval and transfer is completely hidden within these connectors, which can be deployed and operational with just a few clicks. The following data sources are supported by the Salesforce connectors:

- **Salesforce CRM**: Data Cloud integrates seamlessly with Salesforce CRM, enhancing CRM with a unified data approach. This integration allows for better customer insights, more effective sales strategies, and improved customer service. Configuration-based components permit information from Data Cloud to be easily added to a Salesforce record page, and the venerable Reports and Dashboards apps can now be used to visualize and summarize objects located in Data Cloud.

- **Salesforce Marketing Cloud**: By integrating with Marketing Cloud, Data Cloud enables personalized marketing campaigns. Marketers can leverage the unified customer data to create targeted campaigns that resonate with individual customers. A standard package can be used to ingest customer engagement data from Marketing Cloud, and segments built in Data Cloud can be activated in Data Cloud, where they can serve as the entry source for messaging campaigns.

- **Salesforce Service Cloud**: Sending new insights and data into Service Cloud allows for improved customer support. Service agents have access to comprehensive customer profiles, enabling them to provide more informed and efficient service. Imagine the possibilities of proactive case creation, in which an observation of some condition occurring in Data Cloud invokes a Flow in Service Cloud that results in the assignment of a new case to a service agent, informing them of an opportunity to offer assistance. It's also possible to view customer service engagements via Cases in Data Cloud, opening up an opportunity for greater personalization of customer messaging while they have an open support case.

- **Salesforce Commerce Cloud**: Commerce Cloud integration helps in creating personalized shopping experiences. By understanding customer preferences and behavior, businesses can offer tailored product recommendations and promotions. Both B2C Commerce and B2C Commerce can act as a system of record for product catalog and sales order data, providing Data Cloud with an effortless way to bring in those critical data sources.

- **Einstein Studio**: Its integration with Einstein Studio is particularly significant. Data Cloud provides the enriched data necessary for training and deploying AI models within Einstein Studio. This synergy enables advanced analytics, predictive modeling, and AI-driven insights that drive business innovation.

Benefits of Data Cloud

With all the other cloud giants providing data and AI technology solutions that may seem competitive to Data Cloud, it's important to clarify some of the distinguishing factors that put Data Cloud in a class by itself:

- **Unified data view**: One of the primary benefits of Data Cloud is the creation of a unified data view. By centralizing data from various sources, and mapping to the Customer 360 Data Model as an enterprise-level standard schema, businesses can gain a holistic understanding of their customers and operations and regain access to the data that's been trapped in point solutions and legacy systems.

- **Enhanced decision-making**: With accurate, real-time data at their fingertips, employees at all levels can make more informed and timely decisions. This leads to better business outcomes, increased employee productivity, and a competitive edge in the market.

- **Improved customer experience**: By leveraging unified customer data, businesses can deliver more personalized and engaging customer experiences. This improves customer satisfaction and loyalty.

- **Operational efficiency**: Data Cloud helps streamline business processes and improve operational efficiency. By having a single source of truth, businesses can reduce data redundancies and improve collaboration across departments.

- **Scalability and flexibility**: Data Cloud is designed to scale with the business. Whether you're dealing with increasing data volumes or expanding data sources, Data Cloud can accommodate growth and change.

- **Compliance and security**: With robust compliance and security features, Data Cloud ensures that businesses can manage their data responsibly and meet regulatory requirements.

Key goals and outcomes

Salesforce Data Cloud provides a system of reference for data originating from any source to be put into action on behalf of business goals.

The Customer 360 Data Model is designed to apply to any business and any data-producing system. Mapping data from DLOs to DMOs is a key activity in Data Cloud configuration, and these DMOs act as a layer that's used for activation and analysis.

Now that you've been provided with a broad overview of the themes and issues that can be addressed within the Data Cloud system, let's progress to a more close-up view of what it's like to work with them, starting with a flexible and powerful system for ingesting data from other systems.

Integrating data sources with Data Cloud

Connecting various data sources to Salesforce Data Cloud is the first step in building a unified data repository. This section provides a detailed guide on integrating different data sources, including CRM data, third-party applications, and real-time data streams. We'll discuss data connectors, APIs, and best practices for seamless integration.

Data Cloud's ingestion features permit it to provide many of the capabilities expected in a standalone **extract, load, transform (ELT)** tool. Let's look at the scenarios we'll be considering.

Full integration with source systems

Salesforce products and other popular business applications often have built-in connectors that facilitate seamless data integration. These connectors are designed to extract data, load it into Data Cloud, and map it into the Customer 360 Data Model automatically. By utilizing these pre-built connectors, organizations can quickly integrate their systems without the need for extensive custom development.

For example, integrating Salesforce CRM with Data Cloud allows for automatic synchronization of leads, contacts, and accounts data, ensuring that all customer interactions and transactions are up to date. This integration not only saves time but also reduces the risk of data discrepancies.

Salesforce has recently accelerated the arrival of more of these easy-to-use, pre-built connectors – both for a wider range of Salesforce apps as well as for common enterprise applications from other vendors such as Microsoft, Oracle, SAP, and Veeva.

File-based integration

Using file-based integration methods such as SFTP, AWS S3, and Azure Blob Storage, you can ingest data files into Data Cloud. This method is particularly useful for batch processing and handling large volumes of data that can be updated at periodic intervals. Organizations often use this approach to upload data exports from legacy systems or third-party applications.

Follow these steps to enable file-based integration:

1. **Set up secure file transfer**: Use the data sources in **Data Cloud Setup** to Establish a **Secure File Transfer Protocol (SFTP)** or configure cloud storage services such as AWS S3.

2. **Prepare data files**: Format the data files according to the requirements of Data Cloud, ensuring they are clean and well structured. Using the CSV format is standard and acceptable, but also consider using the Parquet file format, which provides superior compression and types for data fields.

3. **Upload files**: Use the remote system capabilities or automated scripts via a middleware component to upload data files to the designated storage location.

4. **Configure data streams**: Use the **Data Stream** interface in Data Cloud to process and import the uploaded files to a DLO.

To configure the connector to the AWS S3 object storage, you'll need to enter credentials on the following screen:

Figure 5.1 – AWS S3 file storage connection setup

API-based integration

One type of data source is the Data Cloud Ingestion API. This is the gateway to setting up a data stream that receives its contents from external systems who send it via the Ingestion API, which comes in both bulk load and real-time versions. MuleSoft is an example of a middleware system that already has support to send data into the Ingestion API. Use of a middleware system such as MuleSoft enables flexible and real-time data ingestion from just about any system. MuleSoft in particular has connectors that simplify access to a very wide range of enterprise-class software systems where your data might be located.

A second type of real-time API-based integration provided by Data Cloud is the Web and Mobile App Connector. This provides the ability to stream both profile and engagement data into Data Cloud by having developers implement the required SDK on your website or mobile app.

These integrations are ideal for scenarios where continuous data flow is necessary. By leveraging APIs, organizations can create custom data connectors that push data into Data Cloud as it is generated.

The following screenshot shows an Ingestion API endpoint that has been configured so that an external program can provide frequent updates to region-specific weather information, which then appear within a DLO according to a predefined schema definition:

Figure 5.2 – Ingestion API setup

Zero Copy Data Federation

Zero Copy Data Federation, also referred to as **Bring Your Own Lake** (**BYOL**), allows Data Cloud to access data from online data warehouse systems and make it visible for further use, connection, and activation within Data Cloud. The network of participating partners is growing and currently includes Snowflake, Databricks, AWS Redshift, and Google. This approach leverages existing data architectures and reduces data duplication. By establishing connections to these external data warehouses, Data Cloud can query and analyze data directly at the source.

The benefits of Zero Copy Data Federation are as follows:

- **Reduced data movement**: Minimize data transfer between cloud providers, which reduces latency and increases efficiency

- **Cost savings**: Lower storage and processing costs by avoiding data duplication

- **Consistency**: Maintain a single source of truth by accessing data directly from the original systems of record

Configuring data sources and data streams

The overall process of data ingestion begins with configuring the data source within Data Cloud Setup, representing the origin system from which data will be retrieved. You then proceed to configure data streams, each representing a single database table with records ingested from the source. Within large organizations, it's common to require an elevated role of system permissions to create the data source, but non-administrator data analysts can be enabled to perform the work of ingesting and mapping various data streams available within the source.

The following are some of the flexible techniques for data stream configuration:

- In cases of fully integrated sources, including the major Salesforce cloud applications, the mechanics of the data retrieval process are built into the product, and the streams that are created are pre-configured. These are referred to as **data bundles** for common use cases that Salesforce wants to make as easy as possible to acquire. This simplifies the setup process and ensures consistency. Inspecting these automatically to create mappings is a great way to learn the proper usage of the Customer 360 Data Model at a granular level of detail.

- For all other types of data unique to your organization, Data Cloud inspects a sample of incoming data and proposes a storage schema. You need to review and modify that schema to include all necessary attributes and metadata about how the stream will be used.

- Choosing the correct data stream category (either Profile, Engagement, or Other) greatly impacts subsequent usage and configuration of the data stream. An Engagement data stream must contain a timestamp field the platform can use to automatically perform time-based calculations.

Example configuration – Salesforce B2C Commerce orders bundle ingestion

If you run an online storefront using B2C Commerce, you'll be glad to know that the product catalog, hierarchical category structure, and sales order history can all be automatically configured as data streams within Data Cloud with complete faithfulness to the details of the internal organization of these complex objects. One thing to be aware of with this feature is the limited lookback availability. When you first enable the data stream, it will receive only the most recent month of order history. If you want to ingest additional historical data, that will require a different data source and additional effort.

Follow these steps to achieve data integration with B2C Commerce:

1. **Create the data source**: In Data Cloud Setup, create a new connector from the B2C Commerce page. Enter the business manager URL. Authentication will be performed automatically if you're logged in to the production system in another browser tab. Select the site or sites that you wish to use in Data Cloud.

2. **Initiate data bundle ingestion**: From the **Data Streams** page, create a new data stream and select **B2C Commerce**. The following page confirms your B2C Commerce instance and shows you all of the order bundle mappings to be created in the data space.

3. **Configure formula fields:** If you'd like to extend the information that will be landed into the DLOs using a simple formula language, it's possible to modify any of the Order Objects by defining new Formula Fields.

4. **Review security and visibility:** On the following page, you can use filters on the DLO field attributes to set restrictions on how region-specific or brand-specific data is viewed. Data governance may require that you segment this type of data for different viewers within the system. The **Data Spaces** feature provides that capability.

5. **Activate the data bundle**: Upon completion of the configuration steps, you'll see new data streams that define DLOs, each with their mapping to the relevant DMO. While this example focused on B2C Commerce as the source system, Data Cloud provides a similarly easy-to-use process for quite a few other scenarios. Data bundles exist for many Salesforce products, such as Sales, Service, Loyalty, Marketing, and Multichannel Inventory – and additional support for enterprise software from other vendors is arriving with every new release of Data Cloud.

The following screenshot shows the incoming sales order data from B2C Commerce on the left-hand side, as well as how each field is mapped to the Customer 360 data model. All of this configuration is part of the data bundle and can be used as-is or customized as needed:

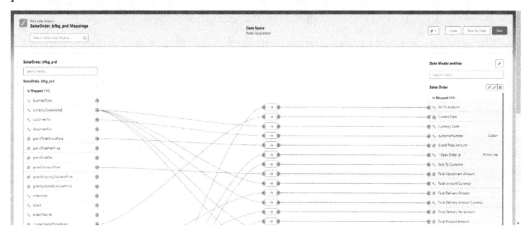

Figure 5.3 – Harmonizing order data from B2C Commerce

Example configuration – using the Ingestion API to stream engagement data

Moving along from the easiest-to-use, out-of-the-box support for data bundles, let's take a look at a more challenging data integration scenario – an enterprise system with no inherent capability to generate a well-defined file-based output, but which provides an API that can be used to retrieve data upon demand or as it is generated. Data Cloud's Ingestion API provides the needed support that a developer can use to connect the two systems.

Follow these steps to enable streaming data ingestion:

1. **Set up the Ingestion API's data source**: Each Ingestion API connection requires the creation of a schema file using the OpenAI text format. This file defines one or more object names, along with the names and types of the attributes of each object.

2. **Share details with your developer**: Data Cloud Setup provides a link to developer documentation, along with API endpoints for each object, which should be shared with your developer.

3. **Configure the data stream**: Create a new data stream, selecting the Ingestion API connection you created in *Step 1* and at least one of the schema objects. As with other data streams, you'll configure how Data Cloud treats this data by specifying the primary key, data stream category, and either the **Record Modified** field (for the **Profile** and **Other** categories) or the **Event Date** field (for the **Engagement** category). Upon completion, you will see one or more data streams, depending on how many schema objects you chose.

4. **Confirm incoming data and map it to DMOs**: When the developer has established API connectivity, data will appear in the data stream. To complete the process, navigate to each data stream and map the API-provided fields to standard Salesforce or custom objects.

While this example shows that data integration can become arbitrarily complicated, depending on the specific use case, the point to take away is that Data Cloud provides multiple pathways to ingest data from any possible backend. The Ingestion API comes in both batch and real-time flavors, and Data Cloud supports another set of similar integration techniques for streaming engagement data from your website or mobile app. The work that's done by the developer to link systems together using the Ingestion API could be hosted and supported within a cloud solutions provider – for example, as an AWS Lambda serverless function. That might be a good approach for a simple use case, but for larger challenges, Salesforce also provides extensive support within their MuleSoft integration platform to retrieve data from hundreds of enterprise software vendors and further simplifies sending it to Data Cloud through the Ingestion API.

Case study 1 – global fashion brand

A global fashion brand selected Data Cloud to create a system of reference for customer data and improve its ability to create targeted customer segments. Their suite of data sources included the following:

- **B2C Commerce orders data bundle**: This provided direct access to order information, enhancing marketing strategies

- **Web and mobile connector**: This replaced a legacy solution for abandoned cart functionality, making clickstream data accessible for broader use

- **Databricks integration**: This enabled access to ERP data for post-purchase order information, crucial for determining customer lifetime value

One challenge that appeared in this implementation was the additional effort required to import a full 2 years of order history. Fortunately, the order totals and product line items were represented in Databricks, and the data engineers were able to prepare a one-time file export of the two years of order history so that it could be ingested to Data Cloud after the B2C Commerce order bundle had already started acquiring new orders.

Case study 2 – heavy equipment sales and service

A company in the construction industry leveraged Data Cloud to analyze the intersection between extreme weather and their customers' construction equipment assets. They licensed a real-time weather stream from a data services provider and built a middleware solution to retrieve and push weather data into Data Cloud using the Streaming Ingestion API.

The following challenges and solutions were identified:

- **Data quality issues**: The focus on finding new uses for the data stored in the company's Salesforce system brought to light several data quality concerns that had been accumulating over time. Accounts, products, and assets were all examples of objects hosted within Salesforce that needed to undergo a data cleansing and validation process as a result of a data quality check that was done before the data bundle ingestion. Data Cloud does provide a toolbox for accomplishing these tasks by declaratively specifying data transformations. But if possible, performing these activities upstream of Data Cloud may be a better solution because other systems may also benefit from the effort to purge unusable data. The product owner decided it would be a good time to use an AppExchange solution that helped to eliminate duplicate and invalid records for contacts, accounts, and products directly within the CRM.

- **Cost of service concerns**: The product owner showed good judgment in relying on their Salesforce AE to iteratively refine estimates and projections of compute and storage fees from Data Cloud. They needed to provide accurate estimates of the data volume and frequency of processing required by the predictive maintenance use case they were designing.

Key goals and outcomes

Data Cloud provides integration capabilities to unlock access not only to the treasure trove of business data within Salesforce products but also to any other systems of record that have earned a place in your enterprise solutions stack.

Depending on which system of record you need to consult, Data Cloud has integration solutions ranging from fully automatic, to "no code" configuration using file-based inputs, to "pro code" integrations that use middleware and APIs.

The best practices for data integration include data preparation, governance, and continuous monitoring to ensure data quality and compliance.

You've now learned about some of the ways that Data Cloud handles the job of retrieving and ingesting data from other systems. Next up, we'll learn how to map the data from its initial form into the standardized Customer 360 Data Model, a process known as harmonization.

Centralizing and harmonizing customer data

The challenge of managing and harmonizing customer data from various sources is a complex yet crucial task that IT departments are quite familiar with. Organizations aiming to leverage their data assets effectively typically employ technical specialists such as data engineers, data architects, and data to make it happen. Salesforce Data Cloud has a lot to offer these employees in the sophisticated suite of tools and design approaches it provides for data integration. Data architects can sleep better at night knowing that their schema is derived from the Customer 360 Data Model, a standards-based design that can be extended and customized as needed, but which provides a very capable storage design relevant to most business activities. In classic Salesforce fashion, the extensible and predefined data model means that even within the activity of building out a large-scale database-backed system, there is a starting point for the activity that lowers the overall risk as compared to beginning from a blank slate.

The Customer 360 Data Model also provides a Data Catalog for all activities that occur downstream of Data Cloud. The powerful metadata management capabilities of the Salesforce platform work in harmony with the Customer 360 Data Model, allowing for a fully documented data dictionary that's essential both for employee productivity as well as data governance.

Data Cloud's transformation and harmonization capabilities allow for the elegant automation of many complex and tedious tasks typically performed by professional data engineers. These tools enable organizations to streamline data workflows, reduce manual intervention, and ensure data consistency and accuracy across the board.

Data transformation

In the previous section, we discussed the mapping process, which moves data out of DLOs and into the "harmonized" DMOs. To employees who work with data every day, whether that work occurs in a spreadsheet or a data warehouse, this concept may seem too simplistic. Typically, any new data source must be modified so that it can be put into the correct "shape" for further analysis. This activity is the "transform" component of the ELT paradigm and is also known as data wrangling. It's estimated that performing this type of work frequently consumes 80% of the time of a data practitioner, leaving only 20% of their time to use the cleaned and organized data for analysis and activation. Data Cloud provides an environment in which these transformations can be configured once and then continue to operate in a fully automated fashion, potentially freeing up time for data analysts and data scientists to do the part of their job they enjoy the most – providing valuable insights to their employer!

Data Cloud provides the following tools and techniques for converting data from one format into another, allowing transformation to occur at different locations within the overall data pipeline:

- **Formula fields on data streams**: The simplest technique is often the most effective. When defining data streams, Data Cloud scans a sample of the incoming data and provides a suggested set of field names and types. These names and types can be modified through configuration, and new derived fields can be defined that use a spreadsheet-like formula language to apply functions to incoming field values. This can be a great way to fill in defaults for missing data, concatenate two fields together, or convert values into a desired standardized output format.

- **Batch data transforms:** This powerful tool allows for open-ended modification of data within the system and offers advanced transformation functionality in a visual editing environment. It can work with DLOs or DMOs, and it can either modify existing objects or create new destination objects with the results of the transformation. However, the most common place for it to be used is to transform an incoming DLO to create a different DLO that can be more easily mapped to the Customer 360 Data Model. It's useful for any type of cleaning or reshaping challenge – for example, going from a wide table format where there are four different phone numbers stored with different field names, into a narrow table format where there is just one phone number column along with a "phone number type" column identifying whether the phone number on the current row represents a business, personal, or mobile phone number.

- **Streaming Data Transforms:** While the batch transform tool is highly capable and offers an easy-to-use flowchart-style user interface, it does have the disadvantage of needing to run on a predefined schedule. When achieving rapid throughput of your data pipeline is important, the Streaming Data Transforms feature can operate on data as it arrives in the source. It's primarily useful for real-time data streams which can be configured using the streaming Ingestion API, or for web and mobile behavioral data (which can be gathered through the Web and Mobile API or the Marketing Cloud Personalization connector). In all these cases, it operates by choosing a source DLO and writing a SQL query that transforms records into a separate DLO for output. Through this familiar declarative language, you can perform common data cleaning tasks such as filtering out rows you don't want to see or applying standardization to specific input attributes.

The following screenshot shows the user experience when applying a batch data transform using the visual editor:

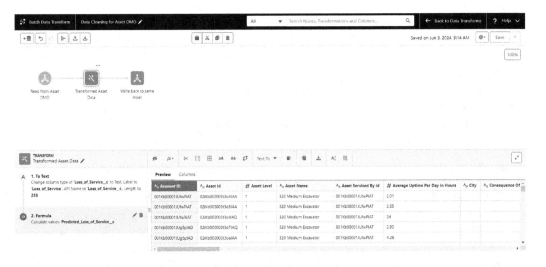

Figure 5.4 – The batch data transform tool at work, applying a simple transformation

The **Transform** node has been added between the source and target, allowing configuration changes to be applied to individual fields.

Data cleansing

Data cleansing is the process of identifying and correcting errors to improve data quality. The aforementioned tools within Data Cloud are available for your use as needed so that a fully automated solution for data cleansing can come together quickly and be ready for production use. The following are some typical issues that need to be fixed to improve data quality:

- Missing values and white spaces
- Inconsistent formatting of dates, addresses, and phone numbers
- Outdated data
- Incorrect data types or inconsistent units
- Irrelevant data

It can certainly be helpful to perform some data analysis outside of Data Cloud to assist in knowing what types of cleansing will be necessary. Data science toolkits and coding practices offer automated exploratory data analysis, which can quickly surface these issues and more. It's also worth asking if there are benefits to applying these types of cleaning steps upstream of Data Cloud. However, it's not always possible – and that's when data transforms in Data Cloud can be a life saver.

Data deduplication

One important feature of Data Cloud we haven't touched on yet is identity resolution. The purpose of identity resolution is to bring together customer profiles originating from different source systems and link them all together under a single unified profile. This matching operation is configured with flexible matching rules that can consider many different attributes and how to identify records that represent the same person using both probabilistic and deterministic matching. It's important to understand that Identity Resolution in Data Cloud is not about merging records, but rather creating relationships and proposing the Unified Individual record that allows the user to review all the different data elements that contributed to this view of the customer.

Salesforce administrators are already aware of how important it is to identify duplicate records within the leads, contacts, and account objects within their Salesforce org. They use standard platform features to configure duplicate and matching rules, which assist with data quality within that instance of Salesforce. Additionally, if data quality has already gone downhill, there are AppExchange partners who can provide automated solutions to assist the administrator with performing cleanup of duplicate records.

For businesses that are focused on data quality, if duplicate records are perpetually a problem within their Sales or Service Cloud instance, it could be advantageous to make use of Data Cloud's identity resolution capabilities to send an event back to the Salesforce organization, based on a **change data capture** (**CDC**) event, to trigger a flow that will merge duplicate records.

The identity resolution capability is often a primary reason to adopt Data Cloud as it provides business-critical functionality that is difficult to achieve any other way. Consider how valuable it can be in a corporate acquisition scenario – driving revenue by prospecting within the other company's customer database or looking for customers who are shared between the two businesses could be a very sensible strategy to pursue. Custom-coded solutions for identity resolution in data warehouses can work but tend to lack the flexibility needed to adapt to ever-changing business requirements. Just to offer one example of the robustness of the Data Cloud solution, Salesforce provides a free set of analytical dashboards that can be installed in Tableau to provide statistics and an exploratory interface around the performance of identity resolution in Data Cloud, permitting the administrator to get vital insights into how well the feature is working across the full range of data sources in the system.

Once the Tableau package has been installed, it can pull the needed information from Data Cloud to display a dashboard, as shown in the following screenshot:

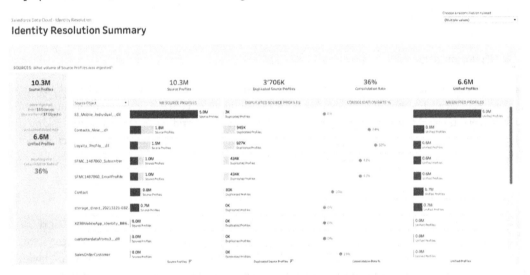

Figure 5.5 – Identity resolution accelerator for Tableau

Harmonizing data from multiple sources

Profile data is just one of the categories of data streams that can be set up in Data Cloud. The others are Engagement (for immutable records that represent an event for a customer that took place on a specific day and time) and Other (for any other type of data not covered in the Profile and Engagement categories).

Making the effort to map your Engagement or other kinds of data into the Customer 360 Data Model can provide the same type of rewards that we saw with identity resolution. Without the concept of a unified data model, it would be much more difficult to derive value from data from multiple backend systems.

As an example from the e-commerce world, a Customer 360 sales order object in Data Cloud allows you to represent the same thing using the same terminology, regardless of whether the system of record for that order happened to be Salesforce Commerce Cloud, SAP Commerce Cloud, Manhattan Omnichannel Commerce, Microsoft Dynamics 365, or an in-house transactional database system. Harmonizing all that order data could be useful in situations such as the following:

- E-commerce orders, shipping updates, and returns information are all private to their respective systems and you need a system of reference to assemble all the order data in one place.

- Online orders are handled by one or more different e-commerce systems, while in-store orders are handled by a completely separate POS. You'd still like to have a unified view of purchasing activity that spans both online and in-store behavior.

Similarly, a service-oriented use case might have to address an environment in which the systems that are used to track customer service are not unified. You can use the Customer 360 Case object in Data Cloud as a mapping destination for customer service cases tracked in ServiceNow, Jira, Salesforce Service Cloud, or other systems. Even if your organization uses more than one of these, you can make use of the same definition of a Case object in Data Cloud to analyze all of them the same way.

Apart from systems unification, there could also be benefits to mapping your data to the Customer 360 Data Model if a set of visualizations exists that was built for Customer 360, and you'd like to make use of them rather than building your own. Salesforce is releasing accelerator packages for Tableau that take this approach, building high-quality reports and dashboards that depend solely on the well-documented Customer 360 Data Model so that they can be used no matter what the original transactional system looks like. And it's not just Tableau that can do this trick – the standard Salesforce Core platform's Reports and Dashboards capabilities can also access the Customer 360 DMOs, and AppExchange developers are likely to be hard at work creating packages of useful data visualizations that answer common business questions. Data Cloud also provides a Query API, which can be used by external systems that want to extract from Data Cloud. Again, using the Customer 360 DMOs or the calculated insights derived from them will lead to the development of standardized and reusable solutions.

The following screenshot shows an example of a high-quality visualization that's been built in Tableau to provide operational details to a customer service manager:

Figure 5.6 – Tableau Service Desk for Data Cloud

Best practices for maintaining data quality

Maintaining excellent data quality is essential for reliable analytics and AI. Data Cloud provides several features and best practices to ensure data integrity:

- **Monitoring**: Ask a Salesforce admin to use the Data Cloud Control and Metadata Change Events to implement Flows that automatically scan this event stream for error conditions, and log errors and notifications when platform jobs do not run as expected.

- **Regular data audits**: Accompany the implementation of Data Cloud with the development of several SQL queries that are used to create data quality checks and gather statistics about record completeness and expected data volume of records over a certain period. These can be periodically run manually or can become the basis for a fully automated system for auditing data quality.

- **Automated data cleansing**: During data stream setup, think defensively about data quality, and implement automated checks to detect and correct errors in real time.

- **Data governance policies**: Establish governance policies to manage data access, usage, and quality. Establish a permissions system of least privilege to prevent unwanted changes to the metadata, and monitor the Metadata Change events to build an audit trail of when new objects and fields are introduced or deleted.

- **Employee training**: Train employees on data management best practices and the importance of data quality.

- **Data spaces**: Use Data Cloud features for the segregation of both records and entire objects by regional business unit or by brand. Similar to the "schema" object of a traditional relational database management system, data spaces allow the Data Cloud administrator to manage role-based permissions on a subset of the overall contents of the Data Cloud instance.

Key goals and outcomes

Harmonizing a wide array of different enterprise data is one of the major value propositions of Data Cloud and its Customer 360 Data Model.

Use the Bulk Data Transform tool to automate the process of cleaning and reshaping incoming DLOs.

The Data Cloud implementer should always assess new data sources and look for the most common quality control issues, which almost always need some attention to detail to make corrections.

With that, you've learned about data harmonization, and hopefully, the value and importance of the Customer 360 Data Model has started to sink in. Having just a single data dictionary that describes all of your enterprise data, even though it may come from dozens of different systems, is a fascinating prospect to data analysts, offering the possibility to use standard queries and other summarization tools against the combined dataset of the entire enterprise. We'll see how to accomplish that activity in the following chapter, which is all about Calculated Insights.

Defining calculated insights on harmonized data

It's important to understand that the Calculated Insights feature is the descendant of a straightforward idea that has proved its merit throughout the history of relational database management systems. The concept of a **materialized view** is extremely familiar to a database administrator, and it simply means that the underlying system provides a means by which the results of a complex query that joins and structures data can be saved into its own table structure, where it can be referenced more efficiently for many other uses that don't require direct access to the underlying data. Essentially, it's a form of caching a query result, and it includes methods for periodically re-running the query to update the materialized view.

In Data Cloud, calculated insights derived from harmonized data play a pivotal role in the process of deriving value from the data, and they work the same way as a classical materialized view. Data Cloud provides tools for creating these insights, allowing businesses to leverage their data for actionable intelligence. This section examines the importance of calculated insights, exploring three approaches to building them: no-code, pro-code using SQL, and streaming insights. Each approach offers unique benefits and caters to different levels of technical expertise.

Why calculated insights are useful

Although Data Cloud gives you a platform that can manage incoming data at the grandest scale, ultimately, the reason to go through the exercise of data ingestion and harmonization is to process that data and derive simple-to-understand insights from it. Calculated Insights is a key enabling technology within Data Cloud that allows administrators to create aggregations and derived calculations that are suitable for reporting and providing high-level summary metrics about customers or other business entities. These insights help identify trends, predict outcomes, and uncover hidden patterns that might not be immediately obvious. By applying calculations to harmonized data, businesses can transform raw data into valuable intelligence that drives growth and innovation.

The use of Calculated Insights can drive both platform efficiency and operational efficiency. After a calculated insight has been defined, it runs on an automated refresh schedule, and it keeps its target object up to date continuously. Data Cloud users then have access to a new object with dimensions and metrics that relate to the primary object, whether it's a Unified Individual, a unified account, or something else. The calculations that are performed can be quite complex, so the calculated insight is a form of encapsulation that allows its output to be taken for granted by everyday users, who don't need to know everything that went into producing the metrics provided by the calculated insight.

Setting up Calculated insights requires understanding the meaning of the terms **dimensions** and **metrics**. These are fundamental concepts in data analysis that serve distinct purposes. Dimensions are qualitative attributes or fields that categorize and provide context to data, such as the unified customer ID, time, location, or product type. They help in segmenting and filtering data to understand different perspectives. Metrics, on the other hand, are quantitative measurements that are used to track performance and outcomes, such as sales figures, revenue, and conversion rates. While dimensions help in organizing and slicing data, metrics provide the numerical values that are analyzed within those categories to derive insights and make data-driven decisions. Successful usage of Calculated Insights in Data Cloud requires explicitly classifying every field you define as one of these two types.

The no-code approach using Visual Builder

Salesforce Data Cloud offers a no-code solution for defining calculated insights through Visual Builder. This tool allows users to create complex calculations and aggregations using a user-friendly interface, making data insights accessible to those without advanced programming skills.

If you're familiar with declarative tools such as the Salesforce Reports and Dashboards builder, the Visual Builder for calculated insights may come as a surprise. It presents the configuration task as being more like the definition of a Flow: a successive series of actions and branching possibilities that allow a data transformation to take place. Reports and Dashboards has a simpler UI since it requires you to choose a report type from which all available data is predefined and joined. In Visual Builder, joining data from different objects present in Data Cloud is a task you must do yourself; however, the tool makes it quite easy to accomplish.

Follow these steps to set this up:

1. **Access Visual Builder**: Navigate to the Calculated Insights app and click the **New** button. Select **Visual Builder** from the list of alternatives and choose **Calculated Insight**.

2. **Select input data**: Choose one of the harmonized DMOs from the resulting list. **Unified Individual** is the most likely suspect, but **Individual** or **Account** may also be good choices, depending on what's in your data.

3. **Join with other data**: Add a **Join** node and select the other tables that should be joined together with your starting table.

4. **Define filters and transforms**:

    *   The **Filter** node allows you to refine query results by defining what to include and what to exclude.

    *   The **Transform** and **Case** nodes exist so that fields in your query can be modified using a declarative interface to associate formula names with their inputs and define the name of a new output field. This allows data cleaning activities to take place when the insight is being built if necessary.

5. **Define the aggregate operation**:

    *   If you try to save the insight that doesn't have an **Aggregate** node, you'll get an error

    *   The **Aggregate** node is where you create the calculated insight.

    *   Define and name your dimensions, which should just be categorical fields that exist in the data you've assembled up to this point.

    *   Define and name your metrics, which consist of an aggregate database operation (such as **Count**, **Sum**, or **Maximum**) applied to one of the fields in your dataset.

    *   The result is the construction of an aggregation query, where the number of rows in the dataset changes by applying the aggregation functions to the group of values within each subset defined by the dimension columns. For example, if your dimension is **Unified Individual**, and your aggregation is **Maximum of Purchase Date**, the resulting calculated insights dataset will have one row for each Unified Individual, and all the purchase data will be replaced by a single field that contains the last purchase date for each person.

6. **Save and run**: After resolving any validation errors, you'll be able to give your calculated insight a name and description and then set up its operational refresh schedule.

The following screenshot shows the process of creating a calculated insight, in which multiple DMOs are being joined together to create a **Last product browse date** variable for all records linked to a single Unified Individual:

Figure 5.7 – Calculated Insights Builder

The pro-code approach using SQL

Visual Builder shows what's possible with a modern user interface that takes maximum advantage of the metadata descriptions and strictly defined schema structure within Data Cloud. Its ease-of-use features include automatically keeping track of all field names from all sources, and automatically applying the correct keys to use to join tables together. Furthermore, it displays a complete menu of all available database functions for transformation and aggregation. Even for data professionals who know SQL, it's worth considering the use of Visual Builder if you will ever need to communicate how your calculated insights are built to a non-technical audience because the visual diagram it produces simplifies the task of understanding what it's doing.

However, for Data Cloud users who are familiar with SQL, a code-based approach might still be advantageous. Some benefits of using SQL include the ability to store text-based queries in a version control system, the ability to rapidly evolve a complex query through interactive experimentation within a database IDE, and the ability to create complex analytical queries that go beyond the current capabilities of Visual Builder.

A recent addition to Data Cloud is a Query Editor that helps users capitalize on the benefits of writing SQL against the Data Cloud objects while greatly simplifying access to metadata through an exploration interface and an autocomplete feature. From the **Query Editor** screen in Data Cloud, you can organize queries into workspaces where they are visible to other users of the platform.

The Query Editor eliminates a lot of the complexity that formerly made the job of SQL authoring more difficult. Before the Query Editor, it was helpful to connect a remote database IDE such as DBeaver to Data Cloud through a JDBC driver and use it to write queries in the same way. The integrated query development environment now provides superior ease-of-use, collaborative query authoring with named workspaces, and integrated browsing of the complex DMO metadata.

The following screenshot shows some built-in example queries that can be accessed using the Query Editor:

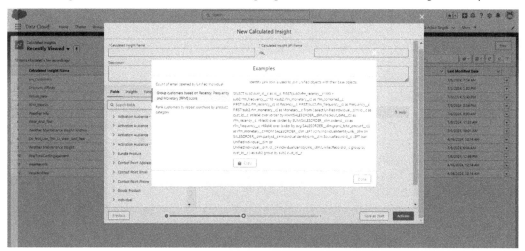

Figure 5.8 – SQL definition for calculated insights

To create a SQL calculated insight, start by writing your SQL query in Query Builder. You'll need to determine in advance which fields you'll be using for dimensions and metrics. The SQL query structure will be declared invalid by the calculated insights builder if it does not meet these specific requirements:

- It must have a GROUP BY clause.
- All fields listed within the GROUP BY clause will be designated as dimension fields. Make sure that all categorical fields, as well as the field you'll use as a reference to your primary object (for example Unified Individual ID), are dimensions by listing them all in the GROUP BY clause.
- All fields in the query results that are not in the GROUP BY clause will be assumed to be your metrics. These will need to be named within the SELECT clause of the SQL statement and must use an aggregate function to calculate their values.

How streaming insights are different

Another option that's available when creating a new insight is a streaming insight. These can be defined using either Visual Builder or by writing a SQL query. The fundamental goal is the same as that of regular calculated insights: to perform an aggregate operation on incoming data so that a higher-level observation can be made about an entire collection of data. Streaming insights differ in that there is an assumption that you're looking at some recent period of data to determine that something has happened. They do not operate on a fixed recurring schedule; instead, they are an "always on" monitoring mechanism that can operate only on the subset of your data sources classified as real-time streaming sources. These include data streams created for web and mobile SDK and Marketing Cloud Personalization. As such, the potential use cases involve near-real-time monitoring of customer interactions on web or mobile channels.

The Streaming Insights feature pairs up nicely with the Data Actions feature in Data Cloud, which allows an event to be delivered to Salesforce CRM, where a Flow can automate the creation of a support case or amend the data on a contact or lead object. As an example, consider monitoring reviews being posted online and automatically creating a support case to drive improvements to customer satisfaction when a low rating is observed. Or how about sending customers a product installation video for a product that they just purchased?

By leveraging the Calculated Insights capabilities of Data Cloud, organizations can unlock the full potential of their data. Calculated insights transform raw data into actionable intelligence, driving informed decision-making and operational efficiency. When taking a thoughtful approach to aligning your most important business use cases with the available features in Data Cloud for an implementation project, calculated insights are very likely to be involved in turning the solution description into the reality of an operational database solution. The insights can also be of great use when you're interacting with generative AI using the Data Graph feature, as we will learn in the next section.

Providing grounding to Prompt Builder using Data Graph

The Data Graph feature in Data Cloud allows the user to easily define a structured collection of data related to a primary DMO, with the intent to package that data together with a prompt to a generative AI model. Data Graph is a technical solution that enhances the capabilities of Prompt Builder in Einstein Studio by grounding prompts in a rich, contextual framework. Through the implementation of Data Graph, organizations can leverage their data more effectively, leading to more accurate and context-aware generative AI interactions. This section explores the creation, management, and application of data graphs within Salesforce Data Cloud, offering a comprehensive guide to harnessing their full potential.

Building a data graph

A data graph is a network of interconnected data entities that represent relationships and hierarchies within your dataset. It is structured to facilitate easy navigation and retrieval of relevant information. In Salesforce Data Cloud, data graphs are constructed by linking data entities based on defined relationships, enabling a more intuitive understanding of complex data structures. The user interface presents the relationships stemming from the primary DMO (such as Unified Individual) in a remarkably simple way. It's extremely easy to define the data graph and preview the JSON-formatted text output that represents one "record" containing nested hierarchical related records. The resulting structured data is perfectly suited to include in a prompt to a large language model, which can easily be used to locate specific information about the customer in question.

Follow these steps to build a data graph:

1. **Access the Data Graph screen in Data Cloud**: Navigate to Salesforce Data Cloud and select **Data Graph** from the tab navigation, then click the **New** button.

2. **Configure the high-level information**: Give the data graph a name and description, and specify the primary DMO. Assuming you're using identity resolution to derive the Unified Individual DMO, you'd probably choose the Unified Individual DMO here.

3. **Establish relationships**: Define the related DMOs and calculated insights you wish to include in the data graph and use the checkboxes to select the attributes that will be useful to provide with the prompt.

4. **Preview the JSON schema**: Use the **Preview** button to see what the overall text structure of the data graph will be, with placeholders for all the actual values. Even before building the data graph, this preview text could be used together with a potential prompt to experiment with the quality of output from a large language model.

5. **Save and build**: After you've verified the structure and reviewed it to make sure it includes every attribute you might need, you're ready to save. A build process will be kicked off and Data Cloud will automatically keep the data graph up to date with changes in the incoming data.

The following screenshot shows how to navigate relationships within the Customer 360 Data Model, starting with all DMOs that are linked to **Unified Individual**:

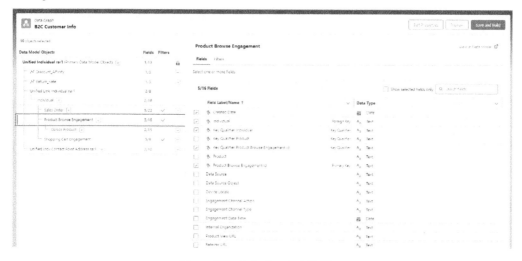

Figure 5.9 – Data Graph definition

Referencing the data graph in Prompt Builder

Finally, we've come to the key point of leverage that Data Cloud provides to businesses that want to use their customer data within every prompt to greatly improve the quality of generative AI output. As you've seen in this chapter, there is a lot to learn and do to implement Data Cloud. However, one of the big payoffs for doing all this setup is that the data graph you've defined can be referenced within Prompt Builder so that a data graph record can be inserted into a prompt. When you think about all the layers of complex technology required to provide rapid access to the data graph within the interactive Copilot experience, it's an impressive achievement that Data Cloud makes this attainable within a mostly declarative and configuration-based environment. Democratization of advanced technology to benefit as many enterprises as possible is one of Salesforce's primary missions, and Prompt Builder's grounding capability delivers on that promise. Integrating data graphs with Prompt Builder enhances the relevance and precision of AI-generated responses. By grounding prompts in the contextual framework of a data graph, Prompt Builder can generate more accurate and context-aware outputs.

You've already seen how to insert input variables and Flow outputs to provide context to the prompt. Including a data graph is an extension of that type of capability and allows you to include data from anywhere in the enterprise within the prompt and the Copilot action.

The prompt that's stored in Prompt Builder can reference data graphs using a simple insertion syntax such as `Write me an outreach email. Using the following data: {{{Data Cloud.Customer Graph}}}`.

Aside from their clear purpose within Einstein Studio for generative AI enhancement, data graphs also have other interesting possibilities, with the potential to include them in activations to Marketing Cloud or the Salesforce Core platform via events. They can also be accessed by external systems using the Data Graphs API, allowing Data Cloud to share its most valuable information in a format that's very easy for application developers to consume. Standard Data Graphs are refreshed every 24 hours, but there are also variations on the feature that support streaming inputs for real-time use cases and record caching to ensure rapid retrieval.

You've now learned some use cases for data graphs, which nicely demonstrates the relationship between Data Cloud and the Einstein Studio features for language generation that we saw earlier in this book. We'll continue learning about how Data Cloud provides the infrastructure that's used to monitor and operationalize the generative AI activity that occurs across the organization.

Auditing generative AI usage with Data Cloud

We're all familiar with the saying "Trust, but verify." Salesforce goes to great lengths to ensure that they deserve the trust of their users, but the concerns and misgivings expressed over the new generative AI technologies are so serious that special verification tools are required to be sure that the generative AI user experience is good and the large language model outputs are properly representing the voice of the business that uses them. The AI audit tools included within Einstein Studio provide a great example of a custom application built on top of Data Cloud, using its extensive capabilities to store audit log data that would have been a struggle to contain within the traditional Salesforce extensible object model. Let's look at its capabilities to see how it can enhance the acceptance of new AI capabilities in your workplace.

Initial setup

Setting up the audit system for generative AI usage in Salesforce involves configuring tracking and logging mechanisms to ensure that all interactions with AI models are recorded. This foundational step is essential for creating an environment of accountability and transparency. Furthermore, it allows Einstein Studio administrators to monitor the thumbs up/thumbs down feedback given by users who interact with Einstein Copilot to do their jobs every day. This ensures that the user experience can be continuously improved.

The feature must initially be enabled to begin its data collection activities. For this, you'll need to navigate to Salesforce Setup and search for `Einstein Feedback`. Then, toggle the switch for **Collect and Store Einstein Generative AI Audit Data**. This results in the creation of a collection of DMOs in Data Cloud that provide the data storage required for the audit functionality.

Reports and dashboards usage

After the Einstein Feedback feature is enabled, you can immediately begin to view the audit tables, such as GenAIGatewayRequest, GenAIGatewayResponse, and GenAIFeedback, in Data Explorer or write queries against them in Query Editor. However, Salesforce also provides a link on the Einstein Feedback setup screen that allows you to install a package of pre-built reports and dashboards to visualize and analyze AI usage data effectively. These tools help you gain insights into AI interactions, performance metrics, and usage patterns, facilitating continuous monitoring and optimization.

Developing automated alert monitoring

Once you've become familiar with the auditing capabilities by manually inspecting them regularly, it's nice to know that it's possible to create an automated monitoring task directly within Data Cloud. To do this, you must create a calculated insight that summarizes the metrics you want to monitor – for example, the number of "BAD" feedback replies accumulated to date by a particular feature, and then create a Record Triggered Flow that is executed when the negative feedback count exceeds a limit. That flow can send an email to your team letting you know that more investigation into the feedback data is necessary to improve the users' experience with their Copilot interactions.

By following these steps, organizations can effectively audit generative AI usage, ensuring compliance, accuracy, and ethical standards are met. Regular monitoring and detailed feedback analysis provide valuable insights, helping to refine and optimize AI deployments for better performance and user satisfaction.

Another fundamental requirement to optimize the quality of AI-generated results is to monitor data quality as it arrives within Data Cloud over time. That's what the next section is all about.

Best practices for data management and quality assurance

Maintaining high data quality is an essential prerequisite for the effectiveness of AI models. In this section, we'll take a quick look at best practices for data management, quality assurance, and ongoing monitoring to ensure data integrity and reliability within Data Cloud.

Continuous data validation

A strategy for continuous data validation helps to ensure that data remains accurate, consistent, and reliable over time. Implementing automated validation rules, real-time data monitoring, and regular audits are essential practices. These measures help Data Cloud administrators detect and correct data issues promptly and be confident they are maintaining data integrity.

Regular audits can be performed on the platform in a few different ways. The simplest is a fully manual process, in which someone is assigned the task of logging in on a regular cadence and reviewing the various screens on which the status of daily jobs is listed. Documentation must be maintained about what a normal state of operation looks like for ongoing processes such as Data Streams, Calculated Insights rebuild, and identity resolution refresh. The user interface displays when an error has prevented normal operation from occurring, and it also provides basic metrics about the number of rows processed by an operation, so this can be an effective way to manually monitor Data Cloud operations.

At a slightly higher level of sophistication and requiring a SQL developer to fully build this out, you can put together a suite of queries that provide automated checks of data counts across different DLO streams, harmonized DMOs, and calculated insights. They can use these queries to get more insight into system operations and perform quality assurance during the initial build-out. Then, the same queries could be turned into metrics on a calculated insight, which can be automatically monitored using the same Data Cloud Triggered Flow approach discussed previously for AI audit monitoring.

Another advanced technique that could unlock the ability to automatically detect and visualize ongoing operations is to take advantage of the Data Cloud Control and Metadata Change Events APIs. These APIs provide the basis for the development of a fully automated support system using Flow. A Salesforce developer could create a Flow for each object that provides monitoring capabilities, and then convert the event produced by Data Cloud into a message to be sent to a cloud-based monitoring and analytics tool for automated analysis or recording. The message could be sent for every update, or it could only monitor for error conditions. The exciting thing about building a solution like this is that the enterprise-level monitoring tools available within sophisticated IT departments will probably apply AI of its own to automatically build up a picture of what "normal operation" looks like, and intelligently decide when an anomalous condition has arisen. It could potentially even alert you to details such as a longer-than-expected runtime for a processing job.

Strategies for ensuring data integrity and reliability

Ensuring data integrity and reliability involves robust data governance practices and advanced monitoring tools. Key strategies include establishing a data governance framework, building QA dashboards, and using SQL-based quality tests. These measures safeguard data against errors, inconsistencies, and breaches.

Ensuring data integrity and reliability involves implementing robust data governance practices and using advanced tools to monitor and manage data quality. The following measures can be taken to safeguard data against errors, inconsistencies, and breaches:

- **Data governance framework**: Establish a data governance framework to define data management policies, roles, and responsibilities. This framework ensures that data is handled consistently and securely across the organization.

- **Quality assurance (QA) dashboard**: Build a QA dashboard using the standard Reports and Dashboards functionality in Salesforce. This dashboard provides an overview of key metrics for monitoring data quality.

- **SQL-based quality tests**: For teams with SQL expertise, use the JDBC driver to connect a professional database IDE and run SQL queries as unit tests for data loading and calculation processes.

Example: A financial services company implements a data governance framework to ensure consistent data handling practices, enhancing data quality and security.

Data discoverability and data governance

Incorporating the Salesforce metadata layer into your data management practices can significantly enhance your enterprise data catalog. Adopting a common naming convention aligned with Salesforce standards is crucial for consistency and clarity. Ensure all new objects and fields have detailed descriptions to facilitate understanding and usage. This metadata can be exported via APIs to build a comprehensive documentation website, providing easy access to data definitions and relationships. A well-maintained data catalog promotes data governance, improves data quality, and supports efficient data management across the organization.

Data Cloud is a complex and highly capable system with lots of moving parts. It has much in common with other modern data management platforms, but it has many unique attributes and purposes that set it apart as a truly innovative platform that isn't just another cloud-based data warehouse. Indeed, all the modern big data platforms have vastly simplified the traditional job of the database administrator – issues such as storage management, data modeling, and query performance have all receded into the area of usually just working automatically. But don't be fooled into thinking that operating Data Cloud will be trouble-free – it's always the case that investing resources into automated monitoring and data quality checks will eventually establish a more solid system that can be trusted throughout the enterprise.

One aspect of Data Cloud that isn't different from the core CRM platform is how release management takes place. Even with new features entering the picture with every release, Salesforce provides administrators with extensive release notes and preparation for new releases and ensures that every release to the cloud-hosted system is automatically deployed to all customers. As we'll see in the next section, you'll want to watch those release notes closely and evaluate how you can benefit from additional possibilities with Data Cloud that appear over time.

Future trends and developments in Data Cloud and AI

Salesforce continues to fill its Data Cloud product roadmap with interesting features that it intends to roll out to customers in the near future. Staying informed about future trends and developments in AI and data management is crucial for maximizing the potential of Data Cloud and Einstein Studio. As Salesforce continues to innovate and expand its capabilities, understanding these advancements can help organizations stay ahead of the curve and fully leverage the benefits of AI and data integration.

Potential enhancements to Data Cloud

Salesforce is continuously evolving Data Cloud to provide more robust and scalable data management solutions. Future enhancements to Data Cloud are expected to include the following:

- **Advanced data integration**: As businesses continue to generate vast amounts of data from diverse sources, advanced data integration capabilities will become increasingly important. Salesforce aims to enhance Data Cloud's ability to seamlessly integrate with various data sources, including IoT devices, social media platforms, and external databases. This will enable organizations to create even more comprehensive and dynamic customer profiles. Integrations to automatically pull a standardized dataset from the massive data-backed systems provided by other vendors are particularly exciting as they hold the promise of allowing the Customer 360 Data Model to become the one enterprise schema that data analysts can use to access complex business-oriented data, no matter what system of record originally produced it.

- **Real-time data processing**: Real-time data processing is essential for organizations that require immediate insights and actions. Salesforce is likely to invest in improving Data Cloud's real-time processing capabilities, allowing businesses to analyze and act on data as it is generated. This will be particularly beneficial for industries such as finance and healthcare, where timely decision-making is critical. Additionally, it's likely that even the batch processing capabilities within Data Cloud will gradually be improved so they can execute more rapidly and with a higher frequency as needed.

- **Enhanced data security and privacy**: With the growing focus on data privacy and security, Salesforce is expected to introduce more advanced security features in Data Cloud. These enhancements will likely include stronger encryption methods, more granular access controls, and improved compliance tools to help organizations meet regulatory requirements and protect sensitive data.

- **AI-driven data management**: Leveraging AI to automate and optimize data management processes is a key area of development for Salesforce. Future enhancements may include AI-driven data cleansing, enrichment, and anomaly detection, which will help organizations maintain high data quality and reliability with minimal manual intervention.

- **Unstructured data processing**: Perhaps the most revolutionary feature being talked about in Data Cloud is the vector database, a newly added technology that provides the capability to ingest unstructured data (think along the lines of DocuSign PDF contracts, or email histories by customer), and use it as additional context for generative AI queries. This will truly leverage the power of today's large language models to draw insights and connections from a large search space, all the while keeping the sensitive data assets securely stored within Data Cloud and depending on the Einstein Trust Layer for data security when it is exchanged with the LLM.

Broader AI and data management trends

Beyond specific enhancements to Data Cloud, there are broader AI and data management trends that will shape the future of how organizations use these technologies:

- **Democratization of AI**: One of the most significant trends is the democratization of AI, where AI tools and capabilities become accessible to a broader range of users, regardless of their technical expertise. Salesforce is at the forefront of this trend, integrating AI features directly into its platform to empower all users. This trend will enable organizations to harness AI's power without needing extensive data science resources.

- **Explainable AI**: As AI becomes more integrated into business processes, the need for transparency and explainability in AI models is growing. Explainable AI allows users to understand how AI models make decisions, which is crucial for building trust and ensuring compliance. Salesforce is likely to focus on developing AI models that provide clear explanations and insights into their decision-making processes.

- **AI for personalization**: Personalization remains a key driver for customer engagement and satisfaction. AI's ability to analyze vast amounts of data and deliver personalized experiences will continue to evolve. Future developments will likely include more sophisticated recommendation engines, dynamic content personalization, and predictive analytics that anticipate customer needs.

- **Integrating AI with emerging technologies**: The integration of AI with emerging technologies such as blockchain, **augmented reality** (**AR**), and **virtual reality** (**VR**) is another trend to watch. These integrations will open new possibilities for innovative applications and enhanced user experiences. Salesforce's ongoing research and development efforts are expected to explore these intersections, providing cutting-edge solutions for their users.

The future of Data Cloud and AI holds immense potential for organizations across industries. By staying informed about upcoming trends and developments, businesses can strategically leverage these technologies to drive growth, enhance customer experiences, and maintain a competitive edge. Salesforce's commitment to innovation ensures that Data Cloud and Einstein Studio will continue to evolve, providing powerful tools and capabilities that empower organizations to achieve their goals.

Summary

By mastering Data Cloud and Einstein Studio, businesses can create a centralized, high-quality data repository that drives intelligent, AI-driven interactions. These tools enable organizations to leverage their data effectively, providing insights that can transform business processes and drive innovation.

This chapter has provided a comprehensive guide to understanding, implementing, and optimizing Salesforce Data Cloud and Einstein Studio. All the efforts you've made to learn how Data Cloud facilitates the centralization and harmonization of customer data will be helpful in the next chapter as we examine the Model Builder component of Einstein Studio and learn about how Data Cloud provides the underlying storage for predictive and generative AI model building.

With the skills you've learned in this chapter, you can ensure data integrity, enhance customer experiences, and effectively administer Data Cloud. You've gained an appreciation of why such an elaborate and powerful suite of data management tools is necessary to provide grounding of copilot interactions with accurate and detailed customer data, all to make the copilot provide truly helpful and high-quality interactions with the user.

In summary, this chapter has equipped you with the knowledge and capabilities to transform your business processes using Salesforce Data Cloud and Einstein Studio. Embrace these tools to drive intelligent interactions, improve decision-making, and foster a culture of continuous innovation. Your ability to leverage data and AI effectively will be a key driver of success as the technology industry undergoes a massive realignment of focus, with AI capabilities at the center of every business strategy and every work environment.

Salesforce is seriously preparing for that future with Data Cloud and the Model Builder functionality that we'll tackle in the next chapter. Model Builder is the place where the "Data and AI" story gets real, and you'll see how it facilitates connecting your business data to AI models in an extremely flexible way.

Exploring Functionalities of Model Builder

In the previous chapter, we learned about how Data Cloud is a new generation of technology that is designed to improve scalability and ease of use in the areas of data storage and data integration. Model Builder is a powerful new application that takes advantage of Data Cloud capabilities to bring AI capabilities of all shapes and sizes into the Salesforce ecosystem, where they can assist users in the flow of their daily work. Salesforce has at least a decade of experience with bundling AI capabilities into their primary applications, but now, with Model Builder, administrators and developers have an actual development environment that can handle the deployment of custom-built AI features at any level of complexity. This chapter explores the possibilities inherent to Model Builder. You'll learn why it's important that the platform allows us to configure many different types of AI models, and why it's reasonable to expect that these capabilities will assume ever greater importance within the business software environment for years to come.

In **Artificial Intelligence** (**AI**) and **Machine Learning** (**ML**), the term *model* has a specific conceptual meaning. An AI model is essentially a mathematical representation of a real-world process or system that can make predictions or decisions based on input data. Models are trained on historical data sets to recognize patterns and relationships, enabling them to perform tasks such as classification, prediction of numeric values, and generation of new content. Salesforce's Model Builder within Einstein Studio provides a new environment in which to create, train, and deploy these models, offering businesses powerful tools to harness AI capabilities, seamlessly integrated with their Salesforce ecosystem. When a model is hosted in a non-Salesforce system, Model Builder serves as a dispatcher that manages its integration with Salesforce.

In this chapter, we'll survey Model Builder's capabilities, and then delve into four key hands-on areas you'll use when putting it into practice:

- Defining and interacting with foundation models for generative AI
- Defining and interacting with predictive models

- Preparing data to train a predictive model
- Integrating predictive models with the Salesforce ecosystem

Model Builder capabilities

The following list briefly explains the capabilities of Model Builder:

- **Integration with Salesforce**: Seamlessly integrate models with Salesforce components such as Flow Builder, the Query API, and Einstein Copilot, enabling intelligent automation and enhanced user interactions
- **A user-friendly interface**: Model Builder provides a graphical interface that simplifies the model creation process, allowing users with varying levels of technical expertise to build and deploy models

    I. **Scalability**: Leverage the power of cloud computing to scale model training and deployment, handling large volumes of data and complex computations efficiently

The benefits of using Model Builder

Business and IT leaders should expect the adoption of Model Builder to deliver the following organizational benefits (all of which are considered some of the most desirable outcomes of any digital transformation project):

- **Enhanced decision-making**: Predictive models provide actionable insights that help businesses make data-driven decisions, improving efficiency and effectiveness
- **Automation**: Generative AI models automate content creation and customer interactions, reducing manual effort and increasing productivity
- **Personalization**: AI models enable personalized experiences by understanding customer behavior and preferences, driving higher engagement and satisfaction

Let's distinguish the different types of models that can be addressed within the Einstein Studio environment. Each has a different purpose and a different methodology, and yet the composition of the user interface makes it clear that they all fit the generalized pattern of an *AI model*. Undoubtedly, Salesforce has plans to expand this repertoire over time to include even more techniques that are well known to highly skilled data scientists.

Large language models – generative AI

Large Language Models (**LLMs**) are a prime example of generative AI, capable of understanding and generating human-like text. These models are trained on vast amounts of text data and can perform tasks such as text completion, translation, summarization, and content creation. When you use Salesforce Copilot, by default, your responses are generated by a Salesforce-developed LLM called XGen. However, Salesforce has taken an innovative approach with Einstein Studio to build out an agnostic environment, in which any LLM can be chosen and applied to a particular business problem for which it is well suited. A Salesforce Research group has recently made available an "LLM Benchmark for CRM," which ranks a large collection of LLMs from different vendors across different dimensions as they relate to a particular business task, such as generating a sales email. Accuracy, Cost, Speed, and Trust and Safety are the four different measurement factors considered.

Because cost and performance are relevant concerns and constraints, there is no one "best LLM." Instead, choosing an LLM for a business application should be considered an exercise in optimization, using the factors measured in Salesforce's benchmark. Businesses will increasingly find it necessary to route workloads to the right model for a specific task. Model Builder provides the environment in which this activity can be managed.

LLMs are sometimes described as being the "new UI" for general-purpose work with information systems. It's true that traditional user interfaces and scripting languages, no matter how well designed, can reach forbidding levels of complexity. A simple conversational UI in which an AI partner can respond to questions, with insights drawn from the actual business records under inspection, can be a satisfying experience for a knowledge worker and can enhance productivity at work.

The key features of LLMs

To further pin down exactly what qualifies as an LLM, we can list three key features that we've come to expect from this type of model:

- **Natural Language Understanding (NLU)**: LLMs can comprehend and interpret human language, making them ideal for applications such as chatbots and virtual assistants

- **Content generation**: These models can generate coherent and contextually relevant text, aiding in tasks such as drafting emails, writing reports, or creating marketing content

- **Contextual awareness**: LLMs maintain context across interactions, providing more relevant and personalized responses

In Einstein Studio, connecting to LLMs involves integrating external models or using pre-trained foundation models available within Salesforce. This integration empowers users to deploy advanced generative AI capabilities, with minimal setup and no need to write code against third-party APIs, leveraging the strengths of these powerful models to drive business value.

A predictive model – regression

Regression models are a cornerstone of predictive analytics, used to forecast numerical values based on input data. These models use statistical algorithms to identify the relationships between variables, allowing for accurate predictions of outcomes. In Salesforce, regression models can be applied to various business scenarios, such as sales forecasting, customer lifetime value prediction, and demand planning.

Applications of regression models

There are endless applications of statistical modeling and forecasting, but let's examine a few that are among the most discussed in a business context.

- **Sales forecasting**: Predict future sales based on historical data, helping businesses plan and allocate resources effectively

- **Customer Lifetime Value (CLV)**: Estimate the long-term value of customers to prioritize marketing and retention efforts

- **Demand planning**: Forecast product demand to optimize inventory management and supply chain operations

The agnostic strategy previously discussed with LLMs also applies to predictive models in Einstein Studio. To satisfy the expectations of businesses at all levels of complexity, Salesforce provides the capability to build your own model from scratch, or to connect to external models developed and hosted within professional data science development environments. When using models with Einstein Studio, what stays the same is Data Cloud providing the data storage needed for all different AI model use cases. But if you want to use a model that was trained on data not present in Data Cloud, which is hosted within a cloud environment such as Amazon SageMaker, Einstein Studio provides the connectivity necessary to operationalize that model, allowing it to be used with greater efficiency and to deliver its predictions according to whatever business requirements may dictate.

Creating regression models in Model Builder involves selecting relevant data, configuring model parameters, and training a model to learn from historical patterns. Once trained, these models provide valuable insights that drive data-informed decision-making and strategic planning. We'll go into this process in more detail later in this chapter.

Predictive model – binary classification

Binary classification models are designed to predict one of two possible outcomes, making them ideal for applications where decisions can be reduced to a yes or no prediction. These models are widely used in scenarios such as fraud detection, customer churn prediction, and lead qualification. In Salesforce, binary classification models enable businesses to make informed decisions by predicting outcomes with high accuracy.

Use cases for binary classification

A few examples of where the potential for ROI might lead a business to develop a classification algorithm are as follows:

- **Fraud detection**: Identifying fraudulent transactions or activities by analyzing patterns and anomalies in data

- **Customer churn prediction**: Predicting which customers are likely to leave, allowing businesses to take proactive retention measures
- **Lead qualification**: Classifying leads as hot or cold based on their likelihood to convert, improving sales efficiency and targeting efforts

In Model Builder, creating a binary classification model involves defining the target variable, selecting features (variables that you think will be relevant inputs to make a prediction), and training the model using historical data. The model's performance is evaluated based on metrics such as accuracy, precision, and recall, ensuring that it delivers reliable predictions for real-world applications.

Einstein Studio with Model Builder, as a technology platform, offers compelling opportunities for businesses looking to leverage AI and machine learning. By providing a platform to manage the complex interactions between existing Salesforce solutions and AI models of all types, it allows organizations to unlock the full potential of their data, driving innovation and competitive advantage.

The rest of this chapter will illustrate what it's like to work within Model Builder, providing examples of the following interactions that will become part of the process of managing AI models.

Working with generative AI models

If you already have an agreement in place with OpenAI for professional or corporate use of ChatGPT, then you can easily use Salesforce to make use of all the models available through OpenAI. Similarly, Microsoft Azure customers may have negotiated usage fees for OpenAI models directly with Microsoft, and those models can also be used in concert with Salesforce. If neither of the preceding is true, then you'll have access to LLMs trained by Salesforce and governed by your Salesforce licensing and limits. In this section, we'll look at how Model Builder provides these configuration selections.

Connecting a new foundation model

Connecting a new foundation model in Einstein Studio is a straightforward process designed to leverage advanced AI capabilities with minimal setup. Foundation models, including pre-trained LLMs, can be integrated to enhance various business processes, from customer service to content generation. The Einstein Studio UI uses the term *Foundation Model* because before you can use generative AI, you need to specify a Foundation Model and define a specific configuration for it to use.

Follow these steps to connect a new foundation model:

1. **Access Einstein Studio**:

   - The Einstein Studio tab is located within the Data Cloud app. You can navigate to it by entering Einstein Studio in the App Launcher. Model Builder is not labeled separately within the app navigation, which can be a bit confusing, but it is one of the capabilities accessible through the Einstein Studio starting point.

2. **Select a model**:

- Choose a foundation model from the available options. A list of "Salesforce-enabled" models comes preconfigured for use with Prompt Builder, and you can see all of those here on the Model Library screen, including the newest LLMs from OpenAI and Azure.

- For a greater degree of customization, you can click the **Add Foundation Model** button. This requires you to select between OpenAI and Azure for hosting and enter your connection details, such as the API endpoint and key. You can also specify that this model has been fine-tuned on a specific dataset to better perform a given task.

3. **Configuration**:

- Configure the selected foundation model by pressing the **New Configuration** button on its detail screen. There are three "hyperparameters" that can be tuned to modify the type of output that the LLM will produce. You can use a sliding scale to adjust factors such as creativity versus predictability, the likelihood of repetitiveness of generated words, and the number of unique words in a response.

- Once the foundation model is connected and configured, it is ready to be utilized across various Salesforce applications, but you should first spend some time testing it out.

The following screenshot demonstrates the setup of a new LLM in Einstein Studio:

Figure 6.1 – Connecting a new Foundation Model

Testing with Model Playground

After connecting a foundation model and creating a new configuration, the next step is to test the model and adjust it using Model Playground. This is a feature within Einstein Studio that allows users to experiment with model settings and assess performance in a controlled environment, where requests can be sent to the model to preview the style of its text generation.

Follow these steps for model configuration and testing:

1. **Access Model Playground**:

   - In Einstein Studio, navigate to the Model Library and choose a foundation model, and then choose a configuration of the model by clicking on its name to see the detailed overview. At this point, you can press the **Edit** button, which opens Model Playground directly.

2. **Change the Model Playground settings**:

   - In Model Playground, clicking the **Settings** button brings up a panel where you can adjust the testing environment.

   - You can specify that 1, 2, or 3 responses should be sent back by the LLM to each request.

   - You can enter stop sequences, which allows a response to be monitored for the language of your choice and terminated at the earliest occurrence of the stop sequence.

   - You can choose to disable the default data masking techniques that apply to all LLM interactions in Einstein Studio. This should be considered useful for testing purposes only, and if you have masking disabled, you should be careful not to expose sensitive data in your LLM interactions.

3. **Test**:

   - Input sample data to test the model's predictions and outputs. Model Playground allows you to simulate real-world scenarios and evaluate the model's accuracy and reliability.

   - Utilize the interactive interface to chat with the LLM and determine whether any adjustments to the hyperparameters would lead to an improved experience. You can see immediate feedback on how changes affect model performance.

   - Test different configurations to identify the optimal settings that deliver the best results for your business needs. You can continue testing different outcomes to iteratively refine the model.

In the following screenshot, we can see the complete request and response data for one interaction with the LLM:

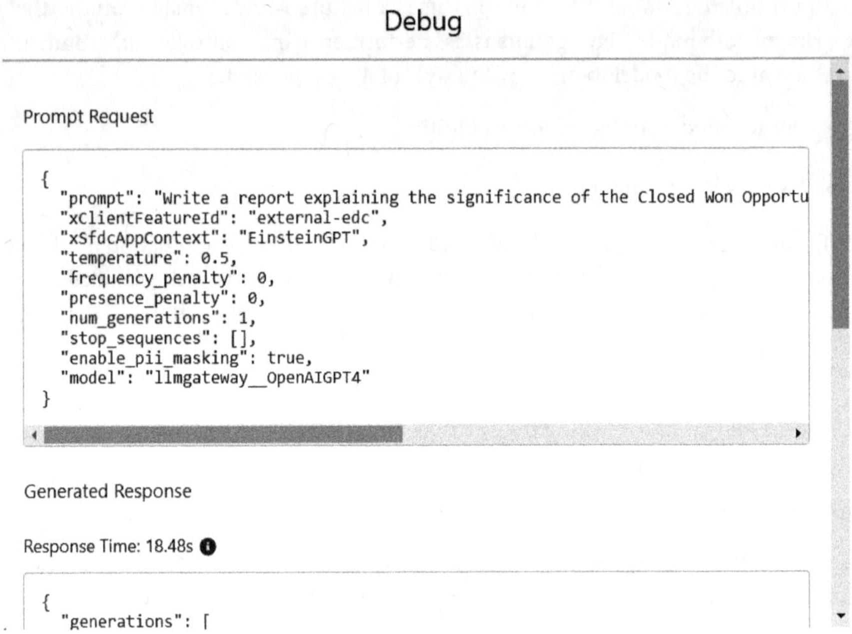

Debug

Prompt Request

```
{
    "prompt": "Write a report explaining the significance of the Closed Won Opportu
    "xClientFeatureId": "external-edc",
    "xSfdcAppContext": "EinsteinGPT",
    "temperature": 0.5,
    "frequency_penalty": 0,
    "presence_penalty": 0,
    "num_generations": 1,
    "stop_sequences": [],
    "enable_pii_masking": true,
    "model": "llmgateway__OpenAIGPT4"
}
```

Generated Response

Response Time: 18.48s ⓘ

```
{
    "generations": [
```

Figure 6.2 – Model Playground

Monitoring Model Activity

From the foundational model display page, it's possible to access an **Activity** tab where monitoring of model usage can be done. Within the **Inferences** section, the **Activity** tab displays a snapshot of the total requests sent to all model configurations during the specified time period. Additionally, the **Errors** section provides summary statistics on interactions with a model. As with any API connection, network timeouts or remote system unavailability can interfere with normal operations and can be measured on this page. Errors triggered by the Einstein Trust Layer also appear here, when it detects inaccurate or biased responses that shouldn't be allowed to continue.

Assigning a generative AI model in Prompt Builder

The Prompt Builder interface, which *Chapter 3* explored in detail, is tightly integrated with the AI model management capabilities of Einstein Studio. Any LLM in the list of standard and custom models, which can be viewed and managed in the Model Library screen of Einstein Studio, can also be selected as the active LLM for a prompt in Prompt Builder. When that prompt is subsequently used, the inference request will be routed to the correct LLM. This gives Salesforce administrators a flexible and powerful means to steadily improve the performance of LLM-driven use cases on the platform, by making it possible to experiment with and upgrade to a different or more heavily customized LLM in specific scenarios, as warranted. Administrators can assign generative AI models to specific tasks, enhancing automated processes and customer interactions. This feature simplifies the deployment of AI capabilities within business workflows and ensures that building use cases within Einstein Studio will not hit any evolutionary dead ends.

In the following screenshot, you can see how a specific prompt is linked to one of the LLMs defined in Model Builder:

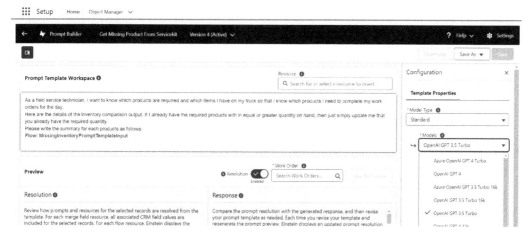

Figure 6.3 – LLM selection in Prompt Builder

The process of working with generative AI models in Salesforce's Einstein Studio involves connecting foundation models, configuring and testing them in the Model Playground, monitoring their activity, and assigning them in Prompt Builder. By following these steps, businesses can leverage advanced AI capabilities to drive innovation, enhance customer interactions, and streamline operations. Cost and performance optimization of LLM workloads can be pursued because there is no vendor lock-in with your choice of model (or models). The integration of generative AI models into Salesforce not only simplifies complex tasks but also provides a scalable and efficient solution to meet evolving business needs.

Working with predictive models

How to implement predictive machine learning with Model Builder depends on the data science footprint of your organization – either you'll connect to existing hosting environments outside of Salesforce, or you'll use Model Builder to directly train and activate a custom model with no external dependencies.

Connecting to external predictive models

With Einstein Studio, Salesforce intends to reassure its customers that their existing investments in machine learning and predictive modeling can be leveraged so that the value they return to a business will increase. In cases where professional data science teams have already done the hard work of training, testing, and improving a predictive model, there is no reason to consider reimplementing it. The Salesforce **Bring Your Own Model** (BYOM) approach in Data Cloud and Einstein Studio is that it effectively rises to the challenge of integrating the model's predictions with the Salesforce environment, where employees are working every day, and gives it access to the entire enterprise's systems of record via the Data Cloud harmonized data model.

Currently, three of the leading AI model deployment environments can connect seamlessly with Einstein Studio using the BYOM methodology. These are Databricks, Google Vertex AI, and Amazon SageMaker. These are all professional data science development and deployment environments that provide the cloud hosting, connectivity, and management required to operationalize an ML model at scale.

From the same Einstein Studio tab we've been looking at, the **Add Predictive Model** button presents a choice between those three external platforms. You'll subsequently need to provide API connection credentials, which you can get from the administrator of the external platform.

Once your external model is connected, you'll be able to use it for any of the predictive AI use cases, exactly like the predictive models created within Einstein Studio and hosted within Salesforce.

Creating a model from scratch

Creating a predictive model from scratch in Einstein Studio involves several steps, from data selection to model training. This section will provide an overview of the process, focusing on the use case of wanting to predict the eventual CLV of a cohort of newly acquired customers.

Follow these steps to create a predictive model:

1. **Select the data:**

    -   Get started by clicking the **Add Predictive Model** button in Einstein Studio and choosing **Create a model from scratch**.

    -   Identify and select the training data source. This must be a specially prepared DMO that contains all relevant variables that you believe could affect the prediction, such as information about an initial purchase or customer demographic information.

    -   The training data source must also contain the prediction target – the actual outcome that you'd like to be able to predict with incomplete datasets in the future. This data will be used to train the model to predict CLV.

- For example, if Data Cloud contains a transaction history, you could create a training data set consisting of customers whose first purchase occurred between 12 and 13 months ago, and the target variable would be their current lifetime value. This would allow the model to predict the 12-month value of a cohort of newly acquired customers.

2. **Configure the model**:

   - Set the goal of the prediction by identifying the target variable that you'd like the model to predict values for. If this variable is numeric, then Model Builder will create a regression model; otherwise, if there are only two values present (such as `True` and `False`), then a binary classification model will be created.

   - Use the Model Builder interface to select the variables you want to use. A minimum of 3 and a maximum of 50 variables can be selected. For predicting CLV, the key variables might include location, email engagement measurement, product categories purchased to date, total amount spent, and frequency of engagement.

   - Model Builder recommends the best ML algorithm to use, but you can override its selection and make your own selection from the following options:

     - **General Linear Model (GLM)**
     - **Gradient Boosting Machines (GBM)**
     - **Extreme Gradient Boosting (XGBoost)**

   - It's not necessary to understand how these algorithms do their job of training the model, but you should know they do represent the most used and well-respected model-building techniques used by data scientists.

A note for the curious

If you wish to learn more about the theory behind predictive modeling, check out a very fun YouTube channel called StatQuest.

---

3. **Train the model**:

   - When the configuration is complete, saving the model causes its initial training to take place.

4. **Evaluate the model's performance**:

   - Once training is complete, click the **View Training Metrics** button to evaluate the model's performance, using a variety of statistical metrics. These metrics will help determine the model's effectiveness in predicting CLV.

   - The metrics displayed help to answer the question, is this a good model? You'll be able to review how your model was trained and understand the quality of your model, giving you confidence in your decision to activate it or not.

- You can see whether the overall accuracy of your model is performant, too low, or too high. Examine the four-fold cross-validation results table to understand how the model performed during testing, measured by repeatedly splitting the dataset into training and validation subsets. Other charts help to visualize metrics of model quality and form your opinion of whether the model is adequately trained.

- If the metrics don't look good enough, you can decide to modify your training data – either the amount provided or the specific variables selected. You can also test out a different algorithm to achieve higher performance.

- This process is another great leap forward in the automation of the traditional process of developing an ML solution. Data science domain experts have mastered coding practices in languages such as R and Python to perform not only the training but also the evaluation and refinement of models like this. It's quite impressive that the Model Builder UI provides a no-code, hand-holding process to take you from training data to a completed and trusted predictive model.

5. **Activate the model**:

- The model needs to be activated before it can start making predictions. In this example story of predicting the 12-month value of a new cohort of customers, a business would want to move forward with using Data Cloud features to make a prediction for customers one month into their engagement timeline, using the outcome to divide the customer cohort into different monetary segments. The segments can then be used to set up personalized marketing campaigns, or they can give customer service agents insight into how the model is evaluating a customer who they're currently chatting with.

Here's a final screenshot of the Model Builder interaction where the ML algorithm selection takes place:

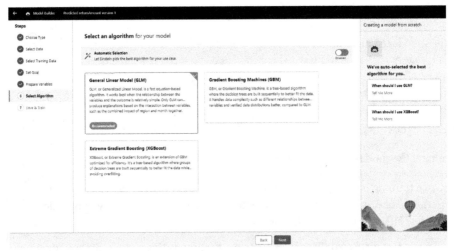

Figure 6.4 – The automated algorithm selection within Model Builder

By following these steps, businesses can create predictive models that provide valuable insights into customer behavior, driving more informed and strategic decisions. Data science teams within big companies can appreciate and use the dependable and scalable environment for AI model deployment offered by Salesforce, while enterprises that haven't yet adopted applied data science can benefit from the no-code environment offered by Model Builder, enabling them to start investigating how ML techniques can assist them with business growth.

Distinguishing Model Builder from other Salesforce ML tools

Salesforce offers several tools to create predictive models, each designed to meet different user needs and technical requirements. Three primary tools are Einstein Studio Model Builder, Einstein Prediction Builder, and Einstein Discovery. Each tool has unique features and is suitable for various scenarios.

Einstein Studio Model Builder

This newly added component of the Einstein family has the following capabilities:

- **Target audience**: Data Cloud administrators and data scientists.

- **Functionality**: Provides a highly customizable environment for creating, training, and deploying ML models. Users can leverage both Salesforce and external models (e.g., Amazon SageMaker and Google Vertex AI) for predictive and generative AI tasks.

- **Flexibility**: Allows you to customize model parameters, integrate external data sources using Data Cloud, and use sophisticated AI techniques.

- **Use cases**: Ideal for complex, large-scale AI projects that require advanced configurations and takes advantage of the harmonized data model within Data Cloud, including customer unification across multiple systems of record.

Einstein Prediction Builder

This slightly older toolkit brought ML capabilities to Salesforce admins:

- **Target audience**: Salesforce administrators, business users, and data analysts.

- **Functionality**: Simplifies the creation of predictive models using a point-and-click interface. Users can build models without needing to write code, making it easily comprehensible for non-technical users.

- **Flexibility**: Prediction Builder has limited customization compared to Model Builder, but it offers an intuitive setup for common use cases. If custom and system attributes have already been used to create a rich picture of standard Salesforce objects such as Lead or Opportunity, Einstein Prediction Builder is a good choice to use to try to find correlations or insights about the data stored on these objects. The ability to reshape or join the data objects within Salesforce is very limited.

- **Use cases**: Suitable for straightforward predictive tasks within the traditional Salesforce CRM object model, such as identifying high-risk opportunities, predicting customer churn, and scoring leads based on conversion likelihood. Works exclusively on data available within the Salesforce Core environment and does not make any use of Data Cloud.

Einstein Discovery

This product is one outcome of Salesforce's strategy for incorporating the acquisition of Tableau:

- **Target audience**: Business analysts, reporting specialists, and data-savvy users who are experts with tools such as CRM Analytics or Tableau.

- **Functionality**: Provides automated insights and recommendations through ML. It helps users understand data patterns and make data-driven decisions without deep technical knowledge.

- **Flexibility**: Combines predictive analytics with actionable insights. Users can explore data, discover patterns, and receive recommendations directly within Salesforce. The CRM Analytics environment (inherited from Tableau) is used as the data storage and processing engine, so Data Cloud is not required.

- **Use cases**: Ideal for use as a more high-powered version of Einstein Prediction Builder, with an increased number of addressable use cases, such as uncovering insights from data, explaining key drivers behind outcomes, and integrating predictive analytics with business workflows for continuous improvement.

Let's compare and summarize the three primary tools:

- **Einstein Studio Model Builder**: Best for scenarios requiring enterprise-wide data that does not already exist in Salesforce, especially when key operational data is already present in Data Cloud. When model predictions need to be integrated into the flow of work, rather than just being part of reporting or analysis, Model Builder is clearly the best choice, due to the flexibility of prediction usage provided in the Data Cloud environment.

- **Einstein Prediction Builder**: Best for Salesforce administrators needing an easy-to-use tool to create basic predictive models that work on a single Salesforce object.

- **Einstein Discovery**: Best for business analysts needing automated insights and recommendations to make informed decisions; it adds simplified ML development within the CRM Analytics and Tableau environments.

Understanding these distinctions helps businesses choose the right tool for their specific needs, ensuring they can effectively leverage AI and predictive analytics within the Salesforce ecosystem.

Working with predictive models in Salesforce's Einstein Studio involves leveraging advanced AI capabilities to enhance business operations. By understanding the capabilities of Model Builder, connecting to external models, and creating models from scratch, businesses can unlock the full potential of their data, connecting it both to LLMs for generative AI applications, and to ML algorithms capable of using data and statistical techniques to predict likely outcomes.

Preparing data to build a predictive model

We've now seen what the overall process of using Model Builder to train and activate a new predictive model looks like. Now, it's time to go into more depth about what it takes to prepare a dataset that will be used for training. The data structure from the Customer 360 data model is highly normalized, meaning that it's organized to eliminate redundancy and ensure that each piece of information is stored only once. Unfortunately, that's not exactly what is required as input to an ML training dataset. A big part of the overall effort expended by the data engineers and data scientists who train and operate predictive models outside of Data Cloud is data preparation, which is required to create a flat and wide data structure that can be used as input to the model. Within Data Cloud, the same types of activities need to take place to reshape complex normalized data into a simpler spreadsheet-style layout, ensuring that it can be easily consumed by the ML algorithm.

Data selection

The first step in preparing data to build a predictive model is selecting the right data. This involves identifying and gathering data sources that contain relevant information for the target prediction. For instance, when predicting the CLV, key data sources might include transaction records, customer interactions, demographic information, and engagement metrics.

Key considerations for data selection

- **Relevance**: Ensure that data is directly or indirectly related to the prediction objective. Irrelevant data can introduce noise and reduce model accuracy.

- **Volume**: Adequate data volume is crucial. The dataset should meet the Model Builder minimum requirement of 400 rows and can contain no more than 20 million rows.

- **Variety**: Include diverse data types (e.g., numerical, categorical, and textual) to capture different aspects of customer behavior.

- **Time scale**: For any type of engagement or event-based data, where the event has a date and time associated with it, it's vitally important to select the right date boundaries for the event data you use for training. In many cases, a cohort-style analysis is necessary, where you begin by identifying a group of customers who are like one another, in terms of when they first enrolled or otherwise engaged with your business.

Example data sources for CLV prediction

- **Transaction data**: Purchase history, average order value, and purchase frequency

- **Customer Interaction Data**: Website visits, customer service interactions, and email engagement

- **Demographic Data**: Age, gender, location, and income level

- **Behavioral Data**: Product reviews, social media interactions, and loyalty program participation

Effective data selection sets the foundation for successful predictive modeling by ensuring that the dataset contains comprehensive and relevant information, as well as that the records used for training have enough logical coherence for the correlations between variables to be accurately identified.

Data quality testing and cleaning

Before beginning the work of feature engineering, it is imperative to perform another round of data quality testing and cleaning. Poor data quality can significantly impair the performance of predictive models, leading to inaccurate or unreliable predictions. Data quality testing and cleaning involve identifying and rectifying issues such as missing values, incorrect data types, duplicates, and inconsistencies.

These are some common data quality issues:

- **Missing values**: Missing data can lead to biased or incomplete models. Identify and handle missing values appropriately, either by imputing them from available context or excluding affected records.

- **Incorrect data types**: Ensure that data types are consistent and correctly formatted (e.g., dates as date types and numerical values as integers or floats). Use the full range of Data Cloud's available data types, such as date, datetime, percent, number, and text, so that Data Cloud can enforce type correctness during ingestion.

- **Duplicates**: Remove duplicate records to prevent skewed model results.

- **Inconsistencies**: Standardize data formats and values to maintain consistency (e.g., standardizing date formats, time zones, currencies, or categorical values).

Hopefully, many of these issues will not be of any concern if due diligence was exercised during the initial data ingestion. To find out whether there are any remaining issues you should be aware of, there are many techniques available, such as inspecting the data in Data Cloud's Data Explorer view, creating reports on the data using Salesforce Reports, or writing exploratory SQL queries in Query Editor. More advanced scripting techniques, using Python or R, can be deployed by data analysts to perform exploratory data analysis on the records in an external tool, perhaps using the Query API to automate the retrieval of records from Data Cloud.

As you identify data quality problems that need to be corrected, you can work within the Batch Transforms tool in Data Cloud to address each of them and build out the transformation pipeline, which moves step by step toward your completed training dataset. Performing these steps ensures that the dataset is clean, consistent, and ready for the next phase of data preparation.

Data preparation and feature engineering

Feature engineering is the process of transforming raw data into meaningful features that enhance the predictive power of ML models. This involves creating new variables, modifying existing ones, and converting data into a format suitable for an algorithm. The goal is to produce a flat, spreadsheet-style dataset with simple numeric, Boolean, or categorical columns that represent various facts about each data observation. In this section, we'll use the term "feature" to indicate a variable in the training dataset that has been selected or formatted in such a way that it is readily usable as input to the ML algorithm. The Batch Transform tool within Data Cloud is designed to facilitate these tasks without requiring coding skills. The main prerequisites to effectively use Batch Transform are like the job requirements for a Data Cloud administrator – an understanding of relational modeling concepts and the Customer 360 data model, along with a talent for using spreadsheet-style formulas to transform individual values or summarize a group of values as a total.

The potential tasks required in data preparation and feature engineering are as follows:

- **Pivoting rows to columns**:

  - Within the Batch Transform, use a Transform step with a window function that can summarize values from multiple rows as a single summary row. By applying this transformation, the total row count is reduced to a simple observation for each subject, which makes the dataset easier to analyze and model.

  - For example, transforming transaction data where each row represents a purchase into a single row per customer with columns for total purchases, average order value, frequency, and a yes/no value for "*Has enrolled in the loyalty program?*".

- **Creating new features**:

  - Generate new features that capture important aspects of data – for instance, creating a `loyalty_score` feature based on the frequency and recency of purchases

  - Use domain knowledge to identify meaningful transformations, such as calculating customer tenure or engagement scores

- **Encoding categorical variables**:

  - Convert categorical variables into numerical formats using techniques such as one-hot encoding or label encoding

  - For example, converting `customer_segment` categories (e.g., `high_value`, `medium_value`, or `low_value`) into a series of binary yes/no columns

- **Scaling and normalization**:

  - Normalize numerical features to ensure that they are on a similar scale. This helps the algorithm to treat each feature equally and improves model performance.

  - Apply techniques such as min-max scaling, which involves rescaling the range of a numerical feature to scale the range in [0, 1] or [−1, 1], or z-score normalization, a version of scaling that represents the number of standard deviations away from the mean.

An example of feature engineering for CLV prediction

- **Customer segmentation**: Create segments based on purchase behavior (e.g., `frequent_buyers` or `occasional_buyers`).

- **Engagement metrics**: Calculate features such as `average_session_duration`, `click_through_rate`, and `email_open_rate`. If you are using the Marketing Cloud Engagement starter data bundle, you can use a particularly valuable data stream called SFMC Einstein Email Scores. This contains many pre-calculated ranking values such as `EmailClickScore` and `EmailClickLikelihood`, some of which are themselves a product of ML analysis that takes place within Marketing Cloud Einstein.

- **Recency, Frequency, and Monetary (RFM) analysis**: Develop features based on the recency of the last purchase, the frequency of purchases, and the monetary value spent. Salesforce publishes some demonstration Calculated Insights that create metrics like these in a GitHub repository.

Data cloud tools for feature engineering

- The Batch Transforms feature in Data Cloud offers a no-code solution to perform complex data transformations. It allows users to reshape data, create new features, and prepare datasets without writing code.

- This tool simplifies the data preparation process, making it accessible to users who may not have extensive coding skills. By providing an intuitive interface and powerful transformation capabilities, Data Cloud enables efficient and effective data engineering.

- You might think of writing SQL in the Calculated Insights tool to perform feature engineering, but you should know that the CIO objects created by Calculated Insights cannot be used as Model Builder inputs. Only DMO objects are acceptable in this context. Although you can't use the Calculated Insight directly as your training data, you can use Batch Transforms to create a DMO containing fields that originate from a previously created CIO.

The benefits of using Data Cloud for data preparation

- **Efficiency**: Streamlines the data preparation process, keeping the transform and clean steps inside the same tool that is used to train and host the ML model. In addition to batch processing, the platform also supports near-real-time use cases in which a data streaming pipeline, with streaming transforms included, can result in updated predictive outputs without waiting for scheduled jobs to run.

- **Accessibility**: Makes data engineering tasks more approachable for non-technical users, allowing them to perform sophisticated transformations without coding.

- **Simplified data integration**: Working with the Customer 360 data model means that the transformation starts from a more harmonious state. Issues around combining data from different sources have already been hashed out during the mapping stage of data ingestion, and using the built-in Batch Transforms means no additional export and import processes are needed. Fewer points of failure make for a more reliable system.

- **Scalability**: Handles large datasets efficiently, ensuring that data preparation activities can scale with business needs.

An example workflow

1. **Ingest the data**: Import raw data into Data Cloud from various sources.
2. **Check the quality of the data**: Perform automated checks to identify and address data quality issues. It's best practice to use formula fields on your data stream definition to perform initial cleaning steps when a data lake object is created.
3. **Transform the data**: Use Batch Transforms to join and pivot DMOs, create new features, and normalize values to get a flattened table with variables suitable for predictive model inputs.
4. **Train the predictive model**: Select the transformed DMO for model training in Einstein Studio, and review the model performance statistics to see whether further iteration is required or whether the model is ready to use.

By following these steps, businesses can prepare high-quality, feature-rich datasets that are ready for ML and allow algorithms to perform prediction tasks successfully. The Batch Transforms tool in Data Cloud requires some getting used to, but the way it presents the entire range of transformation possibilities within a user interface palette makes it a much easier on-ramp than learning how to do data transformation coding. You can focus on planning your ML use case and performing research on what data is available to use to support your prediction, rather than the mechanics of performing the transformation and the challenges of maintaining and deploying source code.

Integrating predictive models with Salesforce components

So, now you know that it's possible to build a high-quality predictive model based on your historical business data, using the configuration-based tools in Model Builder. Or you might work with a data science team that maintains a whole suite of predictive models outside of the Salesforce environment. In either case, it's time to learn how to put the AI model to work. In this section, you'll be introduced to a wide range of different opportunities that exist within the Salesforce platform to integrate the AI model's predictions within your flow of work.

Making predictions within Batch Data Transform

Once you've trained and confirmed the performance of your predictive model, you may want to integrate the request for a predicted value into your overall data flow. Using the Batch Data Transforms feature, you can enrich DMOs with predictive outputs by hooking the AI model into the transformation workflow. Predictive intelligence can, therefore, be added to new observations as they arrive in Data Cloud via ingestion, enabling sophisticated data analysis and visualization in all downstream activities where data is used.

These are the steps to use the AI model node in batch data transforms:

1. **Initiate Data Transforms**:

   I.   In Data Cloud, navigate to Data Transforms and click **New**.

   II. Select **Batch Data Transform**.

2. **Select a data space and the DMO**:

   I.   Click **Data Model Objects** and choose the data space where the output will be stored.

   II. Select the DMO you want to enrich with input data.

3. **Add a transform node**:

   I.   Click the + icon on the DMO to add a transform node.

   II. Select **AI Model** to initiate the data transform node.

4. **Launch the AI model**: Choose the AI model to be used, and then click **Next** to launch it in the transform editor.

5. **Map the fields**: In the **Map Fields** tab, align your model schema fields with the input fields from your DMO.

6. **Modify the output**:

   I.   In the **Modify Output** tab, click **Top Predictors** to include factors with the highest impact on each prediction. This adds a description and impact column to your dataset. Note that this option is available only for Salesforce-created models. It's extremely helpful to be able to present this type of "explainable ML" to end users who view a particular predicted value.

   II. Select up to three predictors for inclusion.

7. **Preview and apply**:

   I.   Preview the data to check the columns in your output DMO.

   II. Click **Apply** to save the prediction outputs to the DMO.

8. **Visualize the data**: To further analyze and visualize your data, use Salesforce Reports and Dashboards, or access the enriched DMO from other visualization applications, such as CRM Analytics or Tableau.

Using the AI model node within Batch Data Transforms simplifies the process of invoking the AI model and storing its predictions alongside the rest of your data, where it can be accessed by all users of the data storage. This is the right technique to use when usage of the AI model is driven by the Data Cloud administrator, or data architect, as part of their idea of what predicted values should be obtainable from the harmonized data storage in Data Cloud, when the prediction remains stable over time, and where it's important to generate the prediction in question for every record arriving from one or more data streams.

Flow Builder

Flow Builder in the Salesforce core platform is the premier low-code tool provided by the platform to create automated workflows, and it has been enhanced with the ability to incorporate predictive insights from AI models. The enormous number of Salesforce admins and developers who know how to work with Flow Builder can now make use of AI models directly from within it.

The types of flows using predictions

- **Screen flows**: Incorporate predictive insights into interactive flows that guide users through a series of screens. For example, a sales representative might see a predicted lead score generated in real time by your custom model to prioritize follow-ups.

- **Record-triggered flows**: Use predictions to trigger automated actions based on changes in records. For instance, if a customer's predicted churn risk exceeds a certain threshold, the system can automatically trigger a retention campaign.

- **Scheduled flows**: Set up flows that run at scheduled intervals to update records with the latest predictions. This ensures that data remains current and actionable.

The key steps to integrate predictions in Flow Builder

1. **Create or open a flow**: Start by creating a new flow or opening an existing one in Flow Builder.

2. **Add a prediction element**: Insert the prediction element into the flow where you want to incorporate AI insights.

3. **Configure the predictions**: Specify the predictive model and the fields that will receive the prediction outputs. Configure the mapping from fields in a flow's environment to the model's required input schema.

4. **Define the actions**: Define the actions that should be taken based on the prediction results. This could include updating records, sending notifications, or triggering other automated processes.

5. **Test and deploy**: Test the flow to ensure that it works as expected, and then deploy it to production. Monitor its performance and adjust as needed.

By integrating predictive insights into Flow Builder, Salesforce ensures that a large number of business and software professionals familiar with using this tool have the chance to work directly with AI models as they are produced for use within a business. Whether by generating a new prediction at the time it's most necessary, or by triggering a custom action workflow when the value of an observed prediction has changed, Flow Builder provides a familiar environment in which to take advantage of the predictive capabilities of Einstein Studio.

The Query API

Data Cloud's Query API provides a way to directly request prediction values from a model to be returned within an API response, without needing to store the prediction results in Data Cloud. This real-time integration is ideal for applications both inside and outside the Salesforce ecosystem that require immediate predictive insights.

The key steps to use the Query API

1. **Set up API access**: Ensure that you have the necessary API access and credentials to interact with the predictive model.

2. **Construct and send an API request**: Create an API request that sends an SQL query to the Query API endpoint. Within this query, the Predict function is used to specify the name of the predictive model, and the necessary input feature values to obtain a prediction result. Since this is done within a SQL query, the input values can either come from the remote application or the harmonized data in Data Cloud, so this mechanism of requesting a prediction is extremely flexible. The query will also process the output of the Predict function, using the `json_extract` function to retrieve the desired value from the AI model's response.

3. **Receive and use a prediction**: The Data Cloud query processor executes the SQL query and invokes the model you requested, and then it returns the prediction value within the API response.

4. **Use the prediction**: Integrate the returned prediction value into your application or workflow as needed.

Data Cloud documentation offers the following example of SQL query syntax that can be used to predict the likelihood of email engagement for a given user (`https://help.salesforce.com/s/articleView?id=sf.c360_a_ad_hoc_get_predictions.htm&type=5`):

```
SELECT cast( JSON_EXTRACT( Predict('Predict_Next_Email_Engagement_
Action_by_user', '003Kb00001XcNDlIAN',1,'send'), '$.predictions[0].
score') as double) as prediction_score
```

Clearly, this technique requires more advanced coding skills. Using the Query API provides software developers with real-time access to predictive insights, enabling immediate action based on model outputs, with the greatest amount of flexibility regarding the execution environment and the origin of the observation for which the prediction is needed. Another benefit of the combination of SQL and predictive modeling is that the API user can potentially request predictions for any number of observations, all within a single API interaction.

Prediction Job in Einstein Studio

The Prediction Job feature in Einstein Studio allows a Salesforce or Data Cloud administrator to set up and manage prediction jobs that generate predictions for large datasets. This feature is designed for scenarios where batch processing is required, and the results need to be stored for further use. It's also appropriate to consider this method when it is important to refresh predicted values over time as their inputs change.

The key steps to set up a Prediction Job

1. **Create a Prediction Job**: In Einstein Studio, click on a model and then click **Model Details**. Proceed to create a new prediction job for this model by specifying the DMO where prediction outputs will be stored.

2. **Configure the job parameters**: Provide a mapping for every field in the model's schema. You can add a DMO and additional related objects to find the origin of the required fields.

3. **Choose a job update type**: Specify whether you prefer batch or streaming mode for the job, whether to run it manually in batch mode or on demand, and whether to update predictions whenever a specified set of fields on the input data has changed.

4. **Create a job**: Specify a name and description and create the job.

5. **Store the predictions**: A new DMO is created to store the predictions for streaming jobs.

Setting up prediction jobs in Einstein Studio allows businesses to automate the generation of predictions for large datasets, ensuring predicted values can remain up to date, even as changes occur to the source data they use to make their inferences.

Copy Field Enrichments

Copy Field Enrichments, a feature accessed through the Salesforce Core platform's Object Manager, allows you to replicate key fields within Data Cloud to make them available to your CRM applications. This capability exists to enhance the Contact, Account, or Lead object users, with fields copied from the Data Cloud object of your choice. The only limitation is that the Data Cloud object must be related to the individual DMO, but you can choose from Calculated Insights objects or Prediction objects created by Model Builder jobs.

The key steps for Copy Field Enrichments

1. **Access Object Manager**: Within the Salesforce Core Setup environment, navigate to Object Manager and choose the Lead, Contact, or Account object.

2. **Select the data objects**: Specify a Data Cloud object – either a Calculated Insight or another object related to the individual DMO.

3. **Copy the predictions to fields**: Use the Copy Field Enrichments feature to map the prediction outputs (or Calculated Insights measures) to specific fields in your CRM data objects. This step integrates predictive insights directly into your existing CRM data structure, enhancing it with valuable information.

4. **Synchronize**: Once saved, the platform performs a one-time full synchronization of the field values, using the Bulk API. In an ongoing operation, incremental syncs will take place, triggered by changes in Data Cloud to the fields that are copied.

By using Copy Field Enrichments, businesses can seamlessly integrate predictive insights into their existing data workflows, enhancing the overall value of their data and improving decision-making processes.

That's certainly a lot of options to consider! The main takeaway here is that the Salesforce platform is designed to maximize the different ways that different user personas have available to interact with AI models, putting their outputs to good use on behalf of the business strategy. You'll want to consult the Data Cloud and Einstein Studio documentation to get the most up-to-date guidance on how to put each of these integration techniques into practice. What they all have in common is the ease of use provided by the AI model hosting capabilities within Model Builder, which has been designed to provide a comprehensive directory of AI models that can be used across an enterprise. By leveraging Model Builder as the interface for all types of AI models, businesses can seamlessly incorporate predictive insights into their operations, while maintaining strict oversight and management of the access to and usage of these powerful tools. Model Builder simplifies the use of AI and advanced predictive analytics, enlisting a diverse range of user personas in an effort to drive more effective and efficient business processes.

Summary

We bring this chapter and the first part of this book to a close by completing a grand tour of the Einstein Studio features that, in combination, deliver on the promise of making AI attainable for the typical Salesforce customer. By recalling what you've learned about Copilot Builder, Prompt Builder, Data Cloud, and Model Builder, it's clear that Einstein Studio comprises a full platform for AI exploration and development. Whether it's building predictive models or creating a conversational AI interface for business-specific tasks, a Salesforce architect or administrator can accomplish their goals both inside and outside of the Salesforce suite of products.

Model Builder is the hub for this idea of an open ecosystem for AI, where it becomes possible to connect to models residing in all the major cloud environments or build your own model, without any external dependencies.

We also explored Batch Data Transforms, another iteration of the same underlying philosophy – if you have external tools and data pipelines available, alongside a data engineering team that prefers to use them, you're encouraged to build on top of that existing infrastructure. If you don't, the built-in transformation tools within Data Cloud ensure that the capabilities you need are still available, without you needing to hire another specialist or license another tool.

As you should be reminded by the frequent appearance of cartoonish images of Einstein the scientist, working with these types of systems does require the application of a scientific method. Model Builder provides the workbench toolkit needed to evaluate and monitor the performance of the AI models that are put into place to serve the needs of a business. Any type of implementation plan needs to include some time to make use of the operational metrics and take at least one pass at refining a model and optimizing its performance.

With your new understanding of the Einstein Studio platform, you should feel confident that businesses of all sizes are free to take part in the AI revolution, bringing enhanced productivity and ease of use to employees and customers alike. The platform truly does offer endless possibilities for innovation.

As we look ahead to the next chapter, it's time to explore how you can further enhance your Salesforce implementations with powerful automation. In Chapter 7, we'll delve into "Leveraging Copilot Actions with Flows & More," where you'll learn to integrate and customize Copilot Actions within Salesforce. This chapter will guide you through setting up intelligent workflows that dynamically respond to user inputs and real-time data, driving greater efficiency and effectiveness in your business processes. Get ready to unlock the full potential of AI-driven automation to streamline operations and elevate user interactions.

7

Leveraging Copilot Actions with Flows and More

The Salesforce Copilot Actions feature represents a significant advancement in AI-driven automation, providing businesses with the tools to create intelligent workflows that enhance operational efficiency and improve customer interactions. This chapter delves into the functionalities and applications of Copilot Actions, guiding you through the process of creating, configuring, and deploying these actions within Salesforce. By leveraging Copilot Actions, organizations can automate complex tasks, streamline workflows, and provide real-time insights that drive better decision-making.

Understanding how to effectively utilize Copilot Actions is crucial for Salesforce administrators and developers looking to maximize the benefits of AI integration. This chapter will cover the key skills needed to navigate the Copilot Actions interface, create and configure actions, integrate them with Salesforce Flows, customize their behavior, evaluate and refine their performance, and utilize analytics for continuous improvement. By mastering these skills, you can ensure that your Copilot Actions are tailored to meet the specific needs of your organization and deliver maximum value.

The business impact of Copilot Actions is profound as they enable companies to automate routine tasks, reduce manual workloads, and enhance customer engagement. By integrating Copilot Actions with Salesforce Flows, businesses can create seamless and efficient processes that improve overall productivity and drive better outcomes. This chapter will provide practical examples and step-by-step guidance to help you implement Copilot Actions effectively.

The key skills to be learned in this chapter include creating and configuring Copilot Actions, integrating them with Salesforce Flows, customizing their actions and responses, testing and refining their performance, and utilizing analytics for continuous improvement. These skills will empower you to design intelligent workflows that enhance business processes and provide superior customer experiences.

In summary, mastering the use of Copilot Actions in Salesforce is a meaningful change for businesses looking to leverage AI to drive efficiency and innovation. This chapter will equip you with the knowledge and skills needed to implement Copilot Actions effectively, ensuring that your Salesforce environment is optimized for maximum impact.

Introduction to Copilot Actions

Salesforce's Copilot Actions offers an advanced method for streamlining workflows and enhancing user interactions within the Salesforce ecosystem. By automating repetitive tasks and providing real-time assistance, Copilot Actions empowers users to focus on high-value activities. This capability not only increases productivity but also enhances the overall efficiency of business processes. The ability to integrate Copilot Actions with Salesforce Flows further amplifies their utility, enabling the creation of sophisticated, AI-driven workflows that can adapt to various business scenarios.

The versatility of Copilot Actions makes it applicable across a wide range of use cases. Whether it's automating lead assignments, providing instant customer support, or generating real-time reports, Copilot Actions can be tailored to meet specific business needs. Its integration with Salesforce ensures that these actions are seamlessly incorporated into existing workflows, providing a cohesive and efficient user experience. This adaptability is crucial for businesses aiming to stay competitive in a rapidly evolving market.

Understanding the fundamentals of Copilot Actions and its integration with Salesforce components is essential for maximizing its potential. By mastering these tools, businesses can unlock new levels of operational efficiency and customer satisfaction. This section provides a comprehensive overview of Copilot Actions, highlighting its features, benefits, and practical applications.

By the end of this section, you will have a clear understanding of how to leverage Copilot Actions to enhance your Salesforce implementations and drive better business outcomes.

Key goals and outcomes

The primary goal of this section is to provide an in-depth understanding of Salesforce Copilot Builder and its capabilities. By the end of this section, you will be able to do the following:

- **Understand the core features and capabilities of Copilot Builder**: Gain insights into the various functionalities that make Copilot Builder a powerful tool for enhancing user interactions and automating tasks
- **Recognize the benefits of using AI-driven copilots**: Learn how these intelligent assistants can streamline workflows, improve efficiency, and provide actionable insights
- **Identify potential applications within your organization**: Explore various use cases where Copilot Builder can be implemented to address specific business needs and challenges

By achieving these goals, you will be well-prepared to leverage Copilot Builder to its full potential. This knowledge will enable you to design and deploy intelligent assistants that address specific business needs, improve operational efficiency, and enhance the overall user experience.

Difference between copilots and Copilot Actions

Understanding the distinction between copilots and Copilot Actions in Salesforce is crucial for effectively leveraging their capabilities within your organization. While both features aim to enhance user interactions and streamline business processes, they serve different purposes and operate in distinct ways. Grasping these differences will enable you to apply each tool appropriately, maximizing their benefits and ensuring they complement your overall CRM strategy.

Salesforce copilots

Copilots in Salesforce are AI-driven assistants designed to perform a wide range of tasks. They can manage complex workflows, provide real-time insights, and automate routine operations, significantly enhancing productivity and efficiency. Copilots are highly customizable, allowing businesses to tailor their functionalities to specific needs. For example, a sales copilot can be configured to manage lead qualifications, track customer interactions, and generate detailed performance reports. This level of customization ensures that copilots can adapt to various business scenarios, delivering precise and actionable support.

Salesforce copilots are AI-driven virtual assistants that are designed to help users navigate the Salesforce platform, automate routine tasks, and provide real-time insights. These copilots leverage machine learning and natural language processing to interact with users conversationally, enabling them to perform various tasks, such as scheduling meetings, generating reports, and updating records. Copilots are particularly valuable for their ability to streamline workflows and reduce the manual effort required for repetitive tasks, thereby allowing users to focus on more strategic activities.

The primary function of Salesforce copilots is to act as an intelligent assistant that can understand and respond to user queries, automate complex workflows, and provide predictive insights based on historical data. Copilots integrate seamlessly with the Salesforce environment, accessing and utilizing data from various Salesforce components to deliver personalized and contextually relevant support. This integration ensures that copilots can operate effectively within existing workflows, enhancing overall user experience and productivity.

Salesforce Copilot Actions

On the other hand, Copilot Actions are more focused and task-specific. They are designed to perform individual, discrete actions within the Salesforce environment, often as part of a larger workflow or process. These actions can include updating records, sending notifications, or triggering specific events based on predefined conditions. Unlike copilots, which can manage multiple tasks and provide broad support, Copilot Actions are typically used to automate specific steps within a workflow, enhancing precision and consistency. This makes them ideal for streamlining repetitive tasks and ensuring that critical actions are performed accurately and efficiently.

The key advantage of Copilot Actions is their ability to provide targeted automation that enhances specific aspects of business operations. Users can configure Copilot Actions to perform a wide range of tasks, from simple data updates to complex multi-step workflows. This capability allows businesses to tailor their automation strategies to meet their unique needs and optimize various processes within the Salesforce environment.

Differences and complementary roles

One of the key differences between copilots and Copilot Actions is their scope and complexity. Copilots are broader in scope, capable of managing entire workflows and interacting with users in a dynamic, conversational manner. They can provide contextual assistance, answer queries, and guide users through complex processes. This makes them suitable for scenarios where continuous, real-time interaction and support are required. In contrast, Copilot Actions are more limited in scope and designed to execute predefined tasks without the need for extensive user interaction. Their simplicity and focus make them highly dependable for automating specific steps within a process, ensuring that these tasks are performed consistently and accurately.

Another important distinction lies in their configuration and deployment. Copilots require a more comprehensive setup, involving the configuration of multiple actions, responses, and integration points. This process often involves a deeper understanding of the business processes, and the user needs to ensure that the copilot operates effectively. In contrast, setting up Copilot Actions is more straightforward as it involves configuring individual tasks within a workflow. This simplicity allows for quicker deployment and easier adjustments, making them an efficient solution for automating specific, repetitive tasks.

The integration capabilities of copilots and Copilot Actions also differ. Copilots can be integrated with a wide range of Salesforce components, including objects, fields, and external data sources. This allows them to provide comprehensive support and insights across various aspects of the business. Copilot Actions, while also capable of integration, are typically more focused on interacting with specific components to perform discrete tasks. This targeted integration ensures that critical actions are seamlessly incorporated into workflows, enhancing overall efficiency and accuracy.

Together, copilots and Copilot Actions complement each other by providing a comprehensive approach to automation and AI-driven support within Salesforce. Copilots offer the flexibility and intelligence to handle a wide range of user interactions and tasks, while Copilot Actions provide the precision and specificity needed to automate processes and responses. By leveraging both tools, businesses can create a robust and efficient Salesforce environment that maximizes the benefits of AI and automation.

In summary, while both copilots and Copilot Actions offer powerful tools for enhancing business processes within Salesforce, they serve different purposes and operate in distinct ways. Copilots provide broad, dynamic support capable of managing complex workflows and interacting with users in real time. Copilot Actions, on the other hand, focus on automating specific, task-oriented actions within a workflow, ensuring precision and consistency. Understanding these differences enables businesses to deploy each tool effectively, leveraging their unique strengths to drive operational efficiency and improve user experiences.

The importance of Copilot Actions

Implementing Copilot Actions can significantly enhance business operations by automating routine tasks and providing real-time insights. These actions help reduce manual workloads, improve accuracy, and ensure that critical tasks are performed consistently and efficiently.

The importance of Copilot Actions in Salesforce cannot be overstated, especially in today's fast-paced business environment, where efficiency and accuracy are paramount. Copilot Actions play a crucial role in automating specific tasks within the Salesforce ecosystem, helping organizations streamline their workflows and improve overall productivity. By automating routine and repetitive tasks, Copilot Actions free up valuable time for employees to focus on more strategic and value-added activities.

One of the primary benefits of Copilot Actions is their ability to enhance consistency and accuracy in task execution. Manual processes are prone to human error, which can lead to inconsistencies and mistakes that affect business outcomes. By automating these tasks, Copilot Actions ensures that they are performed the same way every time, reducing the risk of errors and improving the reliability of business processes. This is particularly important for tasks that require precision, such as data entry, updating records, or sending notifications.

Another significant advantage of Copilot Actions is their contribution to operational efficiency. In a typical business environment, employees often spend a considerable amount of time on routine tasks that could be automated. Copilot Actions help to streamline these tasks, allowing employees to focus on more complex and strategic activities that require human intelligence and creativity. This shift not only improves productivity but also enhances employee satisfaction by reducing the burden of monotonous work.

Copilot Actions also play a vital role in enhancing the responsiveness of business operations. In today's dynamic market, businesses need to be agile and responsive to changing conditions and customer needs. Copilot Actions enable organizations to automate key processes, ensuring that they can respond quickly to added information and evolving circumstances. For example, a Copilot Action could automatically update a customer's status based on their interactions, triggering appropriate follow-up actions in real time. This level of responsiveness is crucial for maintaining a competitive edge and delivering superior customer experiences.

The integration capabilities of Copilot Actions further underscore their importance. Copilot Actions can be seamlessly integrated with various Salesforce components, including objects, fields, and workflows. This integration ensures that automated tasks are well-coordinated with other business processes, creating a cohesive and efficient operational environment. By connecting Copilot Actions with critical components, businesses can ensure that their workflows are streamlined and that key tasks are performed accurately and on time.

Moreover, Copilot Actions contribute to better data management and utilization. In today's data-driven world, having accurate and up-to-date information is critical for making informed business decisions. Copilot Actions help ensure that data is consistently and accurately updated, eliminating the risk of outdated or incorrect information. This improved data integrity enhances the quality of insights derived from the data, enabling businesses to make better decisions and optimize their operations.

The importance of Copilot Actions extends to their role in enhancing compliance and governance. Many industries are subject to stringent regulatory requirements, and maintaining compliance can be a complex and time-consuming task. Copilot Actions can automate compliance-related tasks, ensuring that they are performed consistently and accurately. This not only reduces the risk of non-compliance but also ensures that businesses can meet regulatory requirements efficiently and effectively.

In summary, Copilot Actions are a critical component of the Salesforce ecosystem, offering numerous benefits that enhance business efficiency, accuracy, and responsiveness. By automating routine tasks, Copilot Actions free up valuable time for employees, reduce the risk of errors, and ensure that key processes are performed consistently. Their integration capabilities, contribution to better data management, and role in enhancing compliance further underscore their importance. Leveraging Copilot Actions effectively can drive significant improvements in business operations, enabling organizations to achieve their goals more efficiently and deliver superior customer experiences.

A real-world example for LH&D Manufacturing

At LH&D Manufacturing, implementing Copilot Actions streamlined the lead assignment process, ensuring that leads were automatically distributed to the appropriate sales representatives based on predefined criteria. This automation reduced the time spent on manual lead distribution, allowing the sales team to focus on nurturing and converting leads.

Challenges solved

Here's an overview of the challenges that were solved with this feature:

- **Manual task automation**: Automating routine tasks reduces the need for manual intervention, saving time and reducing errors. For example, lead assignment automation ensures leads are distributed accurately and promptly.

- **Improved workflow efficiency**: By automating key processes, businesses can streamline their operations and eliminate bottlenecks. This leads to faster response times and improves overall efficiency.

- **Consistent task execution**: Automated actions ensure that tasks are performed consistently and according to predefined criteria, reducing variability, and improving reliability.

By addressing these challenges, Copilot Actions helps organizations improve efficiency and accuracy in their operations.

Value provided

This feature provided the following value:

- **Enhanced productivity**: Automating routine tasks frees up employees to focus on more strategic activities, increasing overall productivity. Sales teams can spend more time engaging with leads and customers rather than on administrative tasks.

- **Improved accuracy**: Automated actions reduce the risk of human error, ensuring that tasks are performed accurately and consistently. This improves data quality and enhances decision-making.

- **Better resource allocation**: By streamlining processes and reducing manual workloads, businesses can allocate resources more effectively, optimizing performance and reducing costs.

Overall, Copilot Actions provide significant value by enhancing productivity, accuracy, and resource allocation.

In this section, you learned about Salesforce's Copilot Actions and their significant impact on streamlining workflows and enhancing user interactions. We explored the core features and capabilities of Copilot Actions, understanding how they automate repetitive tasks and provide real-time assistance to improve productivity and operational efficiency. We delved into the differences between copilots and Copilot Actions, recognizing how each serves distinct purposes in the Salesforce ecosystem and complements each other to maximize business outcomes.

By understanding the importance of Copilot Actions, you can appreciate their role in automating routine tasks, enhancing accuracy, and ensuring consistent execution. The real-world example of LH&D Manufacturing illustrated the practical applications and benefits of Copilot Actions in automating lead assignments, improving workflow efficiency, and enhancing resource allocation.

Next, we will explore the specifics of navigating the Copilot Actions interface, providing detailed steps to implement these powerful tools effectively within your Salesforce environment.

Navigating the Copilot Actions interface

The Copilot Actions interface is designed to be user-friendly and intuitive, making it accessible to users with varying levels of technical expertise. At its core, the interface is divided into several key sections, each dedicated to various aspects of copilot development and management. The main dashboard provides a centralized view where users can manage their copilots, track their performance, and access key metrics. This high-level overview is crucial for maintaining control and ensuring that all copilots are functioning optimally:

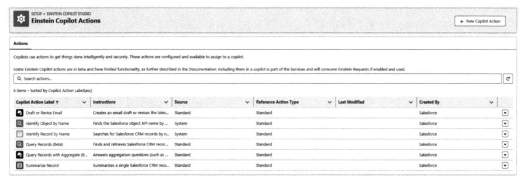

Figure 7.1 – Einstein Copilot Actions list for Copilot Studio

In addition to the dashboard, the interface includes Design Studio, a powerful tool where users can create and customize their copilots. Design Studio offers a range of templates and customization options, allowing users to tailor copilot actions and responses to their specific business needs. This flexibility is essential for creating intelligent assistants that are both effective and aligned with organizational goals. The intuitive drag-and-drop functionality simplifies the customization process, making it easy to design complex workflows without requiring extensive coding knowledge.

Connecting to an existing action (Flow, Apex, or Prompt Template) is another critical component of the Copilot Actions interface. It facilitates the seamless integration of copilots with Salesforce components, such as objects, fields, and workflows. This ensures that copilots can access and utilize relevant data, enhancing their ability to perform tasks and provide insights. By understanding and navigating these key sections effectively, users can maximize the potential of Copilot Actions and drive significant improvements in their Salesforce implementations.

Key goals and outcomes

This section's main goal is to provide a full understanding of the Copilot Actions interface. By the end of this section, you will be able to do the following:

- **Navigate the Copilot Actions interface efficiently**: Learn the layout and key components of the interface to streamline the copilot creation process

- **Utilize key features and tools within the interface**: Understand how to access and use the various tools and features available in Copilot Actions

- **Optimize your workflow within Copilot Actions**: Develop strategies to efficiently create and manage copilots, maximizing productivity.

- Efficiently manage the creation, configuration, and deployment of copilots

- Utilize Analytics Center to monitor and optimize copilot performance

By achieving these goals, you will be well-equipped to leverage the full potential of the Copilot Actions interface. This knowledge will enable you to navigate the tool efficiently, streamline the development process, and create intelligent assistants that deliver significant value to your organization.

Steps to implement

This section delves into the layout of the Copilot Actions interface, as well as how to navigate it, providing a comprehensive overview of its various components. You will learn how to access different sections of the interface, understand the purpose of each component, and navigate the setup pages effectively. Mastering the interface is crucial for efficiently managing and configuring Copilot Actions, ensuring that you can leverage all available tools to their fullest potential.

In this section, we will explore the key features within the Copilot Actions interface that are essential for building effective copilots. You will discover how to utilize the Action Library, configure action settings, and integrate various Salesforce components. Understanding and accessing these features will empower you to create, customize, and deploy intelligent Copilot Actions that enhance your Salesforce environment's functionality and user experience. Follow these steps:

1. **Access the Copilot Actions Setup area**:

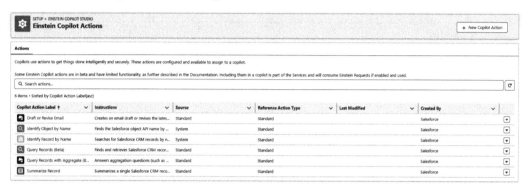

Figure 7.2 – Einstein Copilot Actions list for Copilot Studio

*   **Navigate to Salesforce Setup**: Log in to your Salesforce account and access the **Setup** menu.

*   **Search for Copilot Actions**: In the **Quick Find** box, type `Copilot Actions` and select it from the search results. This will take you to the **Copilot Actions** management page.

*   **Familiarize yourself with the interface**: Explore the various sections of the Copilot Actions **Setup** page, including existing actions, templates, and configuration options. Understanding the layout will help streamline the creation and management of Copilot Actions.

2. **Create a new Copilot Action:**

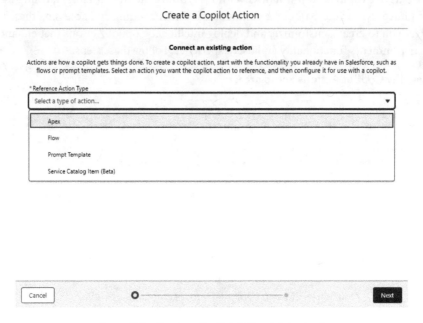

Figure 7.3 – Create a Copilot Action (at startup)

- **Initiate the creation process**: Click on the **New Copilot Action** button to start creating a new action.

- **Choose a reference action type**: Select the appropriate reference action type (**Flow**, **Apex**, or **Prompt Template**) based on the action you want to automate.

- **Select a reference action**: From the available list, choose the specific action that your Copilot Action will execute. This could be a predefined Flow, an Apex method, or a Prompt Template designed for specific interactions.

- **Configure action settings**: Define the parameters and settings for the action. This includes naming the action, setting up triggers, and specifying any conditions under which the action should be executed. Here, you will have to identify the input and output of the action, as well as specify the appropriate options. The following figures break these down in more detail:

Create a Copilot Action

Connect an existing action

Actions are how a copilot gets things done. To create a copilot action, start with the functionality you already have in Salesforce, such as flows or prompt templates. Select an action you want the copilot action to reference, and then configure it for use with a copilot.

* Reference Action Type

Prompt Template ▼

* Reference Action

Top 10 Concert Songs ×

* Copilot Action Label

Top 10 Concert Songs

* Copilot Action API Name

Top_10_Concert_Songs

Cancel   Next

Figure 7.4 – Create a Copilot Action (with selections)

- Let's jump to the final step of creating a copilot action:

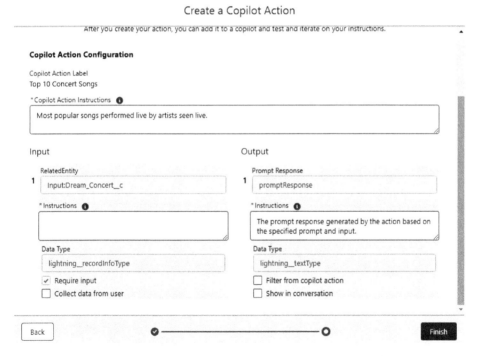

Create a Copilot Action

After you create your action, you can add it to a copilot and test and iterate on your instructions.

Copilot Action Configuration

Copilot Action Label
Top 10 Concert Songs

* Copilot Action Instructions ⓘ

Most popular songs performed live by artists seen live.

Input

RelatedEntity
1   Input:Dream_Concert__c

* Instructions ⓘ

Data Type
lightning__recordInfoType

☑ Require input
☐ Collect data from user

Output

Prompt Response
1   promptResponse

* Instructions ⓘ
The prompt response generated by the action based on the specified prompt and input.

Data Type
lightning__textType

☐ Filter from copilot action
☐ Show in conversation

Back   Finish

Figure 7.5 – Create a Copilot Action (final step – assigning input and output)

3. **Assign the action to a copilot:**

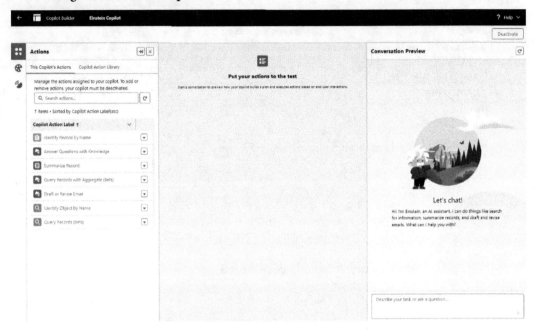

Figure 7.6 – Copilot Builder

- **Navigate to Copilot Builder**: Go to Copilot Builder, the area where you manage your AI-driven copilots.

- **Locate the Action Library**: In the Copilot Builder interface, find the Copilot Action Library, where all available actions are listed.

- **Assign an action:** Select the newly created action from the library and choose **Assign to Copilot**. Specify which copilot will use this action and under what circumstances.

- **Update the copilot configuration**: If necessary, deactivate the copilot temporarily to make configuration changes. After assigning the action, review and update the copilot's settings to ensure it functions as intended with the new action.

4. **Test the Copilot Action**:

Figure 7.7 – Copilot Builder – testing an action

- **Use Conversation Preview**: Utilize the **Conversation Preview** feature in Copilot Builder to simulate interactions with the Copilot.

- **Enter test commands**: Input relevant commands to see how the copilot processes and executes the action. This helps in identifying any issues or areas for improvement.

- **Analyze responses**: Review the copilot's responses and ensure they align with the expected outcomes. This includes checking the accuracy of data retrieval, action execution, and user interaction flow.

- **Adjust**: Based on the test results, fine-tune the action's settings and parameters. This iterative process ensures the action performs optimally before going live.

5. **Deploy the Copilot Action**:

- **Activate the copilot**: Once testing is complete and the action is fine-tuned, reactivate the copilot to deploy it in a live environment.

- **Monitor performance**: After deployment, continuously monitor the copilot's performance. Use analytics and user feedback to assess how well the action is working in real-world scenarios.

- **Gather user feedback**: Encourage users to provide feedback on the copilot's performance. This feedback is crucial for identifying any issues and areas for improvement.

- **Implement improvements**: Based on performance data and user feedback, make necessary adjustments to the action. This ensures the copilot remains effective and continues to deliver value over time.

By following these steps, you will be able to create, customize, and deploy intelligent Copilot Actions that significantly enhance your Salesforce environment's efficiency and user experience. These actions will streamline workflows, provide real-time insights, and ensure that your business processes are more effective and responsive to changing needs.

Action inputs

Action inputs in Salesforce Copilot Actions are essential elements that collect data from users to execute specific tasks. These inputs guide the copilot on what information is needed to act, ensuring that it functions accurately and effectively. Understanding and configuring these inputs correctly is crucial for creating responsive and intelligent copilots that can adapt to various business needs.

Action inputs are the parameters or data points that a copilot requires to execute a specific action within Salesforce. These inputs can range from plain text fields to complex data types, depending on the action's nature. For example, when creating a Copilot Action to update a customer record, inputs might include the customer ID, name, contact details, and other relevant information. These inputs ensure that the copilot has all the necessary data to perform the task accurately.

Let's look at the different types of action inputs:

- **Text inputs**: Plain text fields where users can enter information manually. These are commonly used for names, addresses, and other basic data types.

- **Dropdowns and picklists**: Predefined lists from which users can select an option. These are useful for standardizing responses, such as selecting a country or status.

- **Date and time inputs**: Fields for entering date and time values, ensuring that actions can be scheduled or executed based on specific periods.

- **Checkboxes and toggles**: Binary inputs that allow users to indicate a yes/no or true/false condition. These are useful for options such as enabling or disabling features.

- **Multi-select inputs**: Fields that allow users to select multiple options from a list. These are beneficial for actions that require multiple criteria or selections.

Configuring action inputs

When setting up action inputs, it is essential to define clear and concise labels and provide appropriate help text to guide users on what data is needed. Inputs should be validated to ensure data accuracy and consistency – for instance, ensuring that email addresses follow a standard format or that dates are within a valid range.

Example of configuring action inputs

Consider a scenario where a Copilot Action has been designed to create a new sales opportunity. The action inputs might include the following:

- **Opportunity name (text input)**: The name of the sales opportunity
- **Account name (dropdown)**: A list of existing accounts to associate with the opportunity
- **Close date (date input)**: The expected close date for the opportunity
- **Sales stage (picklist)**: The current stage of the sales process
- **Expected revenue (number input)**: The estimated revenue from the opportunity

These inputs ensure that all the necessary information is collected to create the sales opportunity accurately.

The importance of action inputs

Action inputs play a critical role in the functionality of Copilot Actions. They ensure that the copilot has the necessary data to perform tasks accurately, leading to improved efficiency and user satisfaction. Well-configured action inputs help reduce errors, streamline processes, and enhance the overall user experience by providing relevant and contextually appropriate responses.

In summary, action inputs are vital components of Salesforce Copilot Actions that collect the necessary data to perform specific tasks. Understanding and configuring these inputs correctly ensures that copilots can function effectively, enhancing business processes and user satisfaction. By leveraging various input types and ensuring proper configuration, businesses can create intelligent assistants that provide accurate and relevant support.

A real-world example for LH&D Manufacturing

At LH&D Manufacturing, the sales operations team used the Copilot Actions interface to set up automated workflows for lead nurturing. By efficiently navigating the interface, they were able to quickly configure actions that sent follow-up emails to leads based on specific triggers, improving engagement and conversion rates.

Challenges solved

Here's an overview of the challenges they solved with this feature:

- **Complex interface navigation**: The intuitive interface simplifies navigation, reducing the learning curve for inexperienced users. This allows teams to quickly become proficient and start creating automated actions.

- **Disjointed process management**: The centralized interface ensures cohesive functionality by allowing users to manage all their automated actions in one place. This streamlines process management and improves efficiency.

- **Limited user adoption**: An easy-to-use interface encourages user adoption, ensuring that teams leverage the full capabilities of Copilot Actions. Higher adoption rates lead to better utilization and more effective automation.

By addressing these challenges, the Copilot Actions interface enhances user experience and process management.

Value provided

This feature provided the following value:

- **Streamlined workflow creation**: The user-friendly interface simplifies the process of creating and managing automated actions, saving time and effort. Teams can quickly set up and modify workflows as needed.

- **Enhanced functionality**: The centralized management of automated actions ensures cohesive and effective functionality. This improves the reliability and performance of automated processes.

- **Increased user adoption**: An intuitive interface promotes higher user adoption rates, ensuring that teams fully utilize the capabilities of Copilot Actions. This leads to more effective automation and better business outcomes.

Overall, the Copilot Actions interface provides significant value by streamlining workflow creation, enhancing functionality, and increasing user adoption.

In this section, you learned how to navigate and utilize the Salesforce Copilot Actions interface effectively. We explored key components such as the main dashboard and Design Studio, which are essential for creating, customizing, and managing Copilot Actions. The step-by-step implementation guide provided a detailed walkthrough on accessing the setup, creating new actions, assigning actions to copilots, and then testing and deploying them. This systematic approach ensures that users can leverage the full potential of Copilot Actions, enhancing operational efficiency and productivity.

The real-world example of LH&D Manufacturing illustrated the practical benefits of mastering the Copilot Actions interface. By implementing automated workflows for lead nurturing, the sales operations team significantly improved engagement and conversion rates. The streamlined interface facilitated easy navigation and quick configuration, addressing challenges such as complex navigation, disjointed process management, and limited user adoption. As a result, LH&D Manufacturing experienced enhanced workflow creation, increased functionality, and higher user adoption, leading to more effective automation and better business outcomes.

Creating and configuring Copilot Actions

Creating and configuring AI-driven copilots is a multifaceted process that involves several critical steps, each contributing to the development of a robust and effective assistant. The initial phase focuses on defining the copilot's objectives and scope, which lays the foundation for all subsequent configurations. Clear objectives ensure that the copilot is purpose-built to address specific business needs, whether it's automating routine tasks, providing real-time insights, or enhancing customer interactions. This strategic alignment is crucial for maximizing the copilot's impact and value.

Once the objectives have been defined, Design Studio in Copilot Builder becomes the primary tool for creating the copilot's structure. This involves configuring actions and responses, setting up triggers, and integrating relevant data sources. Design Studio offers a range of customization options, allowing users to tailor the copilot's behavior to their unique requirements. For example, users can define specific conditions under which the copilot should perform certain actions, ensuring that it operates in alignment with business processes. This level of customization is essential for creating a copilot that is both effective and flexible.

The last step in the creation and configuration process involves thorough testing and validation. Before deploying the copilot in a live environment, it is crucial to test its performance in a controlled setting, such as a sandbox. This allows users to identify and resolve any issues, ensuring that the copilot functions as intended. Additionally, gathering feedback from end users during this phase can provide valuable insights into the copilot's effectiveness and usability. By incorporating this feedback into the refinement process, users can optimize the copilot's performance and ensure a seamless deployment.

Key goals and outcomes

This section's main goal is to provide a detailed guide to creating and configuring AI-driven copilots. By the end of this section, you will be able to do the following:

- **Define the purpose and scope of your copilot**: Clearly outline what tasks your copilot will perform and how it will benefit your organization

- **Set up and configure copilot functionalities**: Learn how to customize the copilot's actions and responses to align with your business processes

- **Ensure the copilot meets your business needs**: Tailor the copilot to address specific challenges and opportunities within your organization

- Use Design Studio to create and configure copilots

- Customize copilot actions and responses to meet specific business needs

- Integrate copilots with relevant Salesforce components for cohesive functionality

By achieving these goals, you will be equipped to design and deploy intelligent assistants that enhance efficiency, improve customer interactions, and drive better business outcomes.

A real-world example for LH&D Manufacturing

LH&D Manufacturing used Copilot Actions to automate the approval process for purchase orders. By setting up triggers based on order value thresholds, they ensured that high-value orders were automatically routed to the appropriate approvers. This automation reduced processing times and improved accuracy in the approval workflow.

Challenges solved

Here's an overview of the challenges that were solved with this feature:

- **Manual approval processes**: Automating the approval process reduces the need for manual intervention, speeding up approvals and reducing errors. This ensures the timely processing of purchase orders.

- **Inconsistent workflow execution**: Customizing triggers and conditions ensures that workflows are executed consistently and according to predefined criteria. This improves reliability and reduces variability.

- **Resource bottlenecks**: Automated workflows help alleviate resource bottlenecks by streamlining processes and reducing the workload on employees. This leads to more efficient resource utilization.

By addressing these challenges, Copilot Actions improves workflow efficiency and consistency.

Value provided

This feature provided the following value:

- **Enhanced efficiency**: Automating approval processes and other routine tasks increases operational efficiency. This frees employees to focus on higher-value activities.

- **Improved accuracy**: Customizing triggers and conditions ensure that tasks are performed accurately and consistently. This enhances data quality and decision-making.

- **Better resource utilization**: Streamlined workflows reduce the workload on employees, allowing them to focus on more strategic activities. This optimizes resource allocation and improves overall performance.

Overall, creating and configuring Copilot Actions provides significant value by enhancing efficiency, improving accuracy, and optimizing resource utilization.

In this section, you explored the comprehensive process of creating and configuring AI-driven Copilot Actions in Salesforce. We delved into defining the copilot's objectives and scope, ensuring alignment with business needs to maximize impact. Design Studio was highlighted as a key tool for customizing actions, setting up triggers, and integrating data sources, allowing for precise and flexible configurations. Emphasis was placed on the importance of thorough testing and validation in controlled environments to optimize performance before deployment.

The real-world example of LH&D Manufacturing demonstrated the practical application of Copilot Actions, automating the approval process for purchase orders and addressing challenges such as manual intervention, inconsistent workflow execution, and resource bottlenecks. This automation led to enhanced efficiency, improved accuracy, and better resource utilization, highlighting the significant value that Copilot Actions provide in streamlining business processes and driving better outcomes.

Next, we will delve into integrating Copilot Actions with Salesforce Flows, exploring how this integration can streamline workflows and enhance data accuracy within your Salesforce environment.

Integrating Copilot Actions with Salesforce Flows

Integrating copilots with Salesforce components is a crucial step in ensuring their functionality and effectiveness within your business processes. This integration allows copilots to interact seamlessly with various objects, fields, and workflows in Salesforce, enhancing their ability to perform tasks and provide insights. Effective integration ensures that copilots can leverage the full range of data and functionalities available within Salesforce, making them more versatile and powerful tools for business operations:

Figure 7.8 – Einstein for Flow (Beta)

Copilot Builder facilitates this process by providing a range of tools and options for connecting copilots with Salesforce components. Users can easily configure integration points, ensuring that copilots can access and manipulate the necessary data. For instance, a copilot designed to assist with customer support can be integrated with case management objects, enabling it to provide real-time updates and solutions based on customer inquiries. This seamless integration ensures that copilots operate efficiently within existing workflows, providing consistent and reliable support.

Also, Copilot Builder supports connecting external data sources, allowing businesses to expand their copilots' capabilities further. By integrating external data, users can enhance the copilot's decision-making processes and provide more comprehensive insights. This capability is precious for businesses that rely on diverse data sets to drive their operations. Understanding how to effectively use Copilot Bulder is essential for maximizing the potential of Copilot Actions and ensuring that they deliver significant value to your organization.

Key goals and outcomes

This section's main goal is to provide a comprehensive guide to integrating copilots with Salesforce components. By the end of this section, you will be able to do the following:

- **Understand how copilots interact with Salesforce components**: Learn the integration points and how to leverage them for cohesive functionality to connect copilots with Salesforce objects, fields, and workflows

- **Implement seamless integration with objects, fields, and workflows**: Ensure that your copilots can access and utilize relevant Salesforce data and processes

- **Enhance overall system efficiency**: Optimize the interaction between copilots and Salesforce components to streamline workflows and improve performance

- Ensure cohesive functionality and seamless user experiences

- Leverage integrated copilots to enhance business processes and improve operational efficiency

By achieving these goals, you will be able to create intelligent assistants that operate seamlessly within your Salesforce environment, enhancing their ability to perform tasks and providing valuable insights.

A real-world example for LH&D Manufacturing

At LH&D Manufacturing, integrating Copilot Actions with Salesforce Flows enabled the automation of the order fulfillment process. By connecting Copilot Actions with inventory management and order processing workflows, they ensured that orders were automatically validated, processed, and fulfilled based on real-time inventory data. This integration streamlined the order fulfillment process and reduced the time to delivery.

Challenges solved

Here's an overview of the challenges that were solved with this feature:

- **Disjointed workflow processes**: Integrating Copilot Actions with Salesforce Flows ensures cohesive functionality, eliminating disjointed processes and improving workflow efficiency

- **Manual order processing**: Automating order validation and processing reduces manual intervention, speeding up the order fulfillment process and reducing errors

- **Inconsistent data access**: Seamless integration allows Copilot Actions to access and utilize real-time data, ensuring that workflows are based on accurate and up-to-date information

By addressing these challenges, integrating Copilot Actions with Salesforce Flows enhances workflow efficiency and data accuracy.

Value provided

This feature provided the following value:

- **Streamlined workflow processes**: Integrating Copilot Actions with Salesforce Flows streamlines workflow processes, improving efficiency and reducing processing times. This leads to faster and more reliable outcomes.

- **Reduced manual workloads**: Automating order validation and processing reduces the manual workload on employees, allowing them to focus on higher-value activities. This increases overall productivity.

- **Enhanced data accuracy**: Seamless integration ensures that workflows are based on accurate and up-to-date information, thus improving decision-making and reducing errors.

Overall, integrating Copilot Actions with Salesforce Flows provides significant value by streamlining workflow processes, reducing manual workloads, and enhancing data accuracy.

In this section, you explored the importance of integrating Copilot Actions with Salesforce Flows to enhance their functionality within business processes. We discussed how the Copilot Action interface facilitates seamless connections with Salesforce components, allowing copilots to interact with objects, fields, and workflows. This integration enables automated, real-time responses and improves workflow efficiency.

The real-world example of LH&D Manufacturing illustrated the benefits of automating the order fulfillment process, addressing challenges such as disjointed workflows, manual order processing, and inconsistent data access. Integrating Copilot Actions with Salesforce Flows significantly streamlined processes, reduced manual workloads, and enhanced data accuracy, highlighting the value of seamless integration in driving operational efficiency.

Customizing copilot actions and responses

Customizing copilot actions and responses is a critical aspect of leveraging the full potential of AI-driven assistants within Salesforce. This customization ensures that copilots are not only performing tasks but also providing responses that are contextually relevant and aligned with business objectives. The ability to tailor actions and responses allows businesses to create intelligent assistants that are truly responsive to their needs, enhancing both operational efficiency and user satisfaction.

Copilot Builder offers a comprehensive set of tools for customizing actions and responses. Users can define specific tasks that the copilot should perform, such as sending notifications, updating records, or generating reports. These actions can be configured to trigger based on certain conditions, ensuring that the copilot operates seamlessly within existing workflows. For example, a copilot can be set to automatically update a customer record when the latest information is received, ensuring that data is always current and accurate.

In addition to actions, customizing responses is equally important. Responses can be tailored to provide users with relevant and helpful information, enhancing the overall interaction experience. This involves configuring the copilot to deliver responses that are not only accurate but also timely and contextually appropriate. By leveraging the customization options available in Copilot Builder, businesses can create intelligent assistants that are highly effective and aligned with their specific needs. This level of customization is essential for maximizing the value and impact of Copilot Actions within Salesforce.

Key goals and outcomes

This section's main goal is to provide a detailed guide to customizing copilot actions and responses. By the end of this section, you will be able to do the following:

- **Customize copilot actions so that they align with business processes**: Tailor the tasks and actions performed by your copilots to fit your specific workflows

- **Enhance the relevance and effectiveness of copilot responses**: Ensure that the responses provided by your copilots are accurate, helpful, and contextually appropriate

- **Improve user satisfaction and engagement**: Personalize copilot interactions to enhance the user experience and drive higher satisfaction levels

- Define and configure copilot actions to automate tasks and provide insights

- Customize copilot responses to ensure accuracy and relevance

- Leverage customization options to enhance the performance and effectiveness of your copilots

By achieving these goals, you will be able to create intelligent assistants that are highly effective and tailored to your specific business needs, enhancing operational efficiency and user satisfaction.

Action customization

Customizing copilot actions in Salesforce is a critical step in ensuring that your AI-driven assistants are functional and highly effective in meeting your business needs. This process involves tailoring specific tasks that the copilot should perform, such as sending notifications, updating records, or generating reports, to align with your unique workflows and objectives. By customizing these actions, businesses can create intelligent assistants that deliver precise, contextually relevant support, enhancing both operational efficiency and user satisfaction.

Copilot Builder provides a robust set of tools for action customization. Users can define detailed parameters and conditions for each action, ensuring that the copilot operates seamlessly within the existing business processes. For instance, you can configure an action to automatically update a customer's contact information based on the latest interactions or set up notifications to alert team members about important updates. This level of customization is essential for creating a copilot that can adapt to various business scenarios and provide valuable support.

Customizing actions also involves continuous refinement based on performance data and user feedback. After deploying the copilot, it is crucial to monitor its effectiveness and make necessary adjustments to the actions to ensure optimal performance. This iterative process helps maintain the copilot's relevance and effectiveness over time, ensuring that it continues to meet the evolving needs of the business.

A real-world example for LH&D Manufacturing

LH&D Manufacturing customized their Copilot Actions to automate the customer feedback collection process. By configuring the actions to send personalized survey invitations based on specific customer interactions, they were able to gather valuable feedback and improve their customer service processes. Customizing the responses ensured that customers received timely and relevant follow-ups, enhancing their overall experience.

Challenges solved

Here's an overview of the challenges that were solved with this feature:

- **Generic actions**: Customizing Copilot Actions ensures that they are relevant and aligned with business needs. This increases the effectiveness of automated workflows.
- **Ineffective customer engagement**: Tailoring Copilot responses improves their accuracy and relevance, enhancing customer engagement and satisfaction.
- **Manual feedback collection**: Automating the feedback collection process reduces manual workloads and ensures timely follow-ups, improving the efficiency of customer service operations.

By addressing these challenges, customizing Copilot Actions and responses improves workflow relevance and customer engagement.

Value provided

This feature provided the following value:

- **Relevant and effective actions**: Customizing Copilot Actions ensures that they perform tasks that are relevant and valuable to your business. This enhances the effectiveness of automated workflows.
- **Accurate and helpful responses**: Tailored responses improve the accuracy and helpfulness of copilot interactions, enhancing customer engagement and satisfaction.
- **Efficient feedback collection**: Automating the feedback collection process reduces manual workloads and ensures timely follow-ups, improving the efficiency of customer service operations.

Overall, customizing copilot actions and responses provide significant value by enhancing workflow relevance, improving customer engagement, and increasing operational efficiency.

In this section, you learned how to customize copilot actions and responses in Salesforce to align with specific business needs and workflows. We explored the tools and methods available in Copilot Builder to define and configure tasks such as sending notifications, updating records, and generating reports. By tailoring these actions and responses, businesses can enhance operational efficiency and user satisfaction. We also discussed the importance of continuous refinement based on performance data and user feedback to maintain the copilot's relevance and effectiveness.

Additionally, we examined a real-world example from LH&D Manufacturing, where customizing Copilot Actions for automated customer feedback collection improved workflow relevance and customer engagement. By automating the feedback process and ensuring timely follow-ups, LH&D Manufacturing enhanced its customer service operations. This section highlighted the significant value provided by customization, including relevant and effective actions, accurate and helpful responses, and efficient feedback collection.

Testing and refining copilot performance

Testing and refining copilot performance is a crucial step in ensuring that your AI-driven assistants deliver optimal results. This process involves thoroughly evaluating copilot actions and responses in a controlled environment to identify any issues or areas for improvement. By systematically testing and refining copilots, businesses can enhance their accuracy, reliability, and overall effectiveness, ensuring that they provide consistent value and support.

The initial phase of testing typically involves deploying the copilot in a sandbox environment, where it can operate without impacting live data or workflows. This controlled setting allows users to simulate various scenarios and assess the copilot's performance under different conditions. Any issues or inconsistencies that are identified during this phase can be addressed before the copilot is deployed in a live environment. This initiative-taking approach helps prevent potential disruptions and ensures a smooth implementation.

Refining copilot performance is an ongoing process that extends beyond initial testing. Continuous monitoring and feedback are essential for maintaining ambitious standards of performance and reliability. By regularly reviewing performance metrics and gathering user feedback, businesses can identify new opportunities for improvement and make data-driven adjustments. This iterative process ensures that copilots remain effective and aligned with evolving business needs, maximizing their long-term value and impact.

Key goals and outcomes

This section's main goal is to provide a guide to testing and refining copilot performance. By the end of this section, you will be able to do the following:

- **Implement best practices for testing copilot performance**: Learn how to conduct thorough testing to identify and address performance issues

- **Optimize copilot functionalities for improved outcomes**: Understand how to refine copilot actions and responses to enhance their effectiveness

- **Ensure copilot accuracy and reliability**: Maintain lofty standards of performance and reliability through continuous testing and refinement

- Conduct thorough testing of copilots in a controlled environment

- Identify and resolve performance issues early

- Refine copilot performance based on test results and user feedback

By achieving these goals, you will be able to create intelligent assistants that are highly effective and dependable, enhancing operational efficiency and user satisfaction.

A real-world example for LH&D Manufacturing

At LH&D Manufacturing, the sales team conducted thorough testing of their Copilot Actions in a sandbox environment to identify any performance issues. They used the insights gained from testing to refine the actions and responses, ensuring that the Copilot Actions delivered optimal performance. By incorporating user feedback into the refinement process, LH&D Manufacturing created Copilot Actions that were highly effective and aligned with their business processes.

Challenges solved

Here's an overview of the challenges that were solved with this feature:

- **Performance issues**: Thorough testing identified and resolved performance issues early, ensuring optimal functionality of the Copilot Actions.

- **Ineffective actions**: Refining Copilot Actions based on test results ensured that they were effective and aligned with business needs. This improved the relevance and impact of the automated workflows.

- **User dissatisfaction**: Incorporating user feedback into the refinement process enhanced user satisfaction, ensuring that the Copilot Actions met their needs and expectations.

Addressing these challenges, as well as testing and refining your copilot's performance, ensures its effectiveness and reliability.

Value provided

This feature provided the following value:

- **Optimal performance**: Thorough testing and refinement ensure that Copilot Actions deliver optimal performance. This enhances the effectiveness of automated workflows.

- **Effective and relevant actions**: Refining Copilot Actions based on test results ensures their effectiveness and relevance. This improves the impact of the automated workflows.

- **Enhanced user satisfaction**: Incorporating user feedback into the refinement process enhances user satisfaction and engagement. This ensures that the Copilot Actions meet the needs and expectations of users.

Overall, testing, and refining Copilot performance provides significant value by ensuring optimal performance, improving action relevance, and enhancing user satisfaction.

In this section, you learned about the critical importance of testing and refining Copilot Actions to ensure they deliver optimal results. We discussed the process of evaluating copilot actions and responses in a controlled environment, such as a sandbox, to identify and resolve performance issues before deployment. We also emphasized the necessity of continuous monitoring and feedback to maintain high performance and reliability standards.

We also explored a real-world example from LH&D Manufacturing, where thorough testing and refinement of Copilot Actions led to enhanced effectiveness and alignment with business processes. This initiative-taking approach ensured the actions met user needs and expectations, resulting in increased satisfaction and engagement. By implementing best practices for testing and refinement, businesses can create intelligent assistants that consistently perform at their best, improving operational efficiency and user satisfaction.

Utilizing analytics and troubleshooting copilot issues

Utilizing analytics and troubleshooting copilot issues are essential practices for maintaining the optimal functionality and effectiveness of AI-driven assistants. Analytics provide valuable insights into copilot performance, enabling businesses to measure effectiveness, identify areas for improvement, and make data-driven adjustments. By leveraging these insights, businesses can optimize copilot actions and responses, ensuring that they continue to deliver maximum value.

Copilot Builder includes robust analytics tools that allow users to track key performance metrics and evaluate the impact of their copilots. These metrics can include response times, accuracy rates, user satisfaction scores, and more. Regularly reviewing these metrics helps businesses identify trends and patterns, providing a basis for informed decision-making. For instance, if analytics reveal that a copilot's response times are slower during peak hours, businesses can investigate and address potential bottlenecks.

Troubleshooting is another critical component of maintaining copilot performance. Despite thorough testing and refinement, issues can still arise during live operations. Copilot Builder provides tools and best practices for identifying and resolving these issues quickly. This involves diagnosing the root causes of problems, implementing fixes, and monitoring the results to ensure that the issues are resolved. Effective troubleshooting helps maintain the reliability and effectiveness of copilots, ensuring that they provide consistent support and value.

Key goals and outcomes

This section's main goal is to provide a comprehensive guide to using analytics and troubleshooting copilot issues. By the end of this section, you will be able to do the following:

- **Leverage analytics to track copilot performance**: Use data to measure the effectiveness of your copilots and identify areas for improvement

- **Troubleshoot common copilot issues**: Address and resolve issues quickly to maintain optimal functionality

- **Maintain lofty standards of performance and reliability**: Ensure that your copilots consistently deliver accurate and effective results

- Utilize analytics to measure and optimize copilot performance

- Implement best practices for troubleshooting and resolving issues

- Maintain continuous improvement and reliability of copilot actions

By achieving these goals, you will be able to create intelligent assistants that are highly effective and dependable, enhancing operational efficiency and user satisfaction.

A real-world example for LH&D Manufacturing

LH&D Manufacturing used the analytics tools provided by Copilot Builder to measure the performance of their sales Copilot Actions. They identified areas for improvement and made data-driven adjustments that enhanced the effectiveness of their Copilot Actions. Additionally, they utilized best practices for troubleshooting common issues, ensuring that the Copilot Actions maintained optimal functionality and delivered consistent value. This initiative-taking approach resulted in improved sales performance and user satisfaction.

Challenges solved

Here's an overview of the challenges that were solved with this feature:

- **Performance measurement**: Utilizing analytics tools provided valuable insights into copilot performance, enabling data-driven adjustments. This ensured that the Copilot Actions remained effective and relevant.

- **Identifying improvement areas**: Data-driven adjustments enhanced the effectiveness of the Copilot Actions, ensuring that they continued to deliver optimal results.

- **Maintaining functionality**: Troubleshooting best practices ensured that Copilot Actions maintained optimal functionality, minimizing disruptions, and ensuring consistent value delivery.

Addressing these challenges, utilizing analytics, and troubleshooting Copilot issues ensures that the Copilot Actions remain effective and dependable.

Value Provided

This feature provided the following value:

- **Enhanced Performance**: Utilizing analytics tools and making data-driven adjustments enhances copilot performance. This ensures that the Copilot Actions deliver optimal results.

- **Data-driven optimization**: Identifying and addressing areas for improvement optimizes a copilot's effectiveness. This ensures that the Copilot Actions remain relevant and impactful.

- **Consistent value**: Troubleshooting best practices ensure that Copilot Actions maintain optimal functionality, delivering consistent value. This minimizes disruptions and ensures reliable performance.

Overall, utilizing analytics and troubleshooting copilot issues provides significant value by enhancing performance, optimizing effectiveness, and ensuring consistent value delivery.

In this section, you explored the vital practices of utilizing analytics and troubleshooting copilot issues to maintain the optimal functionality and effectiveness of AI-driven assistants. We highlighted the importance of leveraging analytics tools to track performance metrics such as response times, accuracy rates, and user satisfaction scores, enabling businesses to make data-driven adjustments for continuous improvement.

Additionally, you learned about effective troubleshooting techniques to identify and resolve issues quickly, ensuring that copilots consistently deliver accurate and effective results. The real-world example from LH&D Manufacturing illustrated how these practices led to improved performance and user satisfaction. By implementing these strategies, businesses can ensure that their Copilot Actions remain highly effective, dependable, and valuable over time.

Summary

Integrating and utilizing Salesforce's Copilot Actions is a transformative step for businesses looking to enhance their CRM capabilities with advanced automation. This chapter has provided a comprehensive guide to navigating the Copilot Actions interface, creating and configuring actions, integrating them with Salesforce Flows, customizing them for specific use cases, and testing and refining their performance. By following these guidelines, you can seamlessly integrate Copilot Actions into your existing Salesforce infrastructure, leveraging their powerful capabilities to drive efficiency, innovation, and superior customer experiences.

The advantages of Copilot Actions are manifold. From automating routine tasks and providing actionable insights to enhancing decision-making and improving customer engagement, this tool is designed to elevate your business operations. By customizing Copilot Actions to fit your organization's specific needs, you can ensure that they align perfectly with your business processes and goals. The ability to personalize user settings, create custom reports and dashboards, and configure AI models allows you to extract maximum value from the tool, making your CRM efforts more effective and impactful.

One of the key strengths of Copilot Actions is their ability to evolve and improve over time. Salesforce continuously updates its AI capabilities, incorporating the latest advancements in machine learning and data analytics. To stay updated with the latest features and best practices, it is crucial to leverage Salesforce's extensive resources, including the Salesforce Help and Knowledge Base. These platforms provide a wealth of information, from detailed documentation and troubleshooting guides to expert tips and user forums. Additionally, Salesforce Trailhead offers a range of interactive learning modules that can help you deepen your understanding of Copilot Actions and stay ahead of the curve in AI-driven CRM.

In conclusion, mastering the integration and customization of Copilot Actions is an investment in your organization's future. By harnessing the power of AI, you can transform your Salesforce environment into a dynamic, data-driven ecosystem that drives business success. The skills and knowledge you've gained from this chapter will empower you to implement Copilot Actions with confidence, ensuring a smooth setup and optimal performance. As you continue to explore the capabilities of Copilot Actions, remember to utilize Salesforce's resources and stay engaged with the latest updates and training opportunities. Embrace the potential of AI to revolutionize your CRM strategy and unlock new levels of efficiency, innovation, and customer satisfaction.

In the next few chapters of this book, we're going to highlight the robust feature set of Salesforce's cloud offerings, starting with Sales Cloud, Service Cloud, Marketing Cloud, and Commerce Cloud. These tools represent the forefront of AI integration within Salesforce, offering unparalleled capabilities to customize and optimize your CRM processes. Data Cloud serves as the backbone, ensuring that your AI applications have access to high-quality, real-time data.

These features are invaluable for businesses aiming to stay ahead in the competitive landscape. By leveraging these clouds, you can create a highly responsive and intelligent CRM system that adapts to your unique business needs. The next chapter will focus on Sales Cloud, exploring its capabilities and demonstrating how to integrate and optimize its features to enhance your sales processes and drive business growth.

As you continue reading, you will gain a deep understanding of how to utilize these advanced tools to their fullest potential. Each chapter will provide detailed insights and practical steps to help you implement and customize these features within your Salesforce environment. Embrace the journey ahead, as mastering these tools will significantly elevate your CRM capabilities and drive meaningful business outcomes.

Coming up next in the second half of the book, we'll return to some of the more familiar product areas of Salesforce – Sales, Service, Marketing, and Commerce – and look at how those products are being enhanced to take advantage of the Einstein Studio platform and offer its users incredible new functionality.

Part 2:
Building Use Cases for
GPT Intelligence:
The What of Einstein Copilot

This part of our book shifts the focus from foundational knowledge to practical, real-world applications of Einstein Copilot across various Salesforce clouds. This part delves into how Einstein Copilot can be integrated with Sales Cloud, Service Cloud, Marketing Cloud, and Commerce Cloud to drive innovation and enhance business outcomes.

Chapters 8 and *9* explore how Einstein Copilot enhances Sales Cloud and Service Cloud, transforming the sales processes, improving forecasting, lead management, customer engagement, and revolutionizing customer support through AI-driven automation and insights. These chapters equip sales and service teams with the tools to increase productivity, conversion rates, and customer satisfaction.

Chapters 10 and 11 delve into Marketing Cloud and Commerce Cloud, showcasing how AI optimizes customer segmentation, campaign performance, and the online shopping experience. Readers learn to leverage predictive analytics, dynamic pricing, and proactive engagement to drive ROI, boost sales, and enhance customer satisfaction.

Finally, *Chapter 12* looks ahead at the future of Einstein Copilot, offering predictions about its evolution and how organizations can stay ahead by embracing emerging AI technologies. This forward-looking chapter encourages strategic thinking about the continued integration of AI into your business operations.

> **Note**
>
> We haven't included "Key goals and outcomes" in this part of the book as the approach to implementing these use cases will vary based on the differences in your own ORG configuration, fields, and processes for your business. We feel those differences could drive varying results that can't be accounted for inconsistent outcomes

This part has the following chapters:

- *Chapter 8, Synergy between Einstein Copilot and Sales Cloud*
- *Chapter 9, Integrating Einstein Copilot and Service Cloud*
- *Chapter 10, Integrating Einstein Copilot and Marketing Cloud*
- *Chapter 11, Working with Einstein Copilot and Commerce Cloud*
- *Chapter 12, What's Next With Einstein Copilot?*

8

Synergy between Einstein Copilot and Sales Cloud

Now that we've looked at the mechanics of Einstein Copilot, exploring powerful features such as Prompt Builder, Actions, and Model Builder, it's time to shift our focus to how these tools can be applied within specific Salesforce clouds. In the following chapters, we'll explore how Einstein Copilot can be harnessed to drive efficiency and innovation in Sales Cloud, Service Cloud, and beyond, translating the foundational knowledge we've built into practical, impactful solutions tailored to various business needs.

Salesforce Sales Cloud is a robust platform designed to support and enhance the entire sales life cycle, from lead generation to deal closure. It provides tools and features that help sales teams manage their relationships with potential and existing customers, streamline their sales processes, and ultimately drive revenue growth. With capabilities such as contact management, opportunity tracking, and sales forecasting, Sales Cloud empowers sales professionals to work more efficiently and effectively. The platform's integration with other Salesforce products and its extensive customization options make it a versatile solution for businesses of all sizes and industries.

Einstein Copilot brings a new dimension to the Sales Cloud by integrating advanced **artificial intelligence** (**AI**) into everyday sales activities. Leveraging **machine learning** (**ML**) and **natural language processing** (**NLP**), Einstein Copilot assists sales teams by providing predictive insights, automating routine tasks, and facilitating more informed decision-making. This AI-driven functionality helps sales representatives prioritize leads and opportunities, draft follow-up emails, schedule meetings, and summarize key account information. Doing so frees up valuable time for sales professionals to focus on building relationships and closing deals. Einstein Copilot transforms Sales Cloud into an even more powerful tool, enabling users to harness the full potential of their data and operate at peak efficiency.

The combination of Sales Cloud and Einstein Copilot enhances the capabilities of sales teams. By embedding AI into the core functionalities of the Sales Cloud platform, Einstein Copilot provides actionable insights and automates mundane tasks, allowing sales representatives to be more strategic and proactive. This integration improves individual performance and aligns sales activities with broader business objectives, driving consistent and scalable growth. As businesses increasingly recognize the value of AI, the adoption of Einstein Copilot within Sales Cloud positions them to stay competitive.

Einstein Copilot significantly enhances sales by providing AI-driven insights and automation that streamline and optimize various sales activities. One of the primary ways it does this is through intelligent lead and opportunity management. By analyzing historical data and patterns, Einstein Copilot can prioritize leads and opportunities based on their likelihood to convert, allowing sales teams to focus their efforts where they are most likely to see results. This predictive capability ensures that no valuable leads are overlooked and that sales efforts are strategically aligned with the highest potential returns.

Another enhancement comes from Einstein Copilot's ability to automate routine tasks and provide real-time assistance. For instance, sales representatives can use Einstein Copilot to draft follow-up emails, schedule meetings, and generate summaries of complex opportunities. This not only saves time but also ensures consistency and professionalism in communications. Additionally, by identifying at-risk accounts or suggesting next steps for leads, Einstein Copilot helps sales teams maintain a proactive approach, addressing issues before they escalate and continuously moving prospects through the sales funnel.

Einstein Copilot facilitates better decision-making and strategic planning by providing comprehensive, data-driven insights. Sales managers and executives can leverage these insights to monitor performance, identify trends, and make informed decisions about resource allocation and strategy adjustments. For example, by finding similar closed opportunities, Einstein Copilot can highlight successful strategies that can be replicated for current deals. The integration of Einstein Copilot into the sales process not only boosts efficiency and productivity but also enhances sales teams' overall effectiveness and competitiveness.

In the remainder of this chapter, you will dive into use cases showcasing how Einstein Copilot can be applied within Sales Cloud to maximize efficiency and drive sales success. Each use case is accompanied by illustrative screenshots, demonstrating how to prioritize leads and opportunities, draft follow-up emails, schedule meetings, summarize key account information, and identify at-risk accounts. Custom prompt templates for suggesting next actions and finding similar closed opportunities will also be explored, providing you with tailored strategies to enhance your users' sales processes. By the end of this chapter, you will have a comprehensive understanding of how to leverage Einstein Copilot's capabilities to automate routine tasks, make data-driven decisions, and boost sales performance. This will start you on the path to having the insights and skills needed to implement and customize Einstein Copilot for your users!

> **Please note**
>
> The remainder of this chapter assumes that you have a Salesforce sandbox with Einstein Copilot provisioned and enabled and you have read the chapters in this book about Prompt Builder and Actions.

Exploring out-of-the-box Einstein Copilot

Einstein Copilot offers many **out-of-the-box** (**OOTB**) functionalities designed to effortlessly streamline and enhance various aspects of the sales process. These preconfigured features require minimal setup and are ready to use immediately, enabling sales teams to benefit from AI-driven insights and automation quickly. This chapter guides you through the OOTB capabilities of Einstein Copilot, demonstrating how it can prioritize leads and opportunities, draft follow-up emails, schedule meetings, summarize opportunities, and identify at-risk accounts with just a few simple commands. By understanding and leveraging these built-in features, sales professionals can enhance their productivity and focus more on strategic tasks that drive business growth.

OOTB

As we explore the capabilities of Einstein Copilot within Sales Cloud, it is important to understand the dynamic nature of Einstein Copilot. Salesforce is continuously evolving, and so is Einstein Copilot. What is available OOTB today might be different tomorrow due to ongoing enhancements and updates. This section aims to provide a snapshot of Einstein Copilot's capabilities at the time of writing while also preparing you for potential changes and encouraging a mindset of experimentation and adaptability.

At the time of writing, Einstein Copilot has features designed to streamline sales operations and enhance customer support. These capabilities are intended to provide immediate value with minimal configuration, enabling sales teams to leverage AI to improve efficiency and decision-making quickly. Salesforce frequently releases updates that can introduce new features, enhance existing ones, or modify how certain functionalities are accessed and utilized. As a result, what is considered OOTB will evolve.

For instance, a particular command or prompt that works seamlessly now might require slight adjustments in the future due to changes in the underlying algorithms or the introduction of new capabilities. This is a natural part of the platform's evolution, aimed at continuously improving the **user experience** (**UX**) and expanding the potential of AI-driven service.

You must maintain a flexible and proactive approach to navigate this evolving landscape. If/when encountering scenarios where the OOTB functionality described in this book does not perform as expected, consider the following steps:

- **Verify current capabilities**: Check Salesforce's official documentation and release notes for the latest updates on Einstein Copilot. This will help you stay informed about any new features or changes.

- **Experiment with prompts**: Experiment with different variations if a specific prompt or command does not yield the expected results. Slight modifications in phrasing or additional context can often lead to better outcomes.

- **Leverage community and support**: Engage with the Salesforce community and support channels to share experiences and learn from others. The collective knowledge and insights from other users can be invaluable in adapting to changes.

By embracing this mindset of continuous learning and experimentation, you can maximize the benefits of Einstein Copilot and stay ahead of the curve as Salesforce continues to innovate. The goal is to empower you with the tools and knowledge to effectively leverage AI in service operations, even as the technology evolves.

The following sections will explore specific use cases and demonstrate how to apply Einstein Copilot's OOTB features within Sales Cloud. Keep in mind the dynamic nature of the platform and approach each example with a willingness to adapt and experiment, fully harnessing the power of this transformative AI.

Leads – prioritizing leads

Einstein Copilot revolutionizes lead management by using AI to prioritize leads based on their conversion likelihood. By analyzing various factors such as past interactions, engagement levels, demographic information, and historical sales data, Einstein Copilot assigns scores to each lead, highlighting those with the highest potential. This intelligent prioritization enables sales teams to focus on the most promising prospects, ensuring no valuable lead slips through the cracks. As a result, sales representatives can allocate their time and resources more effectively, increasing the efficiency of their outreach efforts and significantly improving conversion rates.

Step-by-step process

1. Navigate to the **Leads List** view.
2. Click on the Einstein icon on the top right of the screen (if needed).
3. Enter *Please prioritize my leads for me* as the prompt to Einstein Copilot.
4. Click on the Einstein Copilot **Send** icon.

The following screenshot shows how to use Einstein Copilot to prioritize leads:

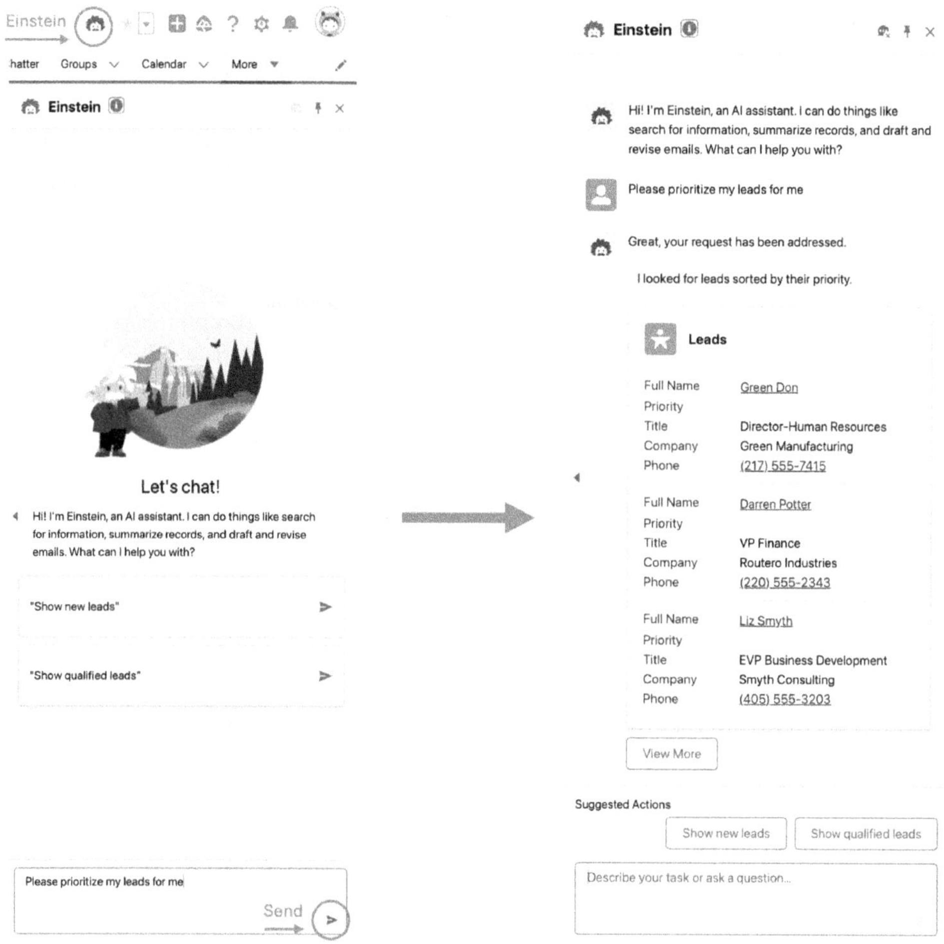

Figure 8.1 – Prioritizing leads

This screenshot illustrates how Einstein Copilot can be leveraged to quickly prioritize leads in Salesforce, showcasing both the simplicity of the query and the intelligent, actionable response.

Einstein Copilot does not produce the exact same response each time because it relies on complex algorithms that generate outputs based on various factors, including the specific input prompt, context, and underlying data models. These models are designed to be adaptive and flexible, ensuring that responses are relevant and tailored to the user's query and current data. The variability in responses also stems from the AI's capability to incorporate real-time data and learning from previous interactions, which means it continuously updates and refines its outputs. This inherent variability enhances the AI's ability to provide nuanced, contextually appropriate, and valuable insights, making each interaction more personalized and effective.

When a user prompts Einstein Copilot with *Please prioritize my leads for me*, they receive a dynamically generated list of leads ranked based on their likelihood to convert. This prioritized list is created using advanced AI algorithms that analyze various factors such as previous interactions, engagement metrics, demographic data, and historical sales trends. The output includes lead scores or ratings that indicate which leads are most promising and should be pursued first. This insightful prioritization allows sales representatives to efficiently target their efforts, focusing on high-potential leads, optimizing their workflow, and increasing the chances of successfully closing deals.

Business benefits

Einstein Copilot's lead prioritization functionality enhances lead management by using AI to score leads based on their conversion likelihood. This allows sales teams to focus on the most promising prospects, ensuring efficient resource allocation and improved conversion rates:

- **Increased efficiency**: Sales representatives can focus on high-potential leads, optimizing their outreach efforts

- **Improved conversion rates**: Prioritizing leads based on AI-driven insights leads to higher success in converting prospects

- **Better resource utilization**: Time and resources are allocated more effectively, driving greater revenue growth

Considerations

While the OOTB prioritization provided by Einstein Copilot is a powerful tool that leverages predefined algorithms to rank leads based on their conversion potential, this functionality can be further refined to meet specific business needs by creating a custom solution. Businesses can achieve an even more precise and effective prioritization by tailoring the prioritization criteria to include unique factors relevant to the organization, such as custom lead attributes, industry-specific indicators, or proprietary engagement metrics. This customization ensures that the AI-driven insights align closely with the organization's sales strategies and goals, ultimately enhancing lead-scoring accuracy and the efficiency of sales efforts. Leveraging Salesforce's customization capabilities, teams can build a prioritization model that reflects their unique business context, leading to better targeted outreach and higher conversion rates.

Leads – writing a follow-up email

Drafting follow-up emails is critical to maintaining momentum in the sales process and ensuring that potential leads remain engaged. With Einstein Copilot, this task becomes significantly easier and more efficient. By leveraging NLP and AI, Einstein Copilot can generate well-crafted, personalized follow-up emails based on the specific context of each lead interaction. When prompted, the AI reviews the lead's history and engagement data to produce an email draft that addresses their needs and encourages further communication. This capability saves sales representatives valuable time and ensures that follow-up communications are consistent, professional, and tailored to the individual lead, thereby increasing the chances of advancing the sales conversation.

Step-by-step process

1. Navigate to a **Lead** page.

2. Click on the Einstein icon on the top right of the screen (if needed).

3. Enter *Please draft a follow-up email for me* as the prompt to Einstein Copilot.

4. Click on the Einstein Copilot **Send** icon.

The following screenshot shows how to use Einstein Copilot to draft a follow-up email:

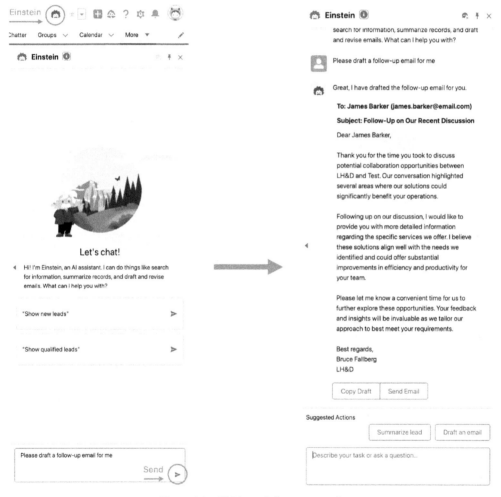

Figure 8.2 – Writing a follow-up email

This screenshot demonstrates how Einstein Copilot can effortlessly generate a personalized follow-up email to a lead in Salesforce, highlighting its ability to streamline communication with just a simple request.

Business benefits

Using Einstein Copilot to write follow-up emails offers numerous benefits, particularly in terms of time savings and maintaining consistency with leads. By automating the drafting process, sales representatives can quickly generate personalized and relevant follow-up emails, freeing up time better spent on high-value activities such as building relationships and closing deals. This automation ensures that follow-ups are sent promptly, reducing the risk of leads losing interest due to delayed responses. Additionally, Einstein Copilot ensures that the content of these emails is consistent, professional, and aligned with the company's messaging standards. This consistency helps to build trust and rapport with leads, reinforcing the company's reliability and attention to detail:

- **Time savings**: Automates email drafting, allowing sales representatives to focus on high-value activities

- **Enhanced engagement**: Ensures timely and personalized follow-ups, reducing the risk of leads losing interest

- **Consistency and professionalism**: Maintains a high standard of communication, building trust and rapport with leads

Considerations

Using "please" when prompting Einstein Copilot reflects a courteous and professional tone and aligns with best practices for interacting with AI tools. Including polite language such as "please" in prompts can help maintain a positive and respectful environment, which is important when collaborating with technology designed to enhance human productivity. While Einstein Copilot is an AI and does not require politeness, forming habits of respectful communication can improve interactions and set a standard for consistency and professionalism in all forms of digital correspondence. Moreover, using clear and polite prompts ensures that requests are articulated well, potentially leading to more accurate and effective responses from the AI, thereby optimizing the UX and efficiency.

Opportunities – prioritizing opportunities

Einstein Copilot's ability to prioritize opportunities with the highest potential is a game-changer for sales teams seeking to maximize their efficiency and success rates. By analyzing various data points, such as historical sales performance, current engagement levels, and predictive analytics, Einstein Copilot can rank opportunities based on their likelihood to close. This prioritization enables sales representatives to focus on the most promising deals, ensuring that their time and resources are invested where they are most likely to yield results. By concentrating on high-potential opportunities, sales teams can increase productivity, shorten sales cycles, and improve overall win rates. This strategic focus helps in better resource allocation and planning, ensuring that the team's efforts are aligned with the organization's revenue goals.

Step-by-step process

1. Navigate to the **Opportunity List** view.

2. Click on the Einstein icon on the top right of the screen (if needed).

3. Enter *Please prioritize my opportunities that are going to close in August* as the prompt to Einstein Copilot.

4. Click on the Einstein Copilot **Send** icon.

The following screenshot shows how to use Einstein Copilot to prioritize opportunities:

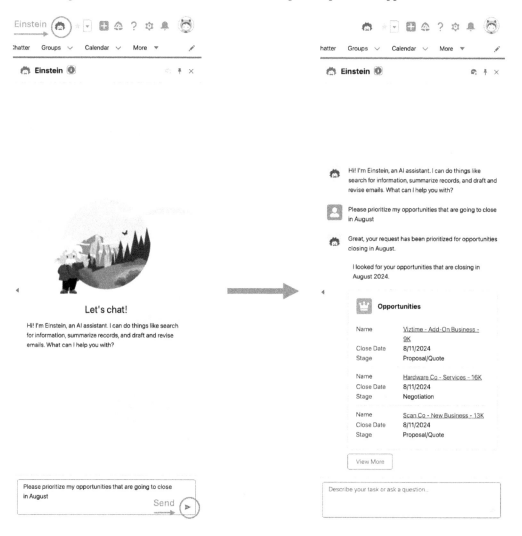

Figure 8.3 – Prioritizing opportunities

This screenshot showcases how Einstein Copilot can efficiently prioritize opportunities in Salesforce, providing a clear, data-driven response to help you focus on the most promising deals.

Business benefits

Einstein Copilot enhances sales outcomes by enabling teams to focus on high-value opportunities with the greatest potential for success. By leveraging AI and data analytics, it analyzes many factors, including past sales data, customer engagement, and market trends, to prioritize opportunities likely to close. This targeted approach ensures efficient allocation of time and resources, improving productivity, shortening sales cycles, and increasing closing rates:

- **Increased productivity**: Focusing on high-potential opportunities maximizes efforts
- **Shortened sales cycles**: Prioritizing the most promising deals accelerates the sales process
- **Improved win rates**: Focusing on top opportunities boosts overall success and aligns with revenue goals

Considerations

Ethical AI usage and data privacy are paramount in leveraging tools such as Einstein Copilot. Salesforce ensures that Einstein Copilot operates within strict ethical guidelines, prioritizing the protection and confidentiality of user data. By adhering to robust data protection regulations and implementing rigorous security measures, Salesforce builds and maintains customer trust. Responsible AI practices safeguard sensitive information and foster transparency and accountability in AI interactions. This commitment to ethical AI usage enhances customer confidence, ensuring that data is handled with the utmost care and respect, ultimately contributing to a more secure and trustworthy AI ecosystem.

Opportunities – writing an email to schedule a meeting

Einstein Copilot streamlines scheduling meetings by automating the creation of email invitations. When a sales representative needs to arrange a meeting, they can simply prompt Einstein Copilot to draft an email request. Using AI, Einstein Copilot considers the sales representative's availability, the context of the opportunity, and previous interactions with the contact to propose suitable meeting times. The generated email is professional, personalized, and includes all necessary details, reducing the back-and-forth typically involved in scheduling. This automation saves valuable time and ensures consistency and accuracy in communications, helping sales representatives secure meetings and maintain momentum in the sales process efficiently.

Step-by-step process

1. Navigate to an **Opportunity** page.
2. Click on the Einstein icon on the top right of the screen (if needed).

3. Enter *Please write an email to request a meeting with the contact for this opportunity. Propose two times that are open on my calendar.* as the prompt to Einstein Copilot.

    Please note: This prompt assumes the user's calendar in Salesforce reflects their schedule.

4. Click on the Einstein Copilot **Send** icon.

The following screenshot shows how to use Einstein Copilot to write an email to request a meeting:

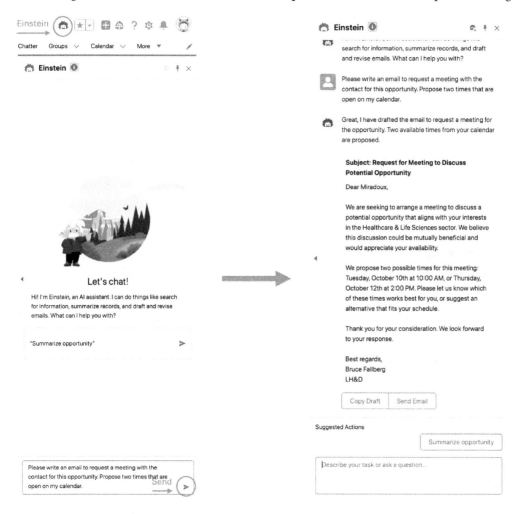

Figure 8.4 – Writing a meeting request email

This screenshot highlights how Einstein Copilot can quickly craft a meeting request email in Salesforce, demonstrating its ability to simplify and expedite scheduling tasks with a single prompt.

Business benefits

Einstein Copilot streamlines the meeting scheduling process by automating email invitations. By automating the creation of meeting invitations, Einstein Copilot eliminates the need for sales representatives to draft and coordinate schedules manually. It intelligently proposes suitable meeting times based on the representative's availability and the context of the opportunity, ensuring that suggestions are both relevant and convenient. This AI-generated email invitation is professional and personalized and proposes suitable meeting times, reducing typical back-and-forth scheduling:

- **Time savings**: Automates email drafting for meeting requests, freeing up valuable time for sales representatives

- **Consistency and accuracy**: Ensures professional and accurate communication, maintaining momentum in the sales process

- **Efficiency in scheduling**: Proposes suitable meeting times based on availability, simplifying the scheduling process

Considerations

Einstein Copilot leverages continuous learning and improvement to stay at the forefront of AI innovation. The AI models underpinning Einstein Copilot are regularly updated with new data and user feedback, allowing the system to adapt and evolve over time. This process ensures that the insights and recommendations remain relevant and accurate and reflect the latest trends and information. Ongoing training and refinement are crucial for maintaining the AI's effectiveness, enabling the system to learn from real-world interactions and continually improve its performance. By embracing a cycle of continuous learning, Einstein Copilot can provide ever-improving support to sales teams, confidently helping them navigate changing market conditions and customer behaviors.

Opportunities – summarizing the opportunity

Einstein Copilot's ability to summarize an opportunity is a powerful tool for sales representatives who need to quickly understand and communicate a sales deal's status and key details. Einstein Copilot generates concise and insightful summaries by analyzing all relevant data within Salesforce, including interactions, notes, and historical context. These summaries highlight critical aspects such as the opportunity's current stage, the main stakeholders involved, recent activities, and any significant changes or updates. This feature saves time by eliminating the need for manual data compilation and ensures that the information presented is comprehensive and easily digestible. Having a clear, succinct summary at their fingertips allows sales professionals to quickly brief colleagues, prepare for meetings, and make informed decisions, ultimately enhancing their ability to manage and close deals efficiently.

Step-by-step process

1. Navigate to an **Opportunity** page.

2. Click on the Einstein icon on the top right of the screen (if needed).

3. Enter *Please summarize this opportunity* as the prompt to Einstein Copilot.

4. Click on the Einstein Copilot **Send** icon.

The following screenshot shows how to use Einstein Copilot to summarize an opportunity:

Figure 8.5 – Summarizing an opportunity

This screenshot illustrates how Einstein Copilot can instantly summarize an opportunity in Salesforce, providing a concise overview to keep you informed and focused.

Business benefits

Using Einstein Copilot to summarize opportunities offers several significant advantages, particularly in providing a quick and comprehensive understanding of each deal, which enhances decision-making. By automatically generating detailed summaries, Einstein Copilot consolidates all pertinent information from various sources within Salesforce, including recent activities, stakeholder interactions, and key changes. This capability saves sales representatives valuable time, as they no longer need to sift through data to compile these details manually. The AI-driven summaries ensure information is accurate, up to date, and presented in a clear, digestible format. This quick access to critical insights allows sales teams to rapidly make informed, strategic decisions, whether preparing for client meetings, updating colleagues, or adjusting sales tactics. Analyzing all relevant data in Salesforce generates concise summaries highlighting critical aspects such as the current stage, main stakeholders, recent activities, and significant updates:

- **Time savings**: Eliminates the need for manual data compilation with quick, automated summaries

- **Enhanced communication**: Provides clear, comprehensive information for briefings and meetings

- **Informed decision-making**: Offers succinct insights, aiding in efficient deal management and closure

Considerations

AI integration and interoperability within the Salesforce ecosystem are key strengths of Einstein Copilot. Seamlessly integrating with other Salesforce products and third-party applications, Einstein Copilot provides a cohesive and comprehensive solution that enhances the capabilities of sales teams. This unified AI approach ensures data flows smoothly across various tools and platforms, enabling more effective collaboration and coordination between departments. By leveraging integrated AI, organizations can streamline their business processes, reduce data silos, and achieve a more holistic view of their operations. This interconnectedness allows for more informed decision-making, improved efficiency, and a greater ability to respond dynamically to customer needs and market changes.

Accounts – identifying at-risk accounts

Using Einstein Copilot to identify at-risk accounts provides sales teams with a proactive approach to account management, allowing them to address potential issues before they escalate. By analyzing various data points such as overdue invoices, declining engagement levels, and changes in purchasing patterns, Einstein Copilot flags accounts that may be in jeopardy. This early warning system enables sales representatives to take timely, corrective actions, such as reaching out to clients to understand their concerns, offering tailored solutions, or adjusting the service approach to better meet their needs. Identifying at-risk accounts helps retain valuable customers and improves overall customer satisfaction by demonstrating a proactive and attentive approach. This functionality ultimately contributes to stronger client relationships, reduced churn rates, and more stable revenue streams.

Step-by-step process

1. Navigate to the **Account List** view.

2. Click on the Einstein icon on the top right of the screen (if needed).

3. Enter *Please list the accounts with overdue invoices* as the prompt for Einstein Copilot.

4. Click on the Einstein Copilot **Send** icon.

The following screenshot shows how to use Einstein Copilot to list accounts with overdue invoices:

Figure 8.6 – Listing opportunities with overdue invoices

This screenshot demonstrates how Einstein Copilot can quickly identify and list opportunities with overdue invoices in Salesforce, enabling you to take prompt action on outstanding payments.

Business benefits

Einstein Copilot's ability to identify at-risk accounts offers sales teams a proactive approach to account management, enabling them to address potential issues before they escalate. Einstein Copilot can analyze overdue invoices, declining engagement, and changes in purchasing patterns to flag accounts that may require attention:

- **Proactive management**: Early identification of at-risk accounts allows timely corrective actions, preventing issues from escalating
- **Customer retention**: Tailored interventions help retain valuable customers and strengthen client relationships
- **Stable revenue**: Reduces churn and ensures more predictable revenue streams through improved customer satisfaction

Considerations

Several emerging technologies and innovations will shape the future of AI in sales. Advancements in NLP will enable more intuitive and conversational interactions with AI, making tools such as Einstein Copilot even more user-friendly and effective. Predictive analytics will continue to evolve, providing deeper insights into customer behavior and sales trends and allowing for more precise forecasting and strategic planning. Personalization will become increasingly sophisticated, with AI delivering highly tailored experiences and recommendations based on individual customer profiles and preferences. Staying informed about these trends will help sales professionals remain competitive, continuously refining their strategies and leveraging the latest AI capabilities to achieve better outcomes. Embracing these innovations will enhance sales performance and drive greater customer satisfaction and loyalty.

Custom prompt templates and actions

Producing custom prompt templates and actions for Einstein Copilot empowers sales teams to tailor AI interactions to their specific workflows and business needs. Organizations can fine-tune responses by creating customized prompts to align with their unique sales strategies and processes. For example, a sales team might develop a template to prompt Einstein Copilot to identify key decision-makers in a lead's organization or suggest the best follow-up timing based on historical engagement data. Custom actions can also be programmed to automate complex tasks or trigger specific workflows, further enhancing efficiency and productivity. This customization ensures that the AI supports general sales activities and addresses the nuanced requirements of different markets and customer segments. As a result, sales professionals can leverage more precise and contextually relevant insights and actions, driving better outcomes and maintaining a competitive edge.

Leads – suggesting next actions

Using Einstein Copilot to suggest the next actions for a lead significantly enhances the effectiveness of sales efforts by providing data-driven recommendations tailored to each unique situation. When a sales representative prompts Einstein Copilot for the next steps, the AI analyzes the lead's historical interactions, engagement patterns, and demographic information to offer personalized action items. These suggestions might include scheduling a follow-up call, sending a targeted email, or offering a specific product or service that matches the lead's needs and interests. By leveraging these intelligent recommendations, sales teams can ensure that their interactions are timely, relevant, and aligned with the lead's journey, ultimately increasing the likelihood of conversion. This proactive approach streamlines the sales process and helps build stronger relationships with potential customers by addressing their needs more effectively and promptly.

> **Please note**
> The following directions assume that you have read the chapters in this book on creating prompt templates and actions.

Step-by-step process

1. Navigate to the **Prompt Builder** page and click on **New Prompt Template**.

2. On **New Prompt Template**, enter these values:

    *   **Prompt Template Type**: **Record Summary**

    *   **Prompt Template Name**: **Lead Next Action**

    *   **API Name**: `Lead_Next_Action`

    *   **Template Description**: **Recommend next actions for a lead**

    *   **Object Type**: **Lead**

3. Click on **Next**.

The following screenshot shows how to start creating a prompt template to suggest lead next actions:

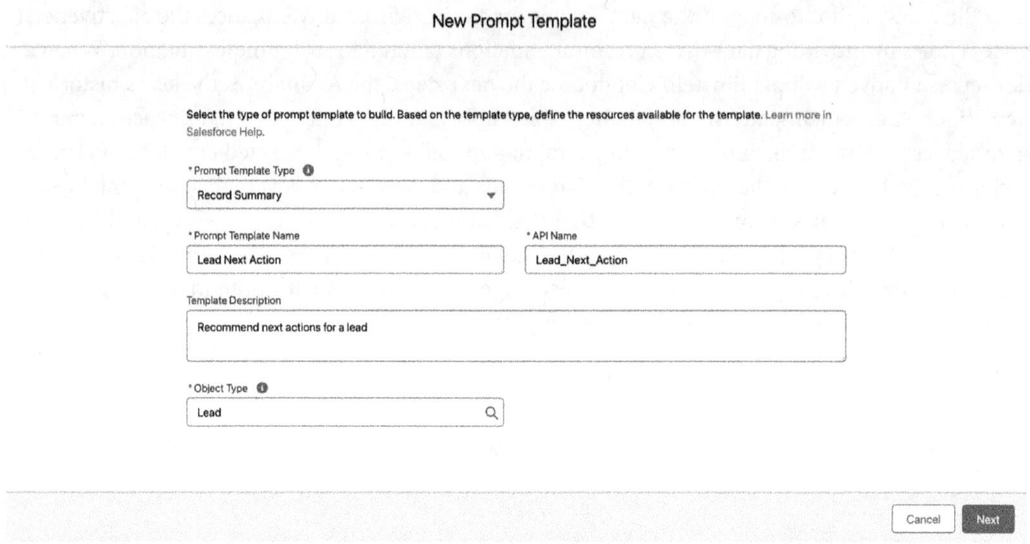

New Prompt Template

Select the type of prompt template to build. Based on the template type, define the resources available for the template. Learn more in Salesforce Help.

* Prompt Template Type ⓘ

Record Summary

* Prompt Template Name

Lead Next Action

* API Name

Lead_Next_Action

Template Description

Recommend next actions for a lead

* Object Type ⓘ

Lead

Cancel   Next

Figure 8.7 – Starting to create a Lead Next Action prompt template

This screenshot shows the creation of a **Lead Next Action** prompt template in Salesforce, illustrating how you can customize AI-driven workflows to suit your specific lead management needs.

1. On the **Prompt Template Workspace** page, set the directions to the following:

    -   **Prompt Template: Suggest Next Actions for a Lead**
    -   **Introduction: Begin with a brief overview of the lead, including the prospect name and current status.**
    -   **Lead Name:** `{!$Input:Lead.FirstName}` `{!$Input:Lead.LastName}`
    -   **Lead Status:** `{!$Input:Lead.Status}`
    -   **Lead Description:** `{!$Input:Lead.Description}`
    -   **Lead Company:** `{!$Input:Lead.Company}`
    -   **Lead Industry:** `{!$Input:Lead.Industry}`
    -   **Lead Annual Revenue:** `{!$Input:Lead.AnnualRevenue}`
    -   **Next Actions: Based on the lead details and current status, suggest the next actions to take. Include specific steps, responsible parties, and deadlines if applicable.**

2. Select a model type.

3. Save and activate the prompt template.

The following screenshot shows how to finish a prompt template to suggest lead next actions:

Figure 8.8 – Adding detail to a Lead Next Action prompt template

This screenshot highlights adding detail to a **Lead Next Action** prompt template in Salesforce, showcasing the ease of refining and enhancing your AI-driven workflows.

1. Navigate to the Einstein Copilot Actions page and click on **New Copilot Action**.

2. On **Connect an existing action**, enter these values:

    - **Reference Action Type: Prompt Template**

    - **Reference Action: Lead Next Action**

    - **Copilot Action Label: Lead Next Action**

    - **Copilot Action API Name:** Lead_Next_Action

3. Click on **Next**.

The following screenshot shows how to start creating an action to suggest lead next actions:

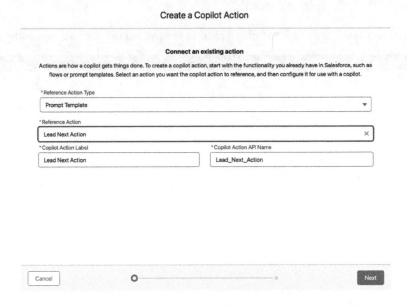

Figure 8.9 – Starting to create a Lead Next Action action

This screenshot illustrates the creation of a **Lead Next Action** action in Salesforce, demonstrating how you can seamlessly set up actionable steps for lead management with AI assistance.

1. On **Copilot Action Configuration**, enter these values:

    *   **Copilot Action Instructions: Recommend next actions to qualify a lead. Provide guidance on what to do next. Help convert a lead to an opportunity.**

    *   **Input**

        *   **Instructions: Get the Lead record ID from the current lead.**

        *   **Require input:** Checked

        *   **Collect data from user:** Unchecked

    *   **Output**

        *   **Instructions: Provide step by step directions on how to qualify the lead and then convert it to an opportunity.**

        *   **Filter from copilot action:** Unchecked

        *   **Show in conversation:** Checked

2. Click on **Finish** (or **Save**).

The following screenshot shows how to finish an action to suggest lead next actions:

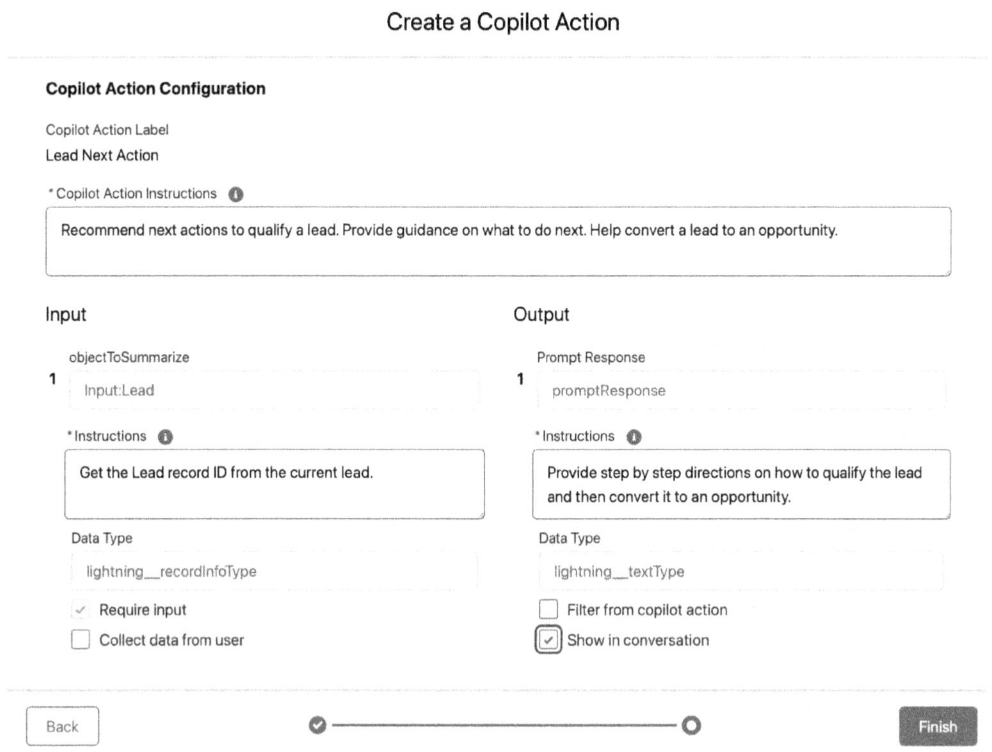

Create a Copilot Action

Copilot Action Configuration

Copilot Action Label
Lead Next Action

* Copilot Action Instructions ⓘ

Recommend next actions to qualify a lead. Provide guidance on what to do next. Help convert a lead to an opportunity.

Input   Output

objectToSummarize   Prompt Response

1   Input:Lead   1   promptResponse

* Instructions ⓘ   * Instructions ⓘ

Get the Lead record ID from the current lead.   Provide step by step directions on how to qualify the lead
                                                       and then convert it to an opportunity.

Data Type   Data Type

lightning__recordInfoType   lightning__textType

✓ Require input   ☐ Filter from copilot action
☐ Collect data from user   ☑ Show in conversation

Back   ⊘─────────────────○   Finish

Figure 8.10 – Adding detail to a Lead Next Action action

This screenshot showcases adding detail to a **Lead Next Action** action in Salesforce, emphasizing the ability to fine-tune tasks with AI precision.

1. Navigate to the Copilot Builder.

2. Deactivate the active copilot (do this at a time when you don't have active users).

3. Navigate to the Copilot Action library.

4. Add the action to the copilot.

5. Activate the copilot.

The following screenshot shows how to add a **Lead Next Action** action to a copilot:

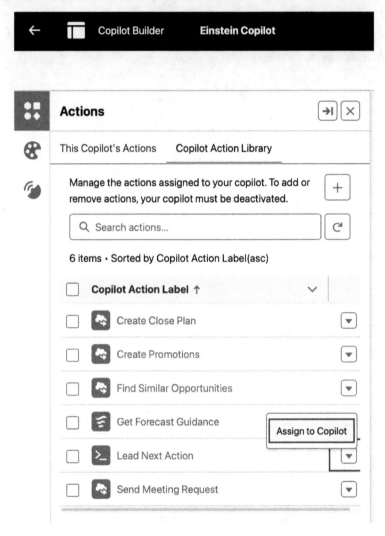

Figure 8.11 – Adding a Lead Next Action action to a copilot

This screenshot demonstrates adding a **Lead Next Action** action to a copilot in Salesforce, highlighting the ease of integrating custom actions into your AI workflows.

1. Navigate to a **Lead** page.

2. Click on the Einstein icon on the top right of the screen (if needed).

3. Enter *Please recommend next actions/steps to take for this lead* as the prompt to Einstein Copilot.

4. Click on the Einstein Copilot **Send** icon.

The following screenshot shows how to use Einstein Copilot to suggest lead next actions:

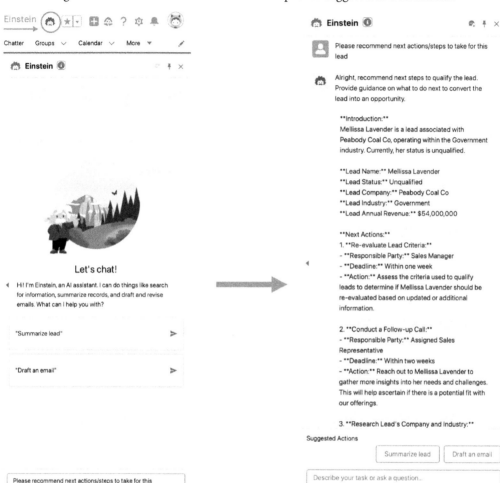

Figure 8.12 – Getting lead next actions

This screenshot illustrates retrieving "lead next actions" in Salesforce, showcasing its ability to provide quick, actionable insights for managing leads effectively.

Producing custom prompt templates and actions for Einstein Copilot empowers sales teams to tailor AI interactions to their specific workflows and business needs. Organizations can fine-tune the AI's responses by creating customized prompts to align with their unique sales strategies and processes. For example, a sales team might develop a template to prompt Einstein Copilot to identify key decision-makers in a lead's organization or suggest the best follow-up timing based on historical engagement data. Custom actions can also be programmed to automate complex tasks or trigger specific workflows, further enhancing efficiency and productivity. This customization ensures that the AI supports general sales activities and addresses the nuanced requirements of different markets and customer segments. As a result, sales professionals can leverage more precise and contextually relevant insights and actions, driving better outcomes and maintaining a competitive edge.

Business benefits

The ability to suggest next actions enhances sales effectiveness by providing data-driven, personalized recommendations tailored to each lead. By analyzing historical interactions, engagement patterns, and demographic information, the AI offers specific action items, such as scheduling calls or sending targeted emails, to align with the lead's journey:

- **Improved lead nurturing**: Data-driven suggestions ensure timely and relevant follow-ups, increasing conversion likelihood

- **Streamlined sales process**: Proactive recommendations simplify decision-making and enhance workflow efficiency

- **Customization and precision**: Tailored prompts and actions align AI responses with specific sales strategies, improving outcomes and maintaining a competitive edge

Opportunities – finding similar closed opportunities

Custom prompt templates and actions for Einstein Copilot can be designed to find similar closed opportunities, offering valuable tips and guidance on successfully closing current opportunities. By analyzing historical data, Einstein Copilot can identify past opportunities with characteristics similar to the current deal, such as industry, company size, product interest, and sales cycle. Once identified, the AI can provide insights into the strategies and actions that led to the successful closure of these past deals. This includes effective communication techniques, optimal follow-up timing, and key decision-makers involved. By leveraging these customized prompts, sales representatives gain actionable intelligence that can be directly applied to their ongoing efforts, increasing their chances of closing the deal. This tailored guidance enhances the sales strategy and reduces the learning curve for new sales team members, promoting a more consistent and effective sales process.

> **Please note**
> The following directions assume that you have read *Chapter 3, Using Prompt Builder*, and *Chapter 4, Working With Copilot Builder*.

Step-by-step process

1. Navigate to the **Prompt Builder** page and click on **New Prompt Template**.

2. On **New Prompt Template**, enter these values:

- **Prompt Template Type**: **Flex**

- **Prompt Template Name**: **Similar Opportunities**

- **API Name**: `Similar_Opportunities`

- **Template Description**: **Find closed opportunities similar to the current opportunity to inform what the user can do to close the current opportunity**

- **Define Sources**

  - **Name: Opportunities**

  - **API Name: Opportunities**

  - **Source Type: Object**

  - **Object: Opportunity**

3. Click on **Next**.

The following screenshot shows how to start creating a prompt template to find similar opportunities:

New Prompt Template

Select the type of prompt template to build. Based on the template type, define the resources available for the template. Learn more in Salesforce Help.

* Prompt Template Type

Flex

* Prompt Template Name

Similar Opportunities

* API Name

Similar_Opportunities

Template Description

Find cloed opportunities similar to the current opportunity to inform what the user can do to close the current opportunity

Define Sources

Define up to 5 sources for your flex template. Assign a unique label, API name, source type, and object, as applicable. Keep in mind that you can't associate an object with String source types.

1. * Name

Opportunities

* API Name

Opportunities

* Source Type

Object

* Object

Opportunity

Add Resources

Cancel   Next

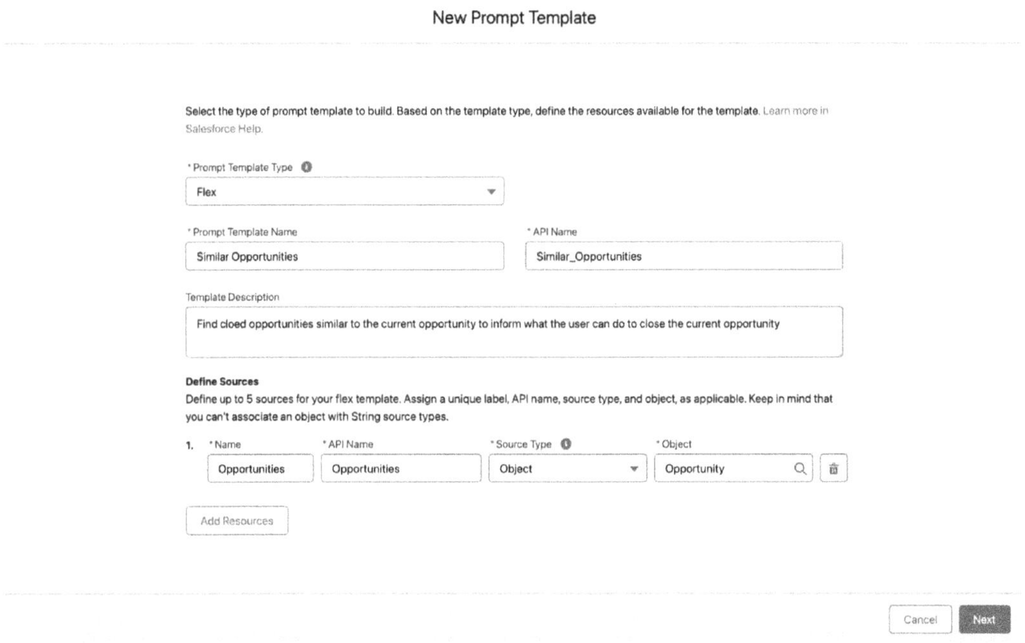

Figure 8.13 – Starting to create a Similar Opportunities prompt template

This screenshot shows initiating the creation of a **Similar Opportunities** prompt template in Salesforce, demonstrating how you can customize AI prompts to enhance opportunity management.

1. On **Prompt Template Workspace**, set the directions to the following:

    -   **Prompt Template: Find closed opportunities similar to the current opportunity to help the user close the current opportunity**

    -   **Introduction: Begin with an overview of the current opportunity**

    -   **Opportunity Name**: {!$Input:Opportunities.Name}

    -   **Opportunity Description**: {!$Input:Opportunities.Description}

    -   **Opportunity Account**: {!$Input:Opportunities.Account.Name}

    -   **Opportunity Amount**: {!$Input:Opportunities.Amount}

    -   **Feedback: Based on the similar opportunities recommend next steps / actions for the user to take.**

2. Select a model type.

3. Save and activate the prompt template.

The following screenshot shows how to finish a prompt template to find similar opportunities:

Figure 8.14 – Adding detail to a Similar Opportunities prompt template

This screenshot highlights adding details to a **Similar Opportunities** prompt template in Salesforce, allowing for more tailored and precise AI-driven insights.

1. Navigate to the **Einstein Copilot Actions** page and click on **New Copilot Action**.

2. On **Connect an existing action**, enter these values:

    - **Reference Action Type: Prompt Template**

    - **Reference Action: Similar Opportunities**

    - **Copilot Action Label: Similar Opportunities**

    - **Copilot Action API Name:** `Similar_Opportunities`

3. Click on **Next**.

The following screenshot shows how to start creating an action to find similar opportunities:

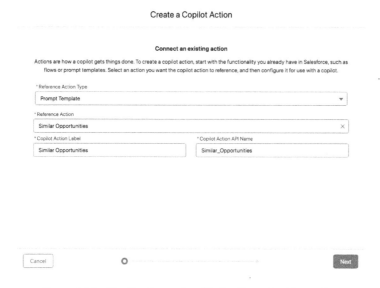

Figure 8.15 – Starting to create a Similar Opportunities action

This screenshot illustrates initiating the creation of a **Similar Opportunities** action in Salesforce, showcasing the ease of setting up customized actions for opportunity management.

1. On **Copilot Action Configuration**, enter these values:

    - **Copilot Action Instructions: Find closed opportunities similar to the current opportunity to inform what the user can do to close the current opportunity**

    - **Input**

      - **Instructions: Get the record ID from the current opportunity**

      - **Require input**: Checked

      - **Collect data from user**: Unchecked

- **Output**

    - **Instructions: Provide information about the similar opportunities and how they were closed can help close the current opportunity**

    - **Filter from copilot action:** Unchecked

    - **Show in conversation:** Checked

2. Click on **Finish** (or **Save**).

The following screenshot shows how to finish an action to find similar opportunities:

Create a Copilot Action

Copilot Action Configuration

Copilot Action Label
Similar Opportunities

* Copilot Action Instructions ℹ️

Find closed opportunities similar to the current opportunity to inform what the user can do to close the current opportunity

Input	Output
Opportunities	Prompt Response
1 Input:Opportunities	1 promptResponse
* Instructions ℹ️	* Instructions ℹ️
Get the record ID from the current opportunity	Provide information about the similar opportunities and how they were closed can help close the current opportunity
Data Type	Data Type
lightning__recordInfoType	lightning__textType
☑ Require input	☐ Filter from copilot action
☐ Collect data from user	☑ Show in conversation

Back ✓————————————————————○ Finish

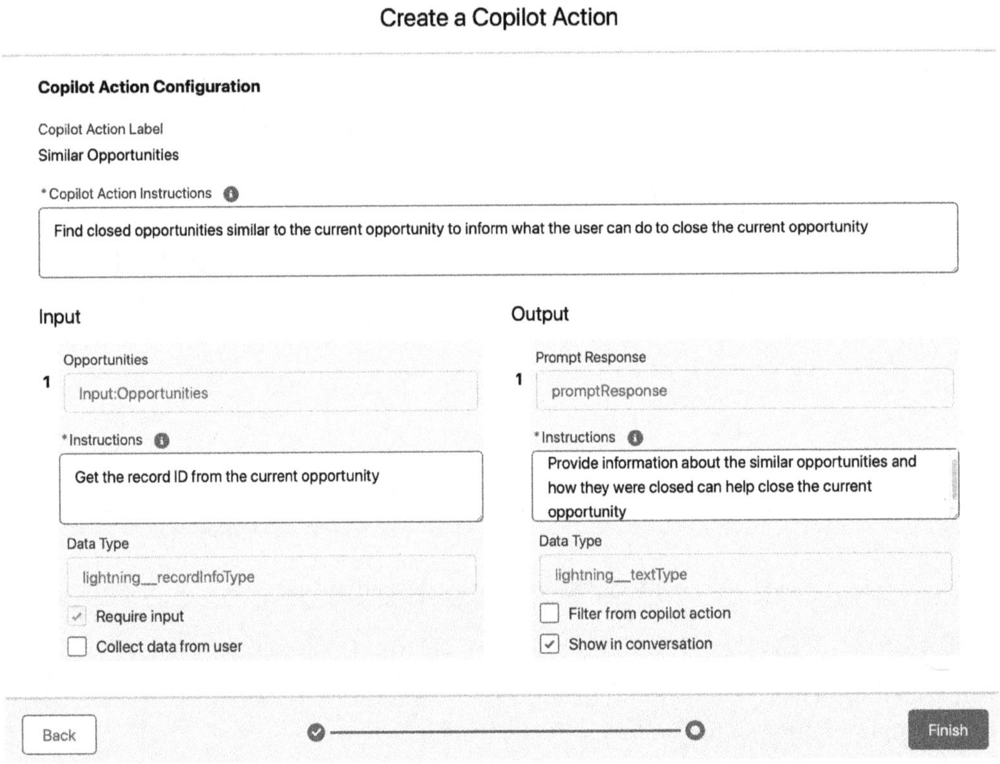

Figure 8.16 – Adding details to the Similar Opportunities action

This screenshot demonstrates adding details to a **Similar Opportunities** action in Salesforce, emphasizing the ability to refine and customize actions for more effective opportunity management.

1. Navigate to the **Copilot Builder**.

2. Deactivate the active copilot (do this at a time when you don't have active users)

3. Navigate to the **Copilot Action Library**.

4.   Add the action to the copilot.

5.   Activate the copilot.

The following screenshot shows how to add a **Find Similar Opportunities** action to a copilot:

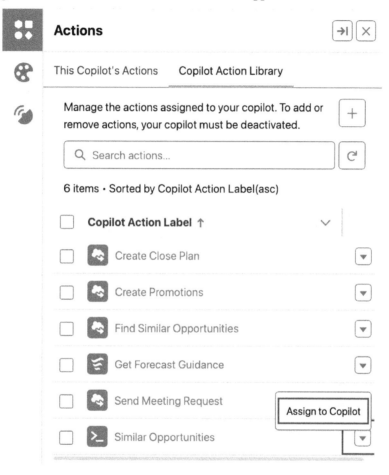

Figure 8.17 – Adding a Find Similar Opportunities action to a copilot

This screenshot shows how to add a **Find Similar Opportunities** action to a copilot in Salesforce, highlighting the seamless integration of customized actions into your AI-driven workflows.

1.   Navigate to an **Opportunity** page.

2.   Click on the Einstein icon on the top right of the screen (if needed).

3.   Enter *Please list three similar opportunities* as the prompt to Einstein Copilot.

4.   Click on the Einstein Copilot **Send** icon.

The following screenshot shows how to use Einstein Copilot to find similar opportunities:

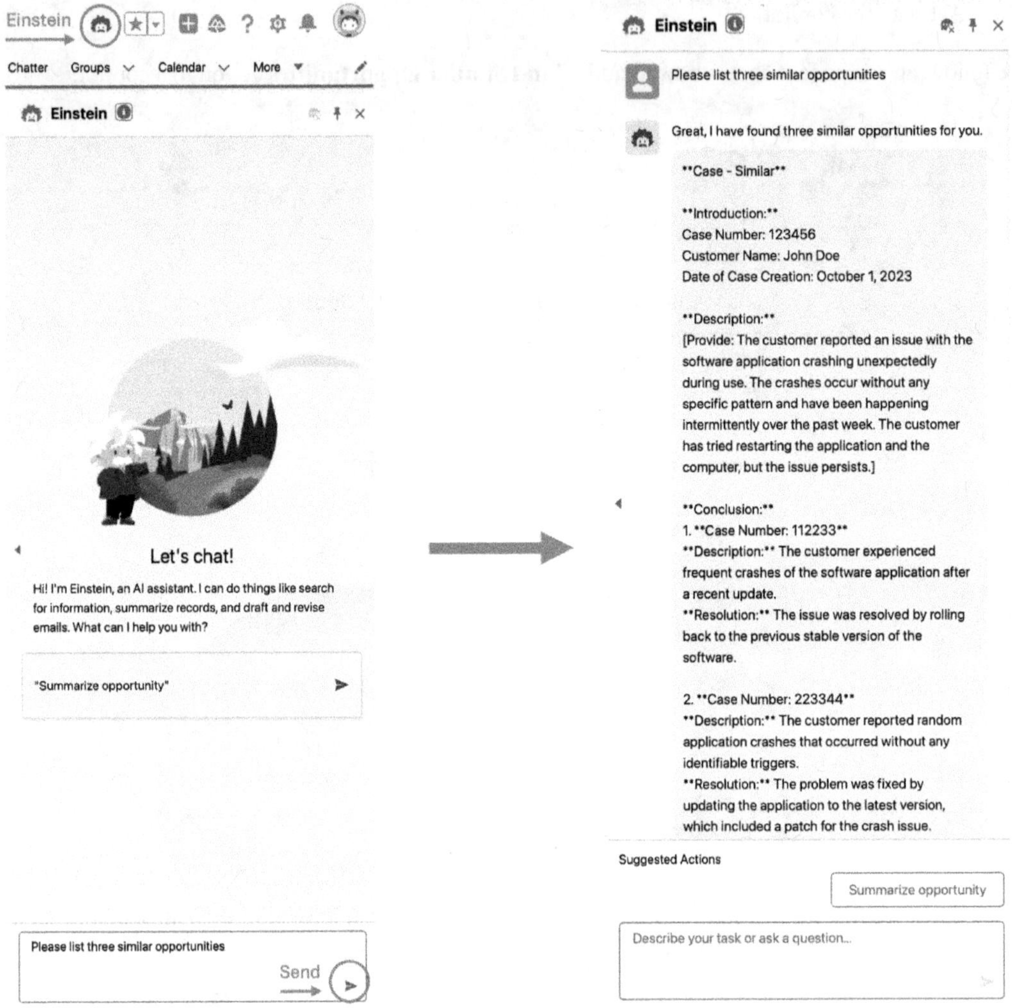

Figure 8.18 – Getting similar opportunities

This screenshot illustrates how to quickly retrieve similar opportunities in Salesforce, showcasing its ability to provide relevant, context-aware insights with a simple query.

Using Einstein Copilot to find similar opportunities offers numerous advantages, particularly in providing actionable insights and strategic guidance to close current deals more effectively. By leveraging AI to identify past opportunities with similar characteristics, sales teams can uncover patterns and strategies that have proven successful in comparable situations. This enables representatives to apply best practices, optimize their approach, and avoid pitfalls previously encountered. Access to this data-driven intelligence helps in tailoring communications, anticipating customer needs, and making informed decisions, ultimately leading to higher conversion rates. Additionally, this capability reduces the time and effort spent on strategizing, allowing sales professionals to focus more on building relationships and closing deals. By drawing on the collective knowledge of past successes, Einstein Copilot empowers sales teams to enhance their performance and achieve better outcomes.

Business benefits

Einstein Copilot's ability to find similar closed opportunities provides sales teams with actionable insights and strategies to close current deals more effectively. By analyzing historical data, the AI identifies past opportunities with similar characteristics, offering guidance on successful strategies, communication techniques, and key decision-makers:

- **Actionable insights**: Provides data-driven strategies based on similar successful deals, increasing the likelihood of closing current opportunities

- **Optimized sales approach**: Helps sales representatives apply best practices and avoid past pitfalls, enhancing their sales tactics

- **Efficiency and consistency**: Reduces time spent on strategizing, allowing for a more consistent and effective sales process benefiting new and experienced team members

Summary

In this chapter, you learned how integrating Salesforce Sales Cloud with Einstein Copilot enhances sales by combining essential CRM tools with AI-driven insights and automation. Sales Cloud provides the foundational capabilities for managing customer relationships, tracking opportunities, and forecasting sales, while Einstein Copilot adds value by prioritizing leads, automating routine tasks, and offering data-driven insights. This synergy allows sales teams to work more efficiently and strategically, focusing on high-potential opportunities and maintaining consistency in communications. The chapter also included practical use cases, showing how to apply these tools to maximize efficiency, improve decision-making, and drive overall sales success.

In the next chapter, you will learn how to harness the power of Einstein Copilot within Salesforce's Service Cloud to enhance customer service operations. The chapter will explore how Einstein Copilot's AI-driven capabilities, such as automating routine tasks, prioritizing cases based on urgency, and providing real-time insights, can significantly improve the efficiency and effectiveness of service agents. You will dive into specific use cases, including case prioritization, summarization, and action recommendations, gaining a comprehensive understanding of how to leverage Einstein Copilot to optimize service delivery, ultimately leading to higher customer satisfaction and operational efficiency.

9
Integrating Einstein Copilot and Service Cloud

Service Cloud, a key component of Salesforce's **customer relationship management** (**CRM**) platform, is designed to help businesses deliver superior customer service. It streamlines case management, facilitates seamless customer interactions, and promptly resolves issues. However, the increasing volume and complexity of customer queries pose a challenge even for well-equipped service teams. Enter Einstein Copilot, Salesforce's cutting-edge AI assistant, transforming service agents' interaction with Service Cloud by providing intelligent, context-aware support.

Einstein Copilot enhances Service Cloud by automating routine tasks, offering real-time insights, and enabling proactive customer service. It uses **natural language processing** (**NLP**) to understand and respond to queries conversationally, making it easier for service agents to navigate the platform and manage cases efficiently. This integration improves operational efficiency and empowers agents to focus on more complex and value-added tasks, ultimately elevating the customer experience.

One of the standout features of Einstein Copilot is its ability to prioritize cases based on urgency and impact, ensuring that high-priority issues are addressed first. This prioritization is crucial in maintaining customer satisfaction, ensuring the most critical problems are resolved swiftly. Additionally, Einstein Copilot can summarize case details, recommend next steps, and even provide insights from similar case resolutions, all of which contribute to a more informed and effective service response.

Einstein Copilot's ability to integrate seamlessly with Service Cloud means leveraging the rich data within Salesforce to provide personalized and relevant assistance. Whether it's listing cases associated with a specific account or suggesting next actions based on historical data, Einstein Copilot acts as a valuable ally to service agents, enhancing their capabilities and productivity.

In this chapter, we will explore how to harness the power of Einstein Copilot within Service Cloud. We will look at specific use cases, such as prioritizing cases, summarizing case details, and recommending next actions. By the end of this chapter, you will clearly understand how to utilize Einstein Copilot to optimize your service operations, leading to improved customer satisfaction and operational efficiency.

Exploring out-of-the-box Einstein Copilot

As we dive into the capabilities of Einstein Copilot within Service Cloud, it is important to understand the dynamic nature of this AI. Salesforce is continuously evolving, and so is Einstein Copilot. What is available **out of the box** (**OOTB**) today might be different tomorrow due to ongoing enhancements and updates. This section aims to provide a snapshot of Einstein Copilot's capabilities at the time of writing while also preparing the reader for potential changes and encouraging a mindset of experimentation and adaptability.

At the time of writing, Einstein Copilot has features designed to streamline service operations and enhance customer support. These OOTB functionalities include case prioritization and case summarization. These capabilities are intended to provide immediate value with minimal configuration, enabling service teams to leverage AI to improve efficiency and decision-making quickly.

Given the rapid pace of innovation at Salesforce, it's essential to recognize that the features in this OOTB section are based on the capabilities available at the time of writing. Salesforce frequently releases updates that can introduce new features, enhance existing ones, or modify how certain functionalities are accessed and utilized. As a result, what is considered OOTB today will evolve.

For instance, a particular command or prompt that works seamlessly now might require slight adjustments in the future due to changes in the underlying algorithms or the introduction of new capabilities. This is a natural part of the platform's evolution, aimed at continuously improving the **user experience** (**UX**) and expanding the potential of AI-driven service.

You must maintain a flexible and proactive approach to navigate this evolving landscape. If/when encountering scenarios where the OOTB functionality described in this book does not perform as expected, consider the following steps:

- **Verify current capabilities**: Check Salesforce's official documentation and release notes for the latest updates on Einstein Copilot. This will help you stay informed about any new features or changes.

- **Experiment with prompts**: Experiment with different variations if a specific prompt or command does not yield the expected results. Slight modifications in phrasing or additional context can often lead to better outcomes.

- **Leverage community and support**: Engage with the Salesforce community and support channels to share experiences and learn from others. The collective knowledge and insights from other users can be invaluable in adapting to changes.

By embracing this mindset of continuous learning and experimentation, you can maximize the benefits of Einstein Copilot and stay ahead of the curve as Salesforce continues to innovate. The goal is to empower you with the tools and knowledge to effectively leverage AI in service operations, even as the technology evolves.

The following sections will explore specific use cases and demonstrate how to apply Einstein Copilot's OOTB features within Service Cloud. Keep in mind the dynamic nature of the platform and approach each example with a willingness to adapt and experiment, fully harnessing the power of this transformative AI.

Case – high-priority cases

One of the standout features of Einstein Copilot in Service Cloud is its ability to swiftly identify high-priority cases, allowing service teams to focus on the most critical issues first. By leveraging advanced AI algorithms and data analysis, Einstein Copilot can scan through case records, assess their urgency based on predefined criteria such as severity, impact, and customer value, and generate a prioritized list. This ensures service agents can allocate their time and resources more effectively, promptly addressing the most pressing concerns. This capability enhances operational efficiency and significantly improves customer satisfaction by promptly resolving urgent issues.

Step-by-step process

1. Navigate to the **Case List** View.
2. Click on the **Einstein** icon on the top right of the screen (if needed).
3. Enter *Please list the high-priority cases* as the prompt to Einstein Copilot.
4. Click on the Einstein Copilot **Send** icon.

The following screenshot shows how to use Einstein Copilot to list high-priority cases:

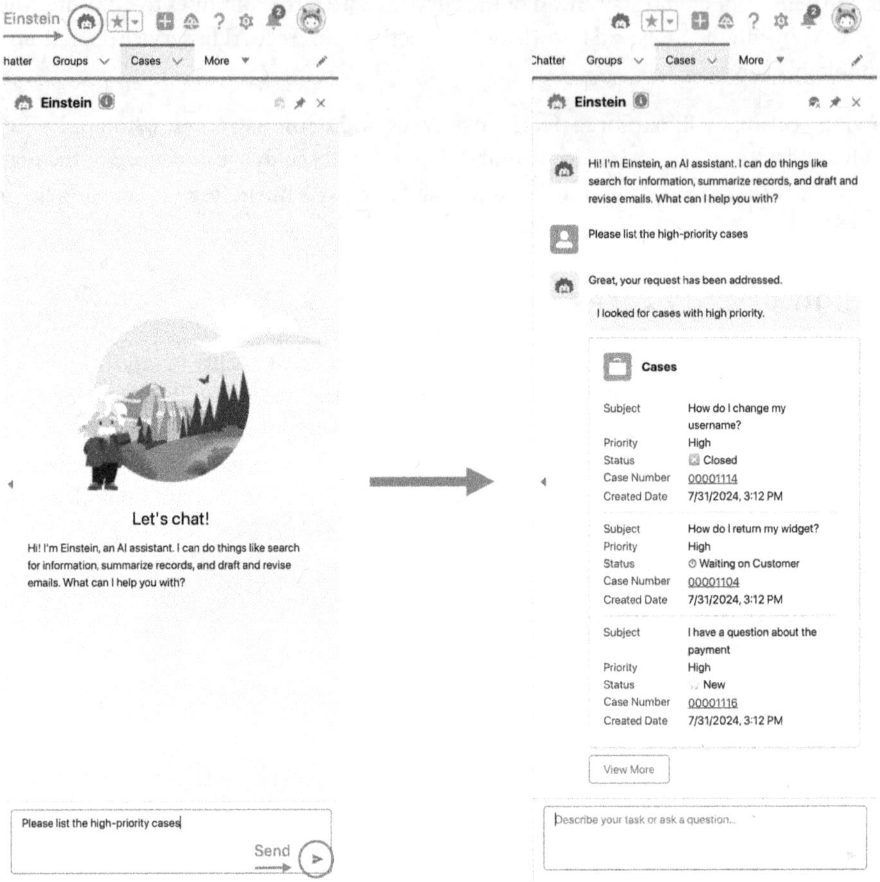

Figure 9.1 – Listing high-priority cases

This screenshot illustrates how Einstein Copilot can quickly list high-priority cases in Salesforce, enabling you to focus on the most urgent customer issues.

Business benefits

Einstein Copilot's ability to identify and prioritize high-priority cases in Service Cloud provides significant business value by enabling service teams to focus on the most critical issues first. By automating the prioritization process, Einstein Copilot enhances operational efficiency, reduces the risk of overlooking urgent cases, and improves customer satisfaction:

- **Improved efficiency**: Automatically prioritizes critical cases, allowing service agents to address urgent issues promptly

- **Enhanced customer satisfaction**: Faster response times lead to quicker resolution of high-impact cases, boosting customer satisfaction

- **Better resource management**: Focused attention on the most pressing cases optimizes the use of time and resources, improving overall service effectiveness

Considerations

Generative AI (**GenAI**), such as Einstein Copilot, is revolutionizing the customer service landscape by delivering faster, more accurate, and highly personalized support. By leveraging advanced **machine learning** (**ML**) algorithms and NLP, Einstein Copilot can understand and respond to customer queries with unprecedented speed and precision. This real-time, AI-driven assistance not only streamlines the resolution of issues but also ensures that responses are tailored to each customer's needs and contexts. The result is a significantly enhanced customer experience characterized by prompt and relevant support, which fosters greater satisfaction and loyalty. As businesses continue to integrate AI into their customer service operations, they can expect to see a marked improvement in customer engagement and retention, ultimately driving long-term success.

Case – writing an email

Einstein Copilot can significantly enhance the process of crafting emails to customers for additional information about their issues. This AI-powered tool leverages NLP to generate clear, concise, and professional email drafts that service agents can use to gather more details. By understanding the context of a case and the specifics of the customer's initial communication, Einstein Copilot can formulate emails tailored to elicit the necessary information, ensuring that the inquiry is relevant and respectful. This saves service agents time and helps maintain a consistent and high-quality communication standard, leading to quicker resolution of customer issues and an improved overall service experience.

Step-by-step process

1. Navigate to a **Case** page.
2. Click on the **Einstein** icon on the top right of the screen (if needed).
3. Enter *Please write an email asking the case contact for more information about the case* as the prompt to Einstein Copilot.
4. Click on the Einstein Copilot **Send** icon.

The following screenshot shows how to use Einstein Copilot to write an email to the case contact:

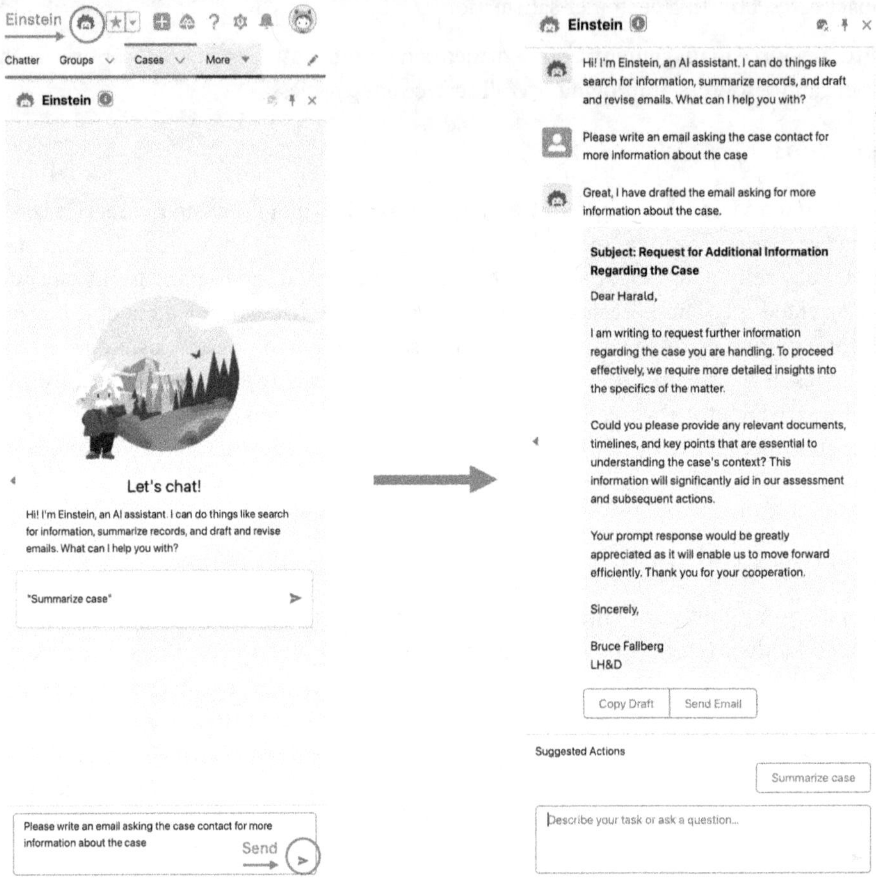

Figure 9.2 – Writing an email

This screenshot demonstrates how Einstein Copilot can draft an email about a case in Salesforce, simplifying communication and ensuring key details are accurately conveyed.

Business benefits

Einstein Copilot significantly enhances the process of email communication within Service Cloud by automating the creation of personalized, professional emails tailored to various customer service scenarios. Whether the service agent needs to request additional information, provide updates on a case, offer solutions, or follow up on a previous interaction, Einstein Copilot leverages AI to generate clear, contextually relevant email drafts. By understanding the specifics of each case, including the customer's history and the nature of the issue, the AI ensures that emails are not only accurate but also resonate with the customer's situation.

This automation saves service agents considerable time, allowing them to focus on resolving more complex issues rather than spending time crafting emails. Moreover, Einstein Copilot maintains a consistent tone, language, and professionalism across all communications, which is crucial for building and maintaining customer trust. By ensuring that all emails are relevant, respectful, and timely, Einstein Copilot helps to improve customer satisfaction, accelerate case resolution, and strengthen the overall customer service experience:

- **Increased efficiency**: Automates drafting various types of emails, freeing up service agents to handle more complex tasks and reducing overall response times

- **Personalized and relevant communication**: Generates emails tailored to the specific context of each customer interaction, whether it's requesting information, providing updates, offering solutions, or following up, thereby enhancing customer satisfaction

- **Consistency and professionalism**: Ensures that all customer communications maintain a high standard of tone and professionalism, reinforcing the brand's reliability and fostering stronger customer relationships

Considerations

AI tools such as Einstein Copilot can significantly boost service agent productivity by automating routine tasks, providing intelligent recommendations, and allowing agents to focus on more complex and value-added activities. By handling repetitive tasks such as case prioritization, data entry, and initial customer queries, AI reduces the workload on service agents, enabling them to concentrate on solving more intricate issues that require human judgment and creativity. Additionally, AI-driven insights and suggestions enhance decision-making processes, helping agents resolve cases more efficiently and effectively. This leads to faster resolution times and fosters a more engaged and satisfied workforce, as agents can dedicate their skills to more meaningful and impactful work, ultimately improving overall service quality and operational efficiency.

Case – summarizing

Einstein Copilot's ability to summarize cases is a powerful feature that streamlines the understanding of complex customer issues. By leveraging NLP and ML, Einstein Copilot can extract key details from lengthy cases to generate concise and informative summaries. This functionality lets service agents quickly grasp a case's essential elements without manually sifting through records. As a result, agents can make more informed decisions and provide faster, more accurate responses to customers. The ability to quickly access a comprehensive case summary enhances productivity and ensures that no critical information is overlooked, leading to more effective and efficient issue resolution.

Step-by-step process

1. Navigate to a **Case** page.

2. Click on the **Einstein** icon on the top right of the screen (if needed).

3. Enter *Please summarize this case* as the prompt to Einstein Copilot.

4. Click on the Einstein Copilot **Send** icon.

The following screenshot shows how to use Einstein Copilot to summarize a case:

Figure 9.3 – Summarizing a case

This screenshot highlights how Einstein Copilot can quickly summarize a case in Salesforce, providing a concise overview to help you stay informed and focused on resolving customer issues.

Business benefits

Einstein Copilot's case summarization feature is a powerful tool that streamlines the process of understanding complex customer issues. By automatically generating concise summaries from detailed case histories and interactions, Einstein Copilot saves service agents valuable time, allowing them to quickly understand a case's context and key points without wading through records. This capability ensures that critical information is readily accessible, reducing the risk of oversight and enabling agents to respond more accurately and promptly to customer inquiries. Moreover, the consistency in the summaries provided by Einstein Copilot helps maintain a high communication standard, ensuring that all relevant details are captured uniformly. Ultimately, this leads to quicker resolution times, improved decision-making, and a more streamlined customer service process, enhancing overall customer satisfaction:

- **Time efficiency**: Automatically generates concise summaries, saving service agents from manually reviewing lengthy case histories

- **Improved accuracy**: Ensures critical information is readily accessible, reducing the risk of oversight and enabling more accurate responses

- **Enhanced productivity**: Facilitates quicker decision-making and issue resolution, leading to a more efficient and effective customer service process and improving overall customer satisfaction

Considerations

AI is pivotal in leveraging vast amounts of data to provide actionable insights and predictive analytics, transforming how businesses make decisions. AI tools such as Einstein Copilot can identify patterns and trends that might not be immediately apparent to human agents by analyzing historical data, customer interactions, and case resolutions. These insights empower businesses to make informed, data-driven decisions, optimizing their operations and strategies. Furthermore, predictive analytics enable companies to anticipate customer needs and issues before they arise, allowing for proactive measures that enhance customer satisfaction and loyalty. This strategic use of data streamlines service operations and drives continuous improvement and innovation within the organization, positioning businesses to stay ahead in a competitive market.

Case – account view

Einstein Copilot can significantly enhance the management and communication of case issues associated with a specific account. By leveraging its advanced AI capabilities, Einstein Copilot can review the cases linked to an account, identify and analyze recurring themes or issues, and generate a summary of notable cases. This summary can then be used to craft a detailed and coherent email to the client, ensuring they are fully informed about specific challenges and plans for remediation. This streamlined approach saves service agents time and provides the client with consistent, accurate, and actionable information, facilitating better decision-making and more effective problem-solving. By integrating Einstein Copilot into this workflow, organizations can improve client communication and continuously improve customer satisfaction.

Step-by-step process

1. Navigate to an **Account** page.

2. Click on the **Einstein** icon on the top right of the screen (if needed).

3. Enter *Please write an email about the notable cases against this account* as the prompt to Einstein Copilot.

4. Click on the Einstein Copilot **Send** icon.

The following screenshot shows how to use Einstein Copilot to write an email about notable cases for an account:

Figure 9.4 – Writing an email about notable cases

This screenshot showcases how Einstein Copilot can draft an email summarizing notable cases for an account in Salesforce, streamlining communication and ensuring key information is effectively conveyed.

Business benefits

Einstein Copilot's Account View feature enhances the management and communication of case issues associated with a specific account. By analyzing linked cases, it identifies recurring themes and generates a summary, which can be used to craft detailed and coherent emails to clients. This process saves service agents time and ensures clients receive consistent, accurate, and actionable information, improving decision-making and problem-solving:

- **Time savings**: Automates the generation of detailed case summaries, reducing the time and effort required by service agents

- **Improved communication**: Ensures consistent, clear, and professional client communication, minimizing the risk of human error

- **Enhanced customer satisfaction**: Facilitates better client collaboration and quicker resolution of issues, leading to an improved overall customer experience

Considerations

The future of GenAI in customer service is brimming with exciting possibilities and advancements. As AI technologies evolve, we can expect even more sophisticated capabilities that enhance customer interactions and service efficiency. Emerging trends include the integration of AI with omnichannel platforms, enabling seamless and consistent customer experiences across various communication channels. Additionally, NLP and ML advancements will lead to more intuitive and human-like interactions, where AI can understand and respond to customer emotions and nuances more effectively.

Another promising development is the incorporation of AI-driven personalization, where customer service can be tailored to individual preferences and past behaviors in real time. This level of customization will not only improve customer satisfaction but also foster deeper customer loyalty. Moreover, the use of AI for predictive maintenance and proactive support is set to become more prevalent, allowing businesses to address issues before they escalate, thus minimizing downtime and enhancing customer trust.

As the landscape of AI technologies continues to shift, businesses must stay informed about these advancements and continuously explore new AI applications. By doing so, they can maintain a competitive edge and ensure their customer service operations are at the forefront of innovation. Encouraging a continuous learning and adaptation culture will be key to leveraging GenAI's full potential, driving operational excellence and exceptional customer experiences.

The OOTB functionality of Einstein Copilot for managing cases in Salesforce Service Cloud offers powerful tools to streamline customer service processes, providing intelligent insights and automating routine tasks. These capabilities are crucial for enhancing productivity and ensuring your service team can focus on resolving customer issues rather than administrative work. However, while the standard features of Einstein Copilot are impressive, the true potential of this tool lies in its customization capabilities. By creating custom prompt templates and defining specific actions tailored to your unique business needs, you can extend the power of Einstein Copilot even further, making it a more personalized and effective tool for your organization. Let's now transition into how you can unlock these advanced features, taking your Salesforce implementation to the next level.

Custom prompt templates and actions

Einstein Copilot's ability to create custom prompt templates and actions tailored to an organization's specific needs is a game-changer in enhancing operational efficiency and service delivery. By developing bespoke prompt templates, businesses can ensure that the AI-driven responses perfectly align with their unique processes, terminology, and customer engagement strategies. This customization allows for more seamless integration of Einstein Copilot into existing workflows, making it easier for service agents to adopt and utilize the tool effectively. Custom prompt templates can be designed to address common scenarios specific to the business, thereby improving the accuracy and relevance of the AI's responses and recommendations.

Furthermore, custom actions enable organizations to automate routine and repetitive tasks unique to their operations, freeing up valuable time for service agents to focus on more complex and high-value activities. For instance, a company can create specific actions to handle frequent customer inquiries, escalate issues based on predefined criteria, or generate detailed reports tailored to different departments. This level of customization enhances productivity and ensures that the AI's output is highly relevant and actionable, leading to quicker issue resolution and improved customer satisfaction.

Organizations can drive continuous improvement and innovation by leveraging Einstein Copilot's capability to develop custom prompt templates and actions. As the business environment and customer expectations evolve, these customizations can be refined to meet new challenges and opportunities. This adaptability ensures that AI remains a valuable asset over time and can support the organization's growth and transformation. Ultimately, the strategic use of custom prompts and actions empowers businesses to deliver a more personalized, efficient, and effective customer service experience, maintaining a competitive edge in an increasingly AI-driven landscape.

Case – suggesting next actions

Einstein Copilot's ability to create custom prompt templates and actions offers a powerful way to enhance case management by suggesting next actions for a case. By developing a tailored prompt template to analyze case details and historical data, Einstein Copilot can provide service agents with intelligent, context-aware recommendations for the next steps. This functionality streamlines the decision-making process and ensures that agents are equipped with the best possible actions to resolve cases efficiently. Whether it involves recommending follow-up tasks, escalating issues, or providing troubleshooting steps, these AI-driven suggestions can significantly improve response times and case outcomes, leading to higher customer satisfaction and more effective service operations.

> **PLEASE NOTE**
>
> The following instructions assume you have read *Chapter 3*, *Using Prompt Builder*, and *Chapter 4*, *Working with Copilot Builder*.

Step-by-step process

1. Navigate to the **Prompt Builder** page and click on **New Prompt Template**.

2. On **New Prompt Template**, enter these values:

   - **Prompt Template Type: Record Summary**

   - **Prompt Template Name: Case Next Action**

   - **API Name:** Case_Next_Action

   - **Template Description: Recommend next actions for service agent to take on a case. Guidance for what to do next. Process for successfully closing the case.**

   - **Object Type: Case**

3. Click on **Next**.

   The following screenshot shows how to start creating a prompt template to suggest case next actions:

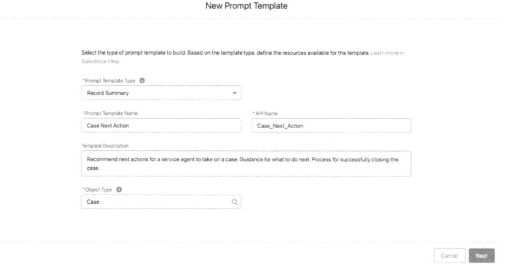

Figure 9.5 – Starting to create a Case Next Action prompt template

This screenshot shows the beginning of a prompt template creation for a **Case Next Action** list in Salesforce, demonstrating how you can customize Einstein Copilot to guide your case management process effectively.

4. After clicking **Next**, the next page is **Prompt Template Workspace**, where the prompt definition continues. On **Prompt Template Workspace**, set the directions to the following:

Prompt Template: Suggest Next Actions for a Case

Introduction: Begin with a brief overview of the case, including the case number, customer name, and current status.

Case Number: {!$Input:Case.CaseNumber}

Case Name: {!$Input:Case.SuppliedName}

Status: {!$Input:Case.Status}

Description: {!$Input:Case.Description}

Next Actions: Based on the case details and current status, suggest the next actions to take. Include specific steps, responsible parties, and deadlines if applicable.

5. Select a model type.

6. Save and activate the prompt template.

The following screenshot shows how to finish a prompt template to suggest case next actions:

Figure 9.6 – Adding detail to a Case Next Action prompt template

This screenshot highlights how you can add detail to a **Case Next Action** prompt template in Salesforce, refining the guidance Einstein Copilot provides for more tailored and effective case management.

1. Navigate to the **Einstein Copilot Actions** page and click on **New Copilot Action**.

2. On **Connect an existing action**, enter these values:

   - **Reference Action Type: Prompt Template**

   - **Reference Action: Case Next Action**

   - **Copilot Action Label: Case Next Action**

   - **Copilot Action API Name**: Case_Next_Action

3. Click on **Next**.

The following screenshot shows how to start creating an action to suggest case next actions:

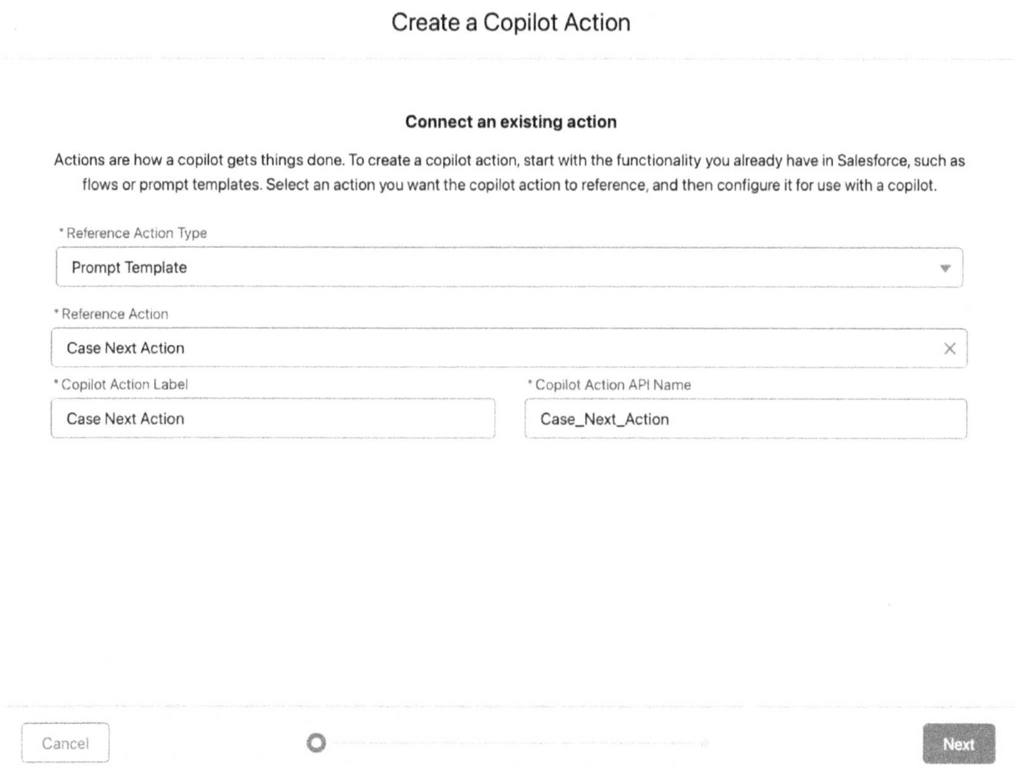

Create a Copilot Action

Connect an existing action

Actions are how a copilot gets things done. To create a copilot action, start with the functionality you already have in Salesforce, such as flows or prompt templates. Select an action you want the copilot action to reference, and then configure it for use with a copilot.

* Reference Action Type

| Prompt Template | ▼ |

* Reference Action

| Case Next Action | × |

| * Copilot Action Label | * Copilot Action API Name |
| Case Next Action | Case_Next_Action |

| Cancel | | Next |

Figure 9.7 – Starting to create a Case Next Action action

This screenshot illustrates the initial steps of creating a Case Next Action action in Salesforce, showcasing how you can set up tailored actions to streamline your case management process.

1. On **Copilot Action Configuration**, enter these values:

    *   **Copilot Action Instructions: Recommend next actions to resolve a Case. Provide guidance on what to do next for the case. Help close a case so the customer is happy with the outcome.**

    *   **Input**

        *   **Instructions: Get the record ID from the current Case.**

        *   **Require input**: Checked

        *   **Collect data from user**: Unchecked

    *   **Output**

        *   **Instructions: Provide step by step directions on what to do next for the case.**

        *   **Filter from copilot action**: Unchecked

        *   **Show in conversation**: Checked

2. Click on **Finish** (or **Save**).

The following screenshot shows how to finish an action to suggest case next actions:

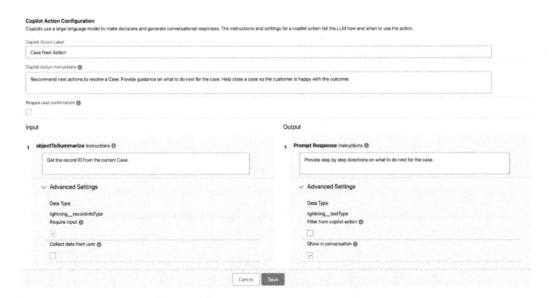

Figure 9.8 – Adding detail to a Case Next Action action

This screenshot demonstrates how you can add detail to a **Case Next Action** action in Salesforce, enhancing the precision and effectiveness of your case management workflows.

1. Navigate to the Copilot Builder.
2. Deactivate the active copilot (do this at a time when you don't have active users).
3. Navigate to **Copilot Action Library**.
4. Add the action to the copilot.
5. Activate the copilot.

The following screenshot shows how to add a **Case Next Action** action to a copilot:

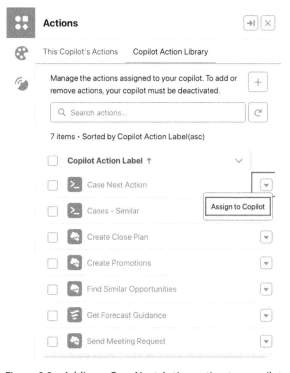

Figure 9.9 – Adding a Case Next Action action to a copilot

This screenshot shows how you can seamlessly add a Case Next Action action to a copilot in Salesforce, integrating customized actions to enhance your case management efficiency.

1. Navigate to a **Case** page.
2. Click on the **Einstein** icon on the top right of the screen (if needed).
3. Enter *Please recommend next actions/steps to take for this case* as the prompt to Einstein Copilot.
4. Click on the Einstein Copilot **Send** icon.

The following screenshot shows how to use Einstein Copilot to suggest case next actions:

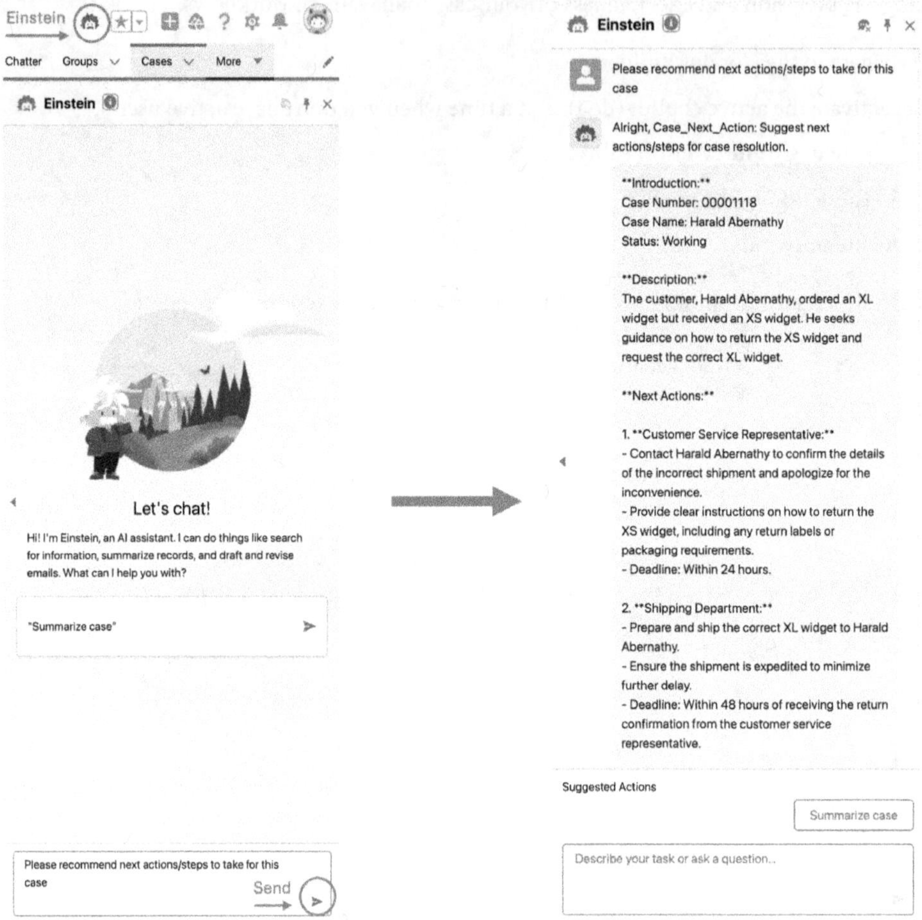

Figure 9.10 – Getting case next actions

This screenshot illustrates how Einstein Copilot can effortlessly provide "next case actions" in Salesforce, guiding you toward the most effective steps for resolving customer issues.

Several strategies can be implemented to extend the solution of using Einstein Copilot to recommend the next steps in case management. Integrating advanced analytics to continuously refine and personalize recommendations based on evolving case patterns and customer feedback can enhance the system's accuracy and relevance. Additionally, incorporating multi-channel data sources, such as social media interactions and chat logs, can provide a more comprehensive view of customer issues, leading to more holistic recommendations. Implementing ML models that learn from agent feedback on recommendations can also improve the system's effectiveness over time. Another extension could be to enable seamless collaboration features, allowing agents to share insights and recommendations within their teams directly through the platform. Finally, expanding the solution to include proactive alerts and notifications for potential issues can help preemptively address problems, further enhancing customer satisfaction and operational efficiency.

Business benefits

Einstein Copilot's ability to suggest next actions for case management provides substantial business value by enhancing decision-making and streamlining service operations. By creating custom prompt templates and actions, service agents receive intelligent, context-specific recommendations based on comprehensive case data. This functionality reduces resolution times, minimizes human error, and ensures consistent and effective case handling, leading to improved customer satisfaction and operational efficiency:

- **Enhanced decision-making**: Provides data-driven, context-specific recommendations that ensure effective case resolution strategies, reducing cognitive load on agents

- **Improved efficiency**: Streamlines the case management process, leading to faster resolution times and higher customer satisfaction

- **Consistency and accuracy**: Automates next-step identification, minimizing human error and ensuring a uniform approach to case handling, fostering greater trust and reliability in service delivery

Case – similar case resolution

Leveraging Einstein Copilot to create a custom feature that looks up cases similar to the current one and lists their resolutions can significantly enhance the efficiency and effectiveness of case management. This feature uses AI to analyze the details of the current case and search through historical case data to identify previous cases with similar issues. By presenting the resolutions of these similar cases, Einstein Copilot provides service agents with valuable insights and proven solutions that can be applied to the current case. This accelerates the resolution process and ensures that agents are equipped with the best practices and successful strategies from past experiences. By utilizing this feature, service teams can reduce resolution times, increase accuracy in handling cases, and ultimately improve customer satisfaction through faster and more reliable service.

Step-by-step process

1. Navigate to the **Prompt Builder** page and click on **New Prompt Template**.
2. On **New Prompt Template**, enter these values:

    - **Prompt Template Type**: Flex

    - **Prompt Template Name: Cases - Similar**

    - **API Name**: Cases_Similar

- **Template Description: Find and summarize similar cases to help with Case resolution**

- **Sources**

  - **Name: Cases - Similar**

  - **API Name:** `Cases_Similar`

  - **Source Type: Object**

  - **Object: Case**

3. Click on **Next**.

The following screenshot shows how to start creating a prompt template to find similar cases:

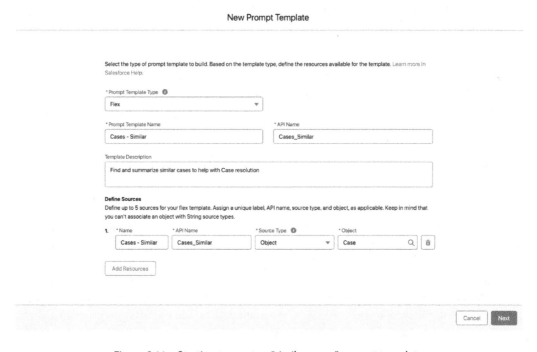

Figure 9.11 – Starting to create a "similar cases" prompt template

This screenshot illustrates the beginning of a prompt template creation for a "similar cases" list in Salesforce, highlighting how you can customize Einstein Copilot to identify related cases efficiently.

1. On **Prompt Template Workspace**, set the directions to the following:

- **Prompt Template: Case - Similar**

- **Introduction: Begin with a brief introduction to the case, including the case number, customer name, and date of case creation.**

- **Description**: {!$Input:Cases_Similar.Description}
- **Conclusion: List up to three similar closed cases based on the description and include the resolution of the case**

2. Select a model type.

3. Save and activate the prompt template.

The following screenshot shows how to finish a prompt template to find similar cases:

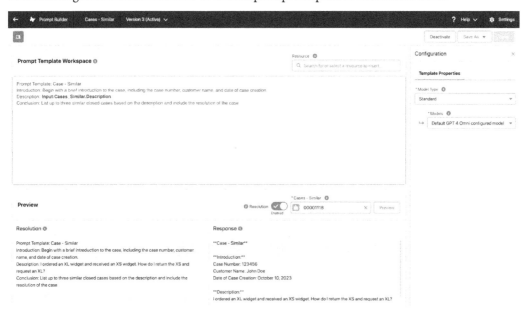

Figure 9.12 – Adding detail to a "similar case" prompt template

This screenshot showcases how you can add detail to a "similar cases" prompt template in Salesforce, refining the criteria to ensure more accurate and relevant case comparisons.

1. Navigate to the **Einstein Copilot Actions** page and click on **New Copilot Action**.

2. On **Connect an existing action**, set the directions to the following:

- **Reference Action Type: Prompt Template**

- **Reference Action: Cases - Similar**

- **Copilot Action Label: Cases - Similar**

- **Copilot Action API Name**: Cases_Similar

3. Click on **Next**.

The following screenshot shows how to start creating an action to find similar cases:

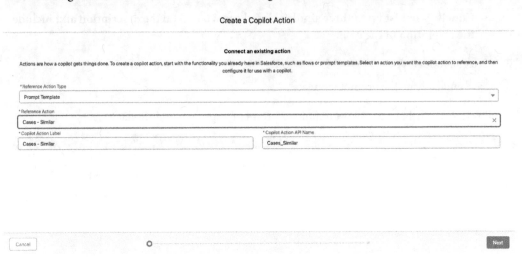

Figure 9.13 – Starting to create a "similar cases" action

This screenshot illustrates the initial steps of creating a "similar cases" action in Salesforce, demonstrating how you can set up actions to quickly identify and manage related cases.

1. On **Copilot Action Configuration**, set the directions to the following:

    *   **Copilot Action Instructions**: Used to find similar cases based on the description
    *   **Input**

        *   **Instructions**: The input is the description field in a specific case record which is used to search for similar cases
        *   **Require input**: Checked
        *   **Collect data from user**: Unchecked

    *   **Output**

        *   **Instructions**: A summary of the specific case along with a list of up to three similar cases
        *   **Filter from copilot action**: Unchecked
        *   **Show in conversation**: Checked

2.   Click on **Finish** (or **Save**).

The following screenshot shows how to finish an action to find similar cases:

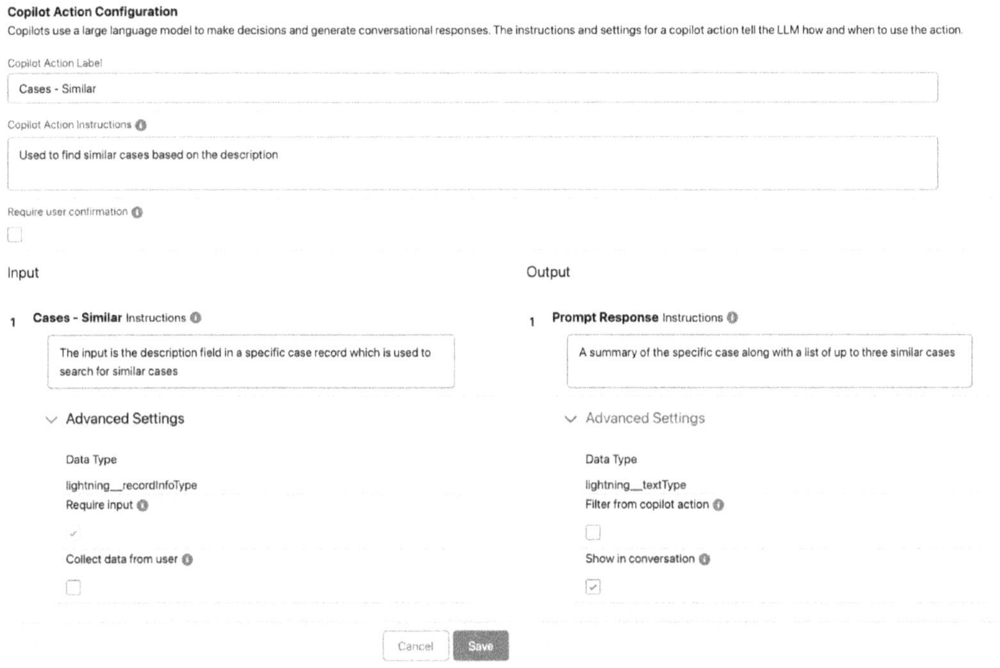

Copilot Action Configuration

Copilots use a large language model to make decisions and generate conversational responses. The instructions and settings for a copilot action tell the LLM how and when to use the action.

Copilot Action Label

> Cases - Similar

Copilot Action Instructions ⓘ

> Used to find similar cases based on the description

Require user confirmation ⓘ

☐

Input

1   **Cases - Similar** Instructions ⓘ

> The input is the description field in a specific case record which is used to search for similar cases

⌄ Advanced Settings

Data Type

lightning__recordInfoType
Require input ⓘ

✓

Collect data from user ⓘ

☐

Output

1   **Prompt Response** Instructions ⓘ

> A summary of the specific case along with a list of up to three similar cases

⌄ Advanced Settings

Data Type

lightning__textType
Filter from copilot action ⓘ

☐

Show in conversation ⓘ

✓

[Cancel] [Save]

Figure 9.14 – Adding detail to a "similar cases" action

This screenshot shows how you can add detail to a "similar cases" action in Salesforce, enhancing the precision and effectiveness of identifying and managing related cases.

1.   Navigate to the Copilot Builder.

2.   Deactivate the active copilot (do this at a time when you don't have active users).

3.   Navigate to **Copilot Action Library**.

4.   Add the action to the copilot.

5.   Activate the copilot.

The following screenshot shows how to add a "find similar cases" action to a copilot:

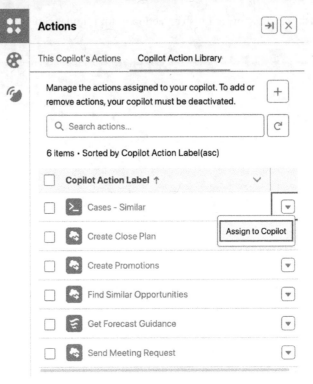

Figure 9.15 – Adding a "similar cases" action to a copilot

This screenshot demonstrates how you can seamlessly add a "similar cases" action to a copilot in Salesforce, integrating customized actions to enhance your case management workflow.

1. Navigate to a **Case** page.
2. Click on the **Einstein** icon on the top right of the screen (if needed).
3. Enter *Please list three similar cases with their resolution* as the prompt to Einstein Copilot.
4. Click on the Einstein Copilot **Send** icon.

The following screenshot shows how to use Einstein Copilot to find similar cases:

Figure 9.16 – Getting similar cases

This screenshot demonstrates how Einstein Copilot can quickly retrieve similar cases in Salesforce, providing relevant insights to help you efficiently resolve customer issues.

The feature of listing resolutions of similar cases using Einstein Copilot can be extended in several impactful ways. One enhancement could involve integrating more advanced ML algorithms to continuously improve the relevance and accuracy of the recommended resolutions by learning from ongoing case outcomes and agent feedback. Additionally, incorporating multi-channel data sources, such as emails, chat logs, and social media interactions, would provide a more comprehensive understanding of customer issues, enriching the recommendations. Another extension could be enabling collaborative functionality, allowing agents to discuss and share insights on similar cases directly within the platform, fostering a more collaborative environment. Furthermore, integrating predictive analytics could help identify potential future issues based on trends observed in similar cases, enabling proactive service measures. These extensions would make the feature more robust and versatile and significantly enhance customer service operations' overall efficiency and effectiveness.

Business benefits

Einstein Copilot's ability to create a custom feature that retrieves and displays resolutions from similar cases significantly enhances case management efficiency and effectiveness. By analyzing current case details and identifying historical cases with similar issues, this feature provides service agents with proven solutions, speeding up the resolution process and improving accuracy. This not only reduces resolution times but also ensures that best practices are consistently applied, leading to higher customer satisfaction and more reliable service outcomes:

- **Accelerated resolution**: Provides quick access to proven solutions from similar past cases, reducing the time needed to resolve current issues

- **Increased accuracy**: Leverages historical data to avoid redundant troubleshooting and apply best practices, enhancing quality of service

- **Consistency and reliability**: Standardizes the resolution process by ensuring all agents have access to the same high-quality information, promoting consistent and reliable customer support

Summary

In this chapter, you learned how to leverage Einstein Copilot within Salesforce Service Cloud to enhance customer service operations through various AI-driven features. You gained insights into identifying high-priority cases, generating case summaries, and using custom prompt templates and actions to recommend next steps and automate routine tasks. Additionally, you understood the value of retrieving and displaying resolutions of similar cases to improve efficiency and consistency in case management. The material also emphasized the dynamic nature of AI capabilities, encouraging a mindset of continuous learning and adaptation. By exploring practical applications and strategic extensions, you are equipped to implement and optimize AI solutions that drive superior customer experiences and operational excellence.

In the next chapter, you will learn how AI and Salesforce Marketing Cloud are transforming digital marketing strategies by providing deeper insights into customer behaviors and enabling more personalized campaigns. The chapter will highlight initial AI-powered features such as Einstein Send Time Optimization and Content Selection, which will improve customer engagement and satisfaction. It will introduce the new generation of Einstein Studio tools, emphasizing their potential to enhance marketing operations through advanced functionalities such as predictive analytics and real-time personalization. Practical use cases will be presented to demonstrate the real-world application of these tools, showing how they can drive strategic decision-making, operational efficiency, and significant value in marketing efforts. By understanding these capabilities, marketers can leverage AI to innovate and optimize their strategies, maintaining a competitive edge in the dynamic market landscape.

10

Integrating Einstein Copilot and Marketing Cloud

Continuing the theme of Copilot-powered use cases, in this chapter, we'll pay attention to the optimization of everyday tasks performed by marketers across the wide range of Salesforce tools they use. You'll see how Data Cloud plays a prominent role in the ever-present challenge of data management within digital marketing. We'll look at how account-based marketing gets a boost from Copilot, and then we'll move off the traditional core platform to the Marketing Cloud Engagement platform and see the latest generative AI enhancements available there. Finally, we'll return to Data Cloud to see the latest advances in analytical power to break down campaign performance according to some straightforward, predefined KPIs.

First, however, it's a good time for a quick review of other AI capabilities built explicitly for marketers that make use of predictive models. While these use cases pre-date the Einstein Studio announcement, all too often, these strengths of the platform have not yet been fully exploited by marketers.

Digital Marketing departments and agencies everywhere are increasingly realizing that AI has become a transformative force in enhancing marketing strategies and operations. AI is already helping businesses to identify deeper insights into customer behaviors, preferences, and trends, enabling them to create more personalized and effective marketing campaigns. Salesforce Marketing Cloud Engagement has been at the forefront of this revolution, integrating AI-powered features such as Einstein Send Time Optimization, Einstein Content Selection, Einstein Messaging Insights, and Einstein Email Recommendations. These first-generation Einstein features in Marketing Cloud are designed as product features that just work, without providing a great deal of customization and without an ability to modify the type of use case they were originally built to support.

These pre-packaged AI use cases have been available within the platform for long enough that they've become standard practice at many companies that have experienced success with using them. For instance, brands using Einstein Send Time Optimization have seen significant improvements in email open rates and customer engagement by sending emails at times when each individual recipient would be most likely to read them. Similarly, Einstein Content Selection has enabled marketers to deliver highly personalized content that resonates with individual customers, leading to increased click-through rates and customer satisfaction. Einstein Messaging Insights provides actionable intelligence on messaging performance, allowing marketers to fine-tune their strategies for better outcomes. Meanwhile, Einstein Email Recommendations leverage machine learning to suggest products or services that customers are likely to be interested in, boosting sales and customer loyalty.

The new generation of Einstein Studio tools promises to take these capabilities even further, empowering marketers to harness the full potential of their enterprise data. With advanced AI functionality, marketers can now create even more sophisticated use cases that drive strategic decision-making and operational efficiency. Whether it's through advanced customer segmentation, predictive analytics for campaign performance, or real-time personalization of customer journeys, Einstein Studio offers a powerful suite of tools that can revolutionize how businesses engage with their customers. As we explore the use cases in this chapter, you'll discover how these cutting-edge AI solutions can unlock new opportunities and drive significant value for your marketing efforts.

Specifically, we'll proceed to highlight the newest Copilot and AI-driven use cases designed to give marketers an edge:

- Customer segmentation in Data Cloud
- Streamlining campaign generation with Copilot for Marketing
- Automating content generation and testing subject line variations
- Improving marketing ROI with Segment Intelligence

Customer segmentation in Data Cloud

Marketers inevitably require a tool that enables them to create customer contact lists by filtering large data sets across a potentially large number of attributes. It's the difficulty of this routine activity that's led to the increasing technical specialization within the digital marketing career path. In this use case, we'll explore how the standard user interface for segment building in Data Cloud has been augmented with a generative AI interface that understands the complexities of the data model and can point the way to defining a complex segment in a fraction of the time.

Einstein Segment Builder, an application of Generative AI within Data Cloud, facilitates interaction with Copilot so that the marketing manager can request automatic generation of customer segments by writing plain text requests such as `I'd like a segment consisting of all people between the ages of 18 and 24 in the UK region who expressed an interest in football`. The associated Copilot action uses its knowledge of the available data within the harmonized Customer 360 data model and builds a query to accomplish this, generates the resulting customer list, and saves it as a segment that can be used for activation in Marketing Cloud or elsewhere. The result is that the marketing manager can more rapidly experiment with their segmentation strategy to enable more effective and targeted marketing campaigns.

Definition of the use case

Using a template for use case documentation helps to fully understand business expectations and rules before an implementation begins.

Requirement

Segment customers based on behavior, preferences, and demographics to enable highly targeted marketing campaigns.

User story

As a marketing manager, I want to use AI to automatically segment customers so that I can create highly targeted marketing campaigns that increase engagement and conversion rates.

Acceptance criteria

Given a set of customer data, when the AI segmentation system processes the data, the customers should be categorized into distinct segments based on behavior, preferences, and demographics.

Given the segmented customer data, when the marketing manager views the segments, the segments should reflect meaningful groupings that can be used for targeted marketing campaigns.

Business value

This use case will enhance marketing efficiency and effectiveness by enabling precise customer segmentation in a self-service manner, leading to more personalized and engaging marketing strategies without the need to submit a ticket to IT requesting the building of a segment.

Technical considerations

- Ensure the AI models can process large volumes of customer data efficiently
- Consider Salesforce governor limits on data processing and API calls
- Consider data privacy and compliance with regulations such as GDPR
- Ensure the harmonization of data from multiple sources is accurate and efficient

Dependencies

- Access to clean, harmonized customer data in Data Cloud (behavioral, preference, and demographic)
- Pre-existing calculated insights and predicted measures within Data Cloud should be sufficient to handle the most important segmentation priorities

Design notes

The Marketing Manager will require 1-2 hours of training in the Einstein Segment Builder UI and the correct language to use to refer to attributes and successfully generate time-based queries.

Discovery references

- Link to business requirements documents
- Gather feedback on current segmentation challenges from both the marketing manager and the IT database administrator
- Analyze customer behavior, preferences, and demographic data

Security and compliance

- Ensure compliance with data protection regulations regarding customer information
- Implement robust user authentication and role-based permissions to protect access to the segmentation system
- Conduct regular audits to ensure data integrity and security

Testing notes

- Test the generation of queries against historical customer data
- Document the test prompts found to consistently create accurate and useful customer segments, along with segment counts and performance metrics for the overall segmentation activity
- Document anti-patterns for prompting that lead to invalid or ambiguous segmentation queries

Mockups and diagrams

Include an entity relationship diagram illustrating the aspects of the data model (DMO names, relationships, and attribute names) that will be most useful during the activity of interacting with Einstein Segment Builder as a reference for the marketing manager.

Discussion log

Keep a running log of key decisions, clarifications, and discussions related to this user story, including dates and participants.

Preparation

As a prerequisite, ensure that Data Cloud and Einstein Segment Creation are available in your Salesforce environment. The Einstein Segment Creation feature must be activated by the Salesforce admin using the **Feature Manager** page in **Setup**. Obtain access to Data Cloud to explore the customer data that is available.

In the following screenshot, the **Enable** button must be pressed next to the **Einstein Segment Creation** section before the new Copilot-based feature will be available within the **Segment Builder** interface. While you're here, go ahead and enable **Approximate Segment Population** too so that you can see a more rapidly updating approximate segment count as you're interactively refining your customer segmentation rules.

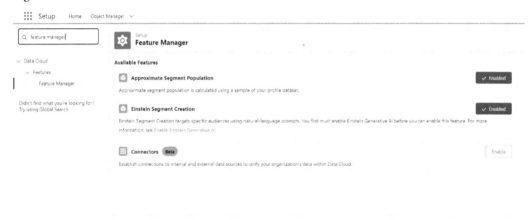

Figure 10.1 – Feature Manager where new Data Cloud features can be enabled

Step-by-step activities to use Einstein Segment Builder

Here's what the **Create Segment with Einstein** interface looks like. The activity begins using the conversational interface with Copilot, which automatically generates as many filter criteria as may be needed.

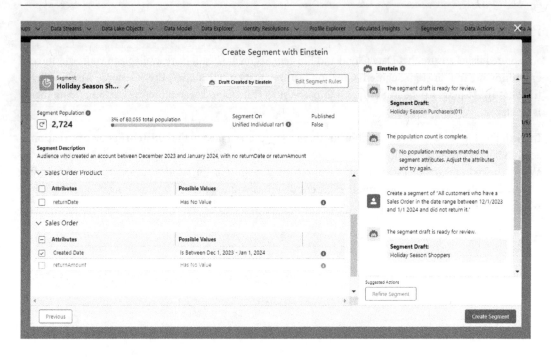

Figure 10.2 – Data types that are useful for segmentation

Are you ready to delegate the chore of creating database queries to Einstein? Read on to see how it's done:

1. **Review data sources**: Ensure your customer data sources are properly connected and synchronized in Data Cloud.

   Example: For LH&D Manufacturing, data sources might include website visits, product reference material downloads, email campaign engagement, and CRM data.

2. **Create a new segment**: To do this, follow these steps:

   I.   Click on **Create Segment** in the Data Cloud interface. Then click on **Einstein Segment Builder**.

   II.   Use natural language to describe the segment criteria, such as `Customers who have placed at least three sales orders in the last year and have not made any returns`.

   III. Here is an example prompt: `Customers who visited the automation solutions page and downloaded at least one brochure in the last three months`.

   IV.   Anything you do know about custom field names or values that are part of your data model can be used to make a more precise prompt. For example, `Create a segment of all Brand='Gibson' customers`.

3. **Refine the segment**: You can do this using the following steps:

    I.   Review the AI-generated segment and refine it, if necessary, by adding more specific criteria or adjusting parameters.

          Example: For LH&D Manufacturing, the marketer might refine the segment to include only customers from specific regions or companies of a certain size.

    II.   You can request a count of the segment population. If it seems too low or is zero, review the various filter criteria that Einstein generated. You can easily make the segment broader by unchecking some of the filters if you feel that they're unnecessary.

    III. If the count is bigger than you want, use the **Refine Segment** button to restate your prompt with additional detail.

    IV.   Use the **Create** button when you're finished refining to build the segment. At this point, it is easy to add an activation that will automate the delivery of the segment to Salesforce Marketing Cloud, or to other marketing automation platforms, via a file drop.

As you can see, the Copilot conversation can really simplify the process of building a complex segment using all aspects of your data model and can even automate the date lookback calculations that are frequently part of list generation. Let's next review some of the most important types of data for segment generation that should be present in your Customer 360 data model.

Customer data – behavior

Behavioral data includes actions customers take on digital platforms. For LH&D Manufacturing, this could involve the following:

- **Website visits**: Tracking which pages customers visit on the B2B website
- **Downloads**: Monitoring downloads of product reference materials, whitepapers, and brochures
- **Email engagement**: Analyzing interactions with email campaigns, such as opens, clicks, and responses

Behavioral data helps in understanding what customers are interested in and how they interact with the company's content. By analyzing these behaviors, Einstein Copilot can group customers with similar behaviors together.

Customer data – preferences

Preferences data includes explicit indications of interest from customers. For LH&D Manufacturing, this could be the following:

- **Subscription lists**: Customers opting in to specific newsletters or product updates

- **Survey responses**: Feedback collected from customer satisfaction surveys indicating interest in certain product lines

- **Event participation**: Attendance at webinars, trade shows, or company-hosted events

This data provides insights into what customers have explicitly expressed interest in, which can be very powerful for segmentation.

Customer data – demographics

Demographic data includes information about the customer's background or the company they work for:

- **Region**: Geographic location of the customer or their company

- **Company size**: Number of employees or revenue size of the customer's company

- **Industry**: The sector the customer's company operates in, such as automotive, aerospace, or energy

Demographic data helps in tailoring marketing efforts to specific segments that are more likely to respond positively to certain messages or offers.

In this use case, we saw how Copilot pops up within the **Segments** tab of Data Cloud to assist with a very specific but very useful task. Since the AI is already familiar with the details of the Customer 360 data model, as well as which elements you are currently making use of, it is quite good at translating your natural language prompts into a query against that data model. Furthermore, it's tightly integrated with the surrounding user interface so that each of the attributes and filter values it proposes are visible and can even be approved or rejected by its human partner. This new type of user interface that relies on the power of large language models offers a true glimpse of the future and provides the marketing manager with a powerful tool with which to rapidly iterate and refine new ideas for segments and campaigns.

Next, we'll consider another generative AI capability for configuration, helping to speed marketers through repetitive tasks.

Streamline campaign generation with Copilot for Marketing

Time is a critical resource, and clicking through traditional user interfaces for putting together a marketing campaign can consume a good part of your day. Marketers often find themselves bogged down by repetitive tasks that consume valuable time and energy, detracting from their ability to perform other important aspects of their role, such as campaign performance analysis and strategic planning. Within the two apps on Salesforce Core designed for marketers, Marketing Cloud Growth Edition and Account Engagement, Copilot is showing up as a generative AI assistant to help with the campaign generation process, enabling marketers to quickly create and deploy campaigns with minimal manual effort. This use case demonstrates how Copilot can streamline the creation of a single email campaign. While this is a simple and predictable task, it can take a frustratingly long time to perform all the necessary setup operations. Since this is often a routine and repetitive type of work that marketers are asked to perform, it's a good example of the efficiency and productivity gains achievable through AI-powered automation.

Definition of the use case

Using a template for use case documentation helps to fully understand business expectations and rules before an implementation begins.

Requirement

Automate the generation of single-send email marketing campaigns to save time and improve efficiency for marketers.

User story

As a marketing specialist, I want to use Copilot for Marketing to quickly generate a single email campaign so that I can focus on strategic tasks and enhance my overall productivity.

Acceptance criteria

Given access to Marketing Cloud Growth Edition or Account Engagement, when the marketer initiates the campaign creation process, then Copilot should generate a campaign brief, a single email, and a draft segment using AI.

Given the AI-generated content, when the marketer reviews the draft, they should then be able to easily edit and finalize the campaign materials.

Business value

This use case will significantly reduce the time marketers spend on repetitive tasks, allowing them to allocate more time to strategy and creativity, thereby improving the overall quality and impact of marketing campaigns.

Technical considerations

- Ensure that Copilot has access to relevant data sources and that AI models are properly configured
- Investigate foundation AI model selection and configuration in Model Builder to ensure that the generated content will adhere to brand guidelines and compliance standards
- Determine whether customization in Prompt Builder or custom Copilot actions could further enhance the accuracy of the AI-generated output

Dependencies

- Access to Marketing Cloud Growth Edition or Account Engagement
- Proper configuration of Copilot and data integration in Marketing Cloud

Discovery references

- Link to business requirements documents
- User feedback on campaign generation challenges
- Analysis of campaign creation processes, time requirements, and pain points

Security and compliance

- Ensure compliance with data protection regulations regarding customer information
- Implement robust user authentication and role-based permissions to govern access to the campaign creation process

Testing notes

- Test the AI model's accuracy in generating relevant and compliant content
- Include edge cases where the campaign criteria might be complex or specific

Discussion log

Keep a running log of key decisions, clarifications, and discussions related to this user story, including dates and participants.

Preparation

This use case is specifically for marketers working within the new Marketing Cloud Growth Edition or Account Engagement (formerly Pardot) apps on Salesforce Core. Data Cloud and Einstein Segment Builder must also be available and enabled.

Step-by-step activities

Excited to experiment with the automated setup of a new campaign? Read on to see how it's done:

1. **Accessing Copilot for Marketing**: Follow these steps:

     I.   **Navigate to the Campaigns tab**: In Marketing Cloud Growth Edition or Account Engagement, go to the **Campaigns** tab.

     II. **Initiate campaign creation**: Click on **New** and choose **Child Campaign**. Provide a name for the campaign and select **All Email Campaigns** as the parent. Next, select the option for **Single email with Einstein**, as demonstrated in this screenshot:

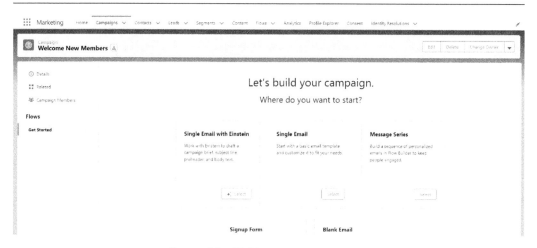

Figure 10.3 – AI-driven campaign creation

2. **Prompting Copilot**: You can do this by following these steps:

I. **Generate Campaign Brief**: Copilot prompts you to provide a brief for the email. Input key details such as the campaign goal, target audience, and any specific messaging guidelines. As an example, in the following screenshot, we asked Copilot to `Promote the new line of industrial machinery to customers in the automotive sector.`

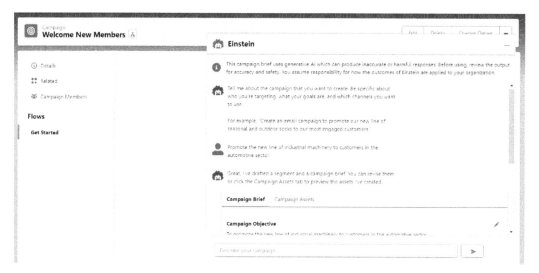

Figure 10.4 – Review the generated text

II.   **Drafting the email content**: Copilot creates a new Campaign record, including the email setup, email subject, preheader text, and message body, based on the provided brief. For example, the generated subject line could be `Discover Our Latest Industrial Machinery Innovations`. The suggested preheader was `Special offer for automotive industry leaders`. The body text could be something such as `Introducing our new line of precision machinery designed to enhance your production capabilities....` In the following screenshot, you'll see how a new email message is presented in the content editor and is ready for further customization.

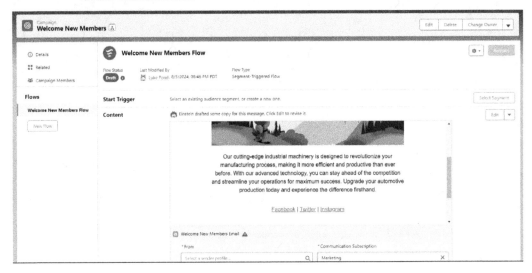

Figure 10.5 – Preview of email content

III.   **Creating the segment**: The new campaign uses entry into a Data Cloud segment to initiate the email send. The **Select Segment** button is used to invoke the Segment Builder (as discussed in the previous use case) to draft a segment for the campaign. Review and edit the segment criteria if necessary. An example prompt for Segment Builder could be `Customers in the automotive sector who have engaged with our content in the last six months`. In this screenshot, you'll see the user experience for editing the segment after Copilot has created the initial version in response to the prompt.

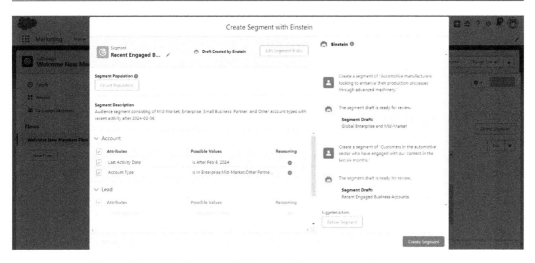

Figure 10.6 – Using Segment Builder to define the campaign entry source

3. **Reviewing and finalizing the campaign**: You can do this by following these steps:

    I.   **Review and edit**: Review the AI-generated campaign components. Make any necessary edits to ensure the content aligns with brand guidelines and campaign objectives. You might want to adjust the messaging tone or add specific details about the promotional offer.

    II. **Finalize and deploy**: Once satisfied with the campaign components, finalize the setup and schedule the email for deployment. The **Single Email** campaign type uses a pre-built Flow for its messaging logic, which is unlikely to need any further customization.

Copilot for Marketing – efficiency and productivity gains

Copilot for Marketing streamlines the campaign creation process by leveraging AI to automate repetitive tasks. For LH&D Manufacturing, this means that instead of manually drafting emails, defining segments, and setting up campaigns, marketers can rely on Copilot to handle these tasks swiftly and accurately. This not only saves time but also ensures consistency and compliance with brand standards.

By using **Natural Language Processing** (**NLP**), Copilot can understand the marketer's brief and generate relevant content for the desired audience. For example, if the marketing team wants to promote a new product line to customers in a specific industry, Copilot can draft an email that highlights key features, benefits, and promotional offers tailored to that audience. It can also create a segment based on engagement history and other relevant criteria, ensuring the campaign reaches the most appropriate audience. While the language aspects are likely to need to be edited by the marketing specialist to have the intended effect, the automation of the multi-step setup process is a great time saver.

In this use case, Copilot for Marketing automates the generation of a single email campaign, saving time and effort for marketers. By handling repetitive tasks such as drafting content and creating segments, Copilot allows marketers to focus on strategic initiatives and creativity, ultimately improving the quality and impact of their campaigns. This AI-powered approach not only enhances efficiency but also ensures that campaigns are consistently aligned with brand guidelines and strategic goals.

That completes our in-depth look at Copilot features in Marketing Cloud Account Engagement and Marketing Cloud Growth on the core platform. Next, we'll turn our attention to Marketing Cloud Engagement to see how similar productivity-enhancing features are making their way into the user experience for marketers using that product.

Automating content generation and testing subject line variations

In the work environment of digital marketing, crafting engaging content and optimizing subject lines are critical tasks performed on a day-in, day-out basis by marketing specialists. The generative AI capabilities within the Salesforce Marketing Cloud Engagement platform, particularly Einstein Copy Insights and other AI-powered tools, significantly enhance this process by automating content creation and testing subject line variations. These features, when used correctly, can accelerate productivity, increase the cohesiveness of the brand voice, and improve engagement rates.

Given that Marketing Cloud Engagement runs on a separate platform with a different technology stack than all the other Salesforce Einstein Studio tools this book has discussed, it isn't able to directly benefit from the Prompt, Copilot, or Model Builder tools. However, the suite of Einstein features within Marketing Cloud Engagement has been under development for many years and continues to receive updates and innovative new capabilities. The only difference is that the features all come built into the platform, so the AI models they use are maintained within the system and are invisible aside from what you can read about them in the product documentation. Be that as it may, the MCE platform includes an impressive slate of different AI functionalities that are all tightly focused on improving the experience and performance of the digital marketer's most frequently encountered challenges.

Definition of the use case

Using a template for use case documentation helps to fully understand business expectations and rules before an implementation begins.

Requirement

Enhance the efficiency of content generation and optimize subject lines to improve engagement rates in email marketing campaigns.

User story

As a marketing specialist, I want to use generative AI to create email content and test subject line variations so that I can enhance email engagement and save time on content creation.

Acceptance criteria

Given access to the Marketing Cloud Engagement platform, when a new email message is created using generative AI features, then the system should generate email content and provide subject line variations for A/B testing.

Given the AI-generated content and subject lines, when the marketer reviews the subject line variations, then they should be able to see a predictive analysis of the effectiveness of each one.

Business value

This use case will improve email engagement rates through optimized content and subject lines, while also reducing the time marketers spend on content creation and testing.

Technical considerations

- Be aware that there is no usage-based pricing; however, the volume of generative AI usage is capped at 10,000 requests per account. Additional usage allowances can be obtained by contacting your Salesforce account executive.

- Use standard email performance reporting to monitor AI-generated content to ensure that it aligns with brand guidelines and compliance standards.

Dependencies

- Access to the Marketing Cloud Engagement platform

- Initial configuration of Brand Settings in Marketing Cloud to enhance and standardize the prompts

Discovery references

- Link to business requirements documents

- User feedback on content generation and subject line testing challenges

- Analysis of email engagement metrics and historical data

Testing notes

- Test the AI model's accuracy in generating relevant and compliant content

- Include edge cases where the content criteria might be complex or specific

- Perform regression testing to ensure existing functionalities are not disrupted

Discussion log

Keep a running log of key decisions, clarifications, and discussions related to this user story, including dates and participants.

Preparation

- **Prerequisites**: Einstein Copy Insights and generative AI features will work best in a Marketing Cloud environment that is already up and running. The Subject Line Testing tool can use up to 90 days of recent subscriber engagement history, and it's safe to assume it won't be well-trained until you have already reached a steady state of normal operations.

- **Setup steps**: From the **Set Up Einstein** screen, activate the Einstein Copy Insights feature and enable Einstein Generative AI. Enter one or more brand personalities and give each one a name. These brand personalities are used to ground the prompts and guide the generated content to align with your brand.

Step-by-step activities

After the Einstein setup mentioned earlier is complete, the Marketing Cloud Engagement user will be able to proceed with AI-guided content experimentation following these steps:

1. **Accessing generative AI features**:

    I. **Navigate to Einstein Copy Insights**: From the Einstein menu, select **Einstein Copy Insights**. Review the dashboard, which presents an overview analysis of the effectiveness of existing subject lines that have been used in previous email campaigns, as seen in the following screenshot:

Figure 10.7 – Einstein Copy Insights dashboard

2. **Configuring content generation**:

I. **Generate subject lines**: Go to the **Subject Line Generation** tab. Enter the key message for this email campaign. Choose one of the preconfigured brand personalities, and optionally, enter a sample subject line. An example interaction with a key message and sample subject line is shown in the following screenshot, along with the five draft subject lines resulting from the Copy Insights model:

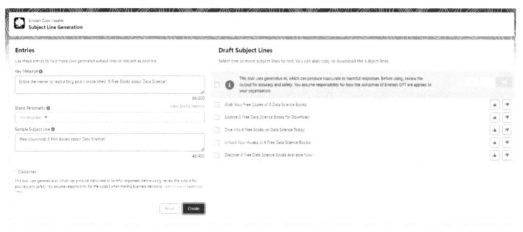

Figure 10.8 – Subject line generation

II. **Test before you send**: Use the **Test** button to navigate to **Einstein Subject Line Tester**. This feature is available only after you opt into global models from Einstein Setup. You will be using a unique version of the global model that's trained using global model data associated with optimized sample weights customized from your Marketing Cloud account. You can test and compare up to 10 different subject lines. The result is a confidence rating from 1 to 5 of each subject line, along with a visual analysis of the language features used that contributed positively or negatively to the rating. Review the insights provided by Einstein, including language factors, emotional tone, and top-performing phrases. For example, insights might show that subject lines with positive tones and specific phrases such as "limited time" perform better.

III. **Drafting the email content**: From the **Body Copy Generation** tab, repeat the steps of entering a key message, choosing a brand personality, and (optionally) entering some test message content. The AI responds with five example text snippets appropriate for use in the email body, each just a couple of sentences in length.

IV. **Refining and finalizing content**: Based on the insights, refine the email content and subject lines to enhance engagement. If there is no consensus on which language variation will be most effective, actual A/B testing can be easily configured within Journey Builder to choose between two or more variations on an email based on actual engagement metrics gathered from a pilot audience.

All behavior of the Copy Insights feature is influenced by the brand personalities configurable in the Marketing Cloud setup. Let's look at examples of how that initial grounding can be specified.

Brand personalities for LH&D Manufacturing used for grounding gen-AI prompts

The CMO of LH&D Manufacturing believes that automating content generation and optimizing subject lines can significantly enhance their email marketing efforts. They decide to create two variations on the brand personality for use within different types of outreach campaigns.

Example 1 – innovative and professional

The Brand Personality configuration used in this example could contain the following text:

- **Tone**: This should be professional, authoritative, and forward-thinking.
- **Language style**: This will be clear, concise, and technical, with an emphasis on innovation and quality.
- **Emotional tone**: A confident, trustworthy, and innovative tone will be used.
- **Description of LH&D Manufacturing**: LH&D Manufacturing is a leader in high-quality industrial equipment and machinery, known for its commitment to innovation and customer satisfaction. With a rich history dating back to 1949, LH&D serves a diverse range of industries including automotive, aerospace, construction, and energy. Our mission is to deliver superior manufacturing solutions that drive industrial innovation and efficiency. We prioritize quality, customer focus, and sustainability in all our operations.
- **Grounded prompt example (key message for subject line generation)**: "Highlight the launch of our new line of precision machinery, emphasizing our cutting-edge technology and commitment to quality."

Example 2 – customer-centric and reliable

The Brand Personality configuration used in this example could contain the following text:

- **Tone**: This should be friendly, supportive, and reliable.
- **Language style**: A warm, approachable, and customer-focused style could be used.
- **Emotional tone**: The tone should be trustworthy, dependable, and service-oriented.
- **Description of LH&D Manufacturing**: LH&D Manufacturing has been a trusted provider of high-quality industrial equipment since 1949. We pride ourselves on our strong customer relationships and our dedication to delivering reliable and efficient solutions. Our products serve various industries, and we are committed to exceeding customer expectations through exceptional service and innovative technology. Our core values include quality, integrity, and sustainability.

- **Grounded prompt example (key message for subject line generation)**: "Invite our customers to explore our new automation solutions, highlighting our commitment to customer satisfaction and support."

The brand personalities are entered one time and can be selected for reuse within the language exploration for each new campaign, ensuring the generated content is consistent with LH&D Manufacturing's image and values.

In this use case, generative AI and Einstein Copy Insights automate the content creation and subject line optimization process, saving significant time and effort for marketers. By handling repetitive tasks and providing valuable insights, these AI-powered tools enable marketers to focus on strategic initiatives and creativity, ultimately improving the quality and impact of their campaigns. This AI-partnered approach enhances efficiency, ensures consistency with brand guidelines, and drives higher engagement rates in email marketing campaigns.

In the next marketing use case, we'll return to the concept of how generative AI enables a rapidly evolving segmentation strategy and see how data-driven feedback can assist marketers to nudge their segment definitions in the right direction.

Improving marketing ROI with Segment Intelligence

Segment Intelligence is an analytics app embedded within Salesforce Data Cloud that enables marketers to gain deep insights into the performance of their activated segments. By combining Data Cloud with the powerful visualization and machine learning capabilities that are the specialty of CRM Analytics, Segment Intelligence provides a comprehensive view of the performance of individual segments across multiple channels, engagement types, and conversion sources. This use case demonstrates how Segment Intelligence can be utilized to build and enhance segments with actionable performance insights, ultimately improving marketing ROI and campaign effectiveness.

Definition of the use case

Using a template for use case documentation helps to fully understand business expectations and rules before an implementation begins.

Requirement

Improve marketing ROI by analyzing segment performance and steadily improving the segmentation process to optimize marketing campaigns.

User story

As a marketing analyst, I expect to use the Einstein Studio Segment Intelligence feature to analyze and optimize the performance of activated segments so that I can improve marketing ROI and campaign effectiveness.

Acceptance criteria

Given access to Segment Intelligence in Data Cloud, when the marketing analyst reviews segment performance, they should see actionable insights on engagement, conversion, and revenue.

Given the performance insights, when the marketing analyst uses Einstein segment creation, then they should be able to build and enhance segments to target more relevant audiences.

Business value

This use case will improve marketing ROI by enabling marketers to make data-driven decisions, optimizing audience targeting and campaign performance.

Technical considerations

- Ensure the data streams required by Segment Intelligence are correctly set up in Data Cloud
- Monitor performance to handle large volumes of data and multiple segment analyses
- Monitor for any anomalies encountered during the data ingestion process
- Ensure compliance with data protection regulations
- Although the Segment Intelligence product makes use of Salesforce CRM Analytics as part of its implementation, it's not required to have any licensing to use CRM Analytics as a product

Dependencies

- Segment Intelligence considers four major data sources: Marketing Cloud Engagement, Salesforce B2C Commerce, Meta Ads, and Google Ads. It's recommended to have access to at least two of these.
- Proper configuration of Data Cloud is a must.

Discovery references

- User feedback on current segmentation challenges
- Existing analysis of marketing campaign performance metrics
- Inventory of existing reports used by the Marketing Analyst to monitor ad spend, revenue, and digital campaign engagement metrics

Security and compliance

- Ensure compliance with data protection regulations regarding customer information
- Analyze roles and responsibilities to differentiate the marketing analyst, marketing specialist, and marketing manager using permission sets in CRM.

Testing notes

- Compare KPIs as delivered by legacy reporting tools against top-level insights provided by Segment Intelligence, including total spend, revenue by campaign

- Determine in advance what system will be best suited for delivering the Marketing ROI metric, to monitor the impact of Segment Intelligence

Discussion log

Keep a running log of key decisions, clarifications, and discussions related to this user story, including dates and participants.

Preparation

- **Prerequisites**: Segment Intelligence assumes a cross-cloud Salesforce environment, where Marketing Cloud and B2C Commerce are the key platforms that support the ecommerce business. Data Cloud is required to use Segment Intelligence, and you should already have at least 30 days of history from segments that you would like to optimize.

- **First-party data setup**: The **Segment Intel Setup** screen in the setup process provides a walkthrough of the initial required steps. The out-of-the-box data connectors must be employed to ingest data bundles from B2C Commerce and Marketing Cloud Engagement. Next, the screen guides you to select the Data Cloud DMO and attribute where the Revenue Metric is located.

- **Second party data setup**: Creating the ROI metric also requires a way to determine total spend on advertising directed by marketing. Using Data Cloud's built-in connector capabilities for Meta Ads and Google Ads, create and map data streams for either or both.

- **Deploy the automated transformations for ads data**: The next prompt from the Segment Intel Setup screen sets up the transformation steps necessary to have a unified view of campaign performance across both Meta and Google. It creates the following DMOs for Meta Ads and Google Ads:

  - Media conversion

  - Media performance

  - Ad group

  - Ad group segment

  - Meta Ads Audience

- **Assign the permission set**: The Data Cloud administrator should view the user record for each of the marketing analysts and must enable their access by assigning them to the Segment Intelligence User permission set.

- **Aggregate the first- and third-party data**: As a final trick, the **Setup** screen prompts you to continue by aggregating your first and third-party data and storing it in DLOs constructed for the purpose of feeding the Segment Intelligence dashboards, which only display aggregated data. The aggregations created will include up to 30 days of first-party data and up to 30 days of third-party data. This is the final step to make the data visible in the Segment Intelligence dashboard.

Step-by-step activities to use Segment Intelligence

After the setup process is complete, the marketing user can proceed to use the new insights as follows.

Reviewing Segment Intelligence results

1. **Use the Segment dashboard**: From the Data Cloud app, click on the **Segment Intelligence** tab to access the dashboard. Review key metrics such as engagement rates, conversion rates, and revenue.

2. **Analyze segment performance**: Access the insights provided by Segment Intelligence to understand how different segments are performing. You'll review metrics such as click-through rates, purchase rates, and revenue generated by each segment.

3. **Use actionable insights**: Utilize the actionable insights provided by Einstein to optimize segments and improve campaign effectiveness. An example of a provided insight might be something such as `Einstein recommends - to improve conversion, prioritize Instagram ads to customers in the Highly Engaged Homeowners` segment. These insights will be especially helpful once the segmentation strategy is in place and undergoing ongoing performance monitoring. If the insight points out a segment that is outperforming others, the marketing team can consider increasing ad spend weighting to increase its outperformance. Optimizing ad spend becomes achievable by using the data and AI-generated insights to continue targeting the most relevant audiences.

4. **Create and enhance segments with Einstein:** Use the Create Segment with Einstein feature to build new segments based on the performance insights whenever you learn something new about what type of customer segment is most likely to take action to engage with your campaigns. As an example, you might create a segment of customers who have high engagement rates but low purchase rates and target them with a special promotion.

Practical application for LH&D Manufacturing

One of the divisions of LH&D Manufacturing supports a replacement parts business that supplies both individual consumers and repair companies ranging in size from 1 to 100 technicians. They have a relatively low opt-in rate for direct email marketing, and consequently, their advertising budget needs to be fairly large to ensure good search placement. They've also questioned the effectiveness of their email marketing campaigns, having lacked a good way to monitor and seek improvement on key metrics such as revenue per campaign. Using Segment Intelligence, they now have the tools they need to perform more rapid experiments with customer segmentation, evolving a larger number of segments for email and ad placement. They set up a monthly review process where they update both their segment definitions and their campaign spend decisions based on feedback provided by Segment Intelligence. Both the marketing analyst and the CMO feel that they've entered a new era of experimentation and innovation, leading to steady improvement against their business goals, with their creativity being unleashed by the new data-driven insights.

In this use case, we've seen how Segment Intelligence enables marketers to gain valuable insights into the performance of their segments, build and enhance segments with actionable insights from Einstein, and optimize their marketing campaigns. With these tools on their side, marketers can improve their marketing ROI, target more relevant audiences, and drive higher engagement and conversion rates. Using Data Cloud to harmonize the large amount of operational data needed to answer these questions solves an enormous data engineering challenge that has held back innovation in countless companies. This AI-driven approach not only enhances efficiency but also ensures that marketing efforts and expenditures are aligned with data-driven insights and strategic goals.

Summary

The advancements in AI-powered tools within Salesforce Marketing Cloud present transformative opportunities for marketers. By learning about the features we've discussed in this chapter and investigating what it would take to implement them within an organization, marketing teams can significantly enhance their efficiency and effectiveness. These tools not only streamline repetitive tasks but also provide deep, actionable insights that drive more informed decision-making at all levels.

In this chapter, we explored several practical use cases demonstrating the impact of AI on digital marketing. From automating customer segmentation and campaign generation to optimizing content and testing subject lines, these AI-driven capabilities empower marketers to deliver more personalized, targeted, and engaging campaigns. The integration of Data Cloud and CRM Analytics further amplifies these benefits by harmonizing large volumes of data, enabling more precise audience targeting, and showing the way to optimize marketing ROI. We learned about this in this chapter. With advanced prebuilt analytics applications such as Segment Intelligence, Salesforce is once again democratizing access to technology, since most businesses won't have the budget to deploy a team of analytics consultants to assemble enterprise data, discover techniques for using it to improve marketing operations, and repeat their analysis on a regular basis to keep it current.

As LH&D Manufacturing and other forward-thinking companies continue to embrace these advanced tools, they are poised to unlock new levels of innovation and performance in their marketing strategies. This is another point we learned about in this chapter. The ability to harness AI for data-driven insights and automation not only enhances marketing outcomes but also frees up valuable time for marketers to focus on creativity and strategic planning, as we learned in this chapter. By staying at the forefront of these technological advancements, businesses can stay competitive by reacting more nimbly to an increasingly dynamic marketplace.

Naturally, marketing activities must be coordinated with merchandising and the shopper experience to really generate results – and in the next chapter, we'll look at how Einstein Copilot lends its capabilities to those activities as well in Salesforce Commerce Cloud.

11

Working with Einstein Copilot and Commerce Cloud

E-commerce product owners and technical leads face the challenge of delivering highly personalized and engaging shopping experiences while managing vast and complex product catalogs. To maintain control over the software and data that coordinate these activities, it's more important than ever to seek out assistive technologies that can enhance efficiency, drive customer satisfaction, and increase conversion rates. Through its integration with Einstein Copilot, Salesforce is continually enhancing the entire Commerce Cloud product suite with advanced AI-driven capabilities that empower businesses to achieve these goals.

An exciting part of watching the evolution of Commerce Cloud is the way that the different Copilot capabilities link together across multiple products. The Copilot for Marketing campaign generation, discussed in the previous chapter, naturally leads to a need for accelerated promotion configuration, which is provided by Copilot for Commerce. And while some of the Copilot features are specific to one product, others – such as generative AI capabilities for chatbot development – can plug into a range of products, including B2C Commerce, B2B Commerce, and Order Management, even when those products are delivered through different Salesforce organizations or (in the case of B2C Commerce) on an entirely different technology stack. The Data Cloud Customer 360 strategy of harmonizing data within an e-commerce data model that is held in common across different verticals and different enterprise applications is the secret ingredient in the flexibility of the Copilot solutions Salesforce is offering. A product catalog, sales order, or inventory allocation can be stored the same way in Data Cloud even when the data itself originates from different enterprise applications. Then, an AI model designed for a specific business purpose can be trained against that data and used to make predictions or generate language output.

Einstein Copilot for Commerce enables businesses to harness the power of AI to automate and optimize various aspects of the e-commerce workflow and user experience. From generating SEO-optimized product descriptions to managing smart promotions and providing personalized shopping assistance, Einstein Copilot is designed to enhance every facet of the e-commerce journey. This AI-driven approach not only improves the quality and engagement of content but also significantly boosts operational efficiency, allowing teams to focus on strategic initiatives. By integrating these AI tools, businesses can ensure that their operational data, such as product catalogs, promotions, and orders, are always up-to-date, detailed, and tailored to meet the unique preferences and behaviors of their customers, driving higher satisfaction and loyalty.

The innovations in Salesforce Commerce Cloud are set to redefine the e-commerce landscape by providing real-time insights and personalized experiences at scale. With features such as AI-powered chatbots, automated order management, and dynamic product recommendations, businesses can create seamless and engaging shopping experiences that resonate with customers. These advancements empower e-commerce leaders to not only meet but exceed customer expectations, ensuring sustained growth and competitive advantage in a rapidly evolving market.

In this chapter, we'll focus on different use cases for Copilot that are all directly focused on accelerating common daily tasks for the team running the e-commerce business and raising the quality of their customer's online shopping experience.

Improving product descriptions with Copilot for Merchandising

Creating compelling and SEO-optimized product descriptions is a crucial task for any e-commerce business, and leveraging AI tools such as Einstein Copilot can significantly enhance both efficiency and quality in this process.

Defining the use case

Using a template for use case documentation helps you fully understand business expectations and rules before implementation begins.

Requirement

Enhance the quality, uniqueness, and specificity of product descriptions by using AI to streamline the merchandising process and improve customer engagement.

User story

As a merchandiser, I want to use AI to generate and refine product descriptions so that they are more engaging, follow the brand voice, and are optimized for search engines, leading to higher conversion rates.

Acceptance criteria

- Given a product in the catalog, when the merchandiser uses the AI tool to generate a product description, the description should be SEO-optimized, written in the brand's voice, and tailored to customer preferences

- Given multiple products selected for description generation, when the AI tool generates descriptions or other product fields, the generated text should reflect the unique attributes specified in the selected product fields used as inputs

Business value

This user story will enhance customer engagement, increase conversion rates, and decrease return rates by improving the quality of product descriptions. It will also improve the efficiency of merchandisers by automating the content creation process. Search engine rankings for product pages will improve with better uniqueness, detail, and keyword integration within product descriptions.

Technical considerations

- Ensure that the prompt is correctly engineered so that the generated text reflects the business goals, the branding values, and any specific SEO requirements

- Estimate the consumption of Data Cloud credits caused by increased usage of generative AI

Dependencies

The availability of detailed product data records in the Salesforce Product2 object to be used as grounding to generate accurate descriptions.

Testing notes

- Test the AI-generated descriptions for accuracy and engagement

- Include edge cases where product attributes might be ambiguous, complex, or missing

- Perform regression testing to ensure existing functionalities are not disrupted

Preparation

- Ensure the Einstein Generative AI capabilities are turned on by using the **Setup** page titled **Einstein Generative AI Setup**

- Ensure the product catalog is loaded into Product2 in readiness for use with B2B Commerce or D2C Commerce

Step-by-step activities

Follow these steps:

1. **Initial navigation**: Navigate to the Product Workspace in the **Commerce - Admin** app. Click through to one product where you'd like to generate improved descriptions.

2. **Configure the prompt**: Click **Edit Page** via the **Setup** menu. Ensure that the Einstein Generative AI Recommendations component has been added to the page; if not, you can add it now. Review the **Product Description** instructions and update them with a prompt that matches your business and brand requirements.

   The following screenshot shows the Lightning App Builder as it's being used to add the Einstein Generative AI Recommendation component to the product detail page:

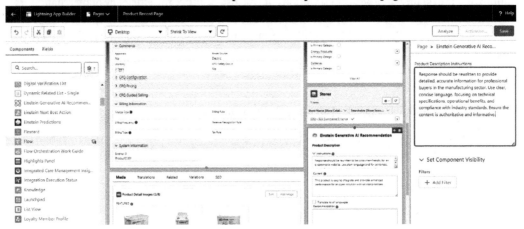

Figure 11.1 – Initial description prompt setup

3. **Improve the product description:** Return to the **Product** page and scroll to view the Einstein component. Choose the language for the generated text or click the **Translate to All Languages** checkbox. Click the **Create** button. Either repeat this process after making improvements to the prompt or description or press the **Accept** button to save the new product description directly to the product record

The following screenshot helps us visualize the generated text for the product description before the **Accept** button has been pressed:

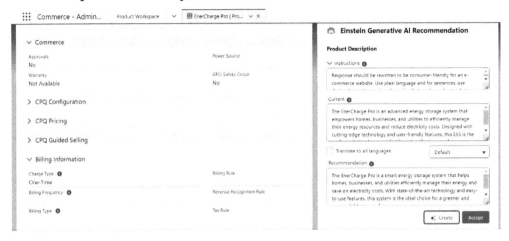

Figure 11.2 – Refining and/or translating the product description

4. **Generate text for a product field in bulk**: Return to the product list view page and select one or more products. From the **Action** select menu, choose **Draft Product Text with Einstein**.

The following screenshot shows the choices available in the Action select menu, all of which can be applied to a multiple-product selection:

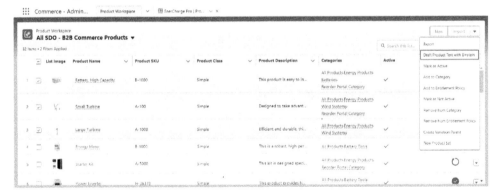

Figure 11.3 – Product selection for Draft Product Text with Einstein

5. **Configure prompt grounding and the destination field**: Choose the field for which you want to generate the description (for example, **Specifications**). Review the default prompt to ensure it is well-written for this task. Specify additional product fields that should be used to ground the AI prompt (for example, **Product Name**, **Features**, **Usage**, and **Materials**). This detailed configuration helps ground the AI so that it generates a description or other text that is not only accurate but also rich in relevant details. Click the **Create All** button.

6. **Review the results**: Check the generated text for accuracy, SEO optimization, and engagement. Make any necessary adjustments before saving the text to the product records.

The following screenshot shows the process of generating product descriptions in bulk, including the capability to fully preview the improved text before it is saved:

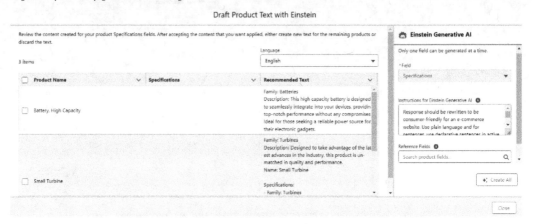

Figure 11.4 – Draft Product Text with Einstein results

Efficiency and scale

One of the major benefits of using AI for product descriptions is increased efficiency. Generating descriptions for thousands of products manually would be a monumental task. With AI integrated into the flow of work, this process is streamlined, allowing a single merchandiser to handle a sizable catalog with ease.

For a company such as LH&D Manufacturing, which offers a wide range of machine parts, this is particularly beneficial. By improving the **Specifications** attribute across their catalog, they can ensure that customers have all the information they need to make informed purchasing decisions. This not only enhances the customer experience and increases their organic search traffic but also reduces the likelihood of returns due to unclear or incomplete product information.

As an example scenario, a merchandiser learns that a new line of industrial pumps has been added to the catalog for resale from a strategic partner. They review the available catalog data fields and notice that while there are multiple detailed data fields containing individual specifications, there is no customer-facing text field that's appropriate and can be displayed on the **Specifications** tab of the website product display page. With the help of Einstein Copilot, within a few hours, they successfully generated and reviewed descriptions for over 100 products, including an additional required translation for Spanish. This task, which would have taken 10 times the effort to complete manually, is now done efficiently and accurately. The merchandiser can now shift their focus to planning a marketing campaign to promote these updated products, leveraging the new, detailed descriptions to highlight the pumps' superior features and benefits.

Moving on to the next use case, we'll see another way that Copilot uses its natural language processing to generate both configuration instructions and customer-friendly text phrases in a different context.

Creating and optimizing promotions with Einstein

Creating and optimizing promotions is a vital aspect of driving sales and customer engagement in e-commerce. This activity is strongly linked with the marketing effort to distinguish addressable customer segments – as the number of segments grows, so too does the expectation of having a uniquely appealing promotional offer for each of them. Salesforce Commerce Cloud's Einstein Copilot offers robust AI-driven tools to automate and enhance this process, making it more efficient and effective.

Defining the use case

Using a template for use case documentation helps us fully understand business expectations and rules before implementation begins.

Requirement

Automate the creation and optimization of promotions using AI to improve efficiency and effectiveness, leading to increased customer engagement and sales.

User story

As an e-commerce specialist, I want to use AI to create and optimize promotions, as recommended by the marketing team, so that they are more targeted, effective, and easier to manage, ultimately driving higher sales and customer satisfaction.

Acceptance criteria

- Given a new promotional campaign, when the e-commerce specialist uses the AI tool to create the promotion, the promotion should be generated with targeted discounts, qualifiers, and compelling text
- Given multiple customer segments, when the AI tool generates promotions, each promotion should be tailored to the specific preferences and behaviors of the segment

Business value

This user story will enhance the efficiency of creating promotions and make them more appealing to customer segments by ensuring they are targeted and relevant. This will lead to increased customer engagement, higher sales, and improved marketing ROI.

Dependencies

- Available to licensed users of B2B Commerce or D2C Commerce
- Einstein Generative AI must be enabled and the EinsteinGPTCommerceAddOn license is required

Testing notes

- Test the AI-generated text for accuracy and relevance
- Carefully review the suggested discounts and qualifiers to ensure the right grouping of products is being specified

Preparation

To enable the functionality of creating and optimizing promotions using AI, follow these steps:

1. **Access Einstein Copilot:** Navigate to the **Commerce** app and the **Store** tab in Salesforce. Select the store you wish to work on. Use the navigation column to select **Promotions**. Click the **Draft with Einstein** button, as shown in the following screenshot:

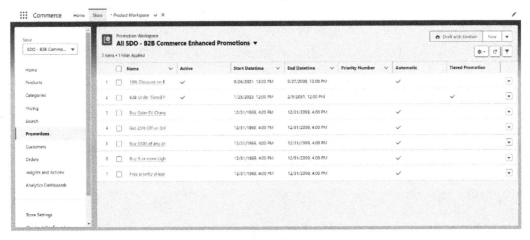

Figure 11.5 – Promotion creation navigation

2. **Enter the prompt**: In the prompt entry form, specify the details of the promotion you want to create. For example, you might include information about the target customer segment or buyer group, the type of discount, and any specific qualifiers. The following screenshot shows the process of entering the prompt:

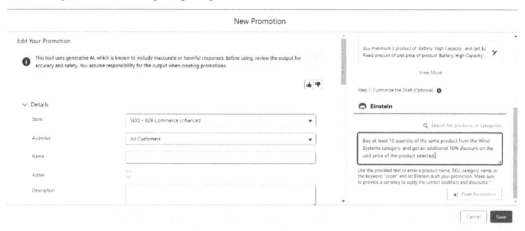

Figure 11.6 – Entering the prompt

3. **Configure action**: Click the **Draft Promotion** button. Review the generated text, buyer group selection, discounts, and qualifiers. Make any necessary adjustments to ensure the promotion aligns with your marketing goals. As usual in these Copilot-assisted interfaces, the generated configuration is displayed transparently, and you can easily add or remove criteria, as shown in the following screenshot:

Figure 11.7 – Automatic promotion configuration

4. **Review the results**: Check the generated promotions for relevance and any misunderstandings of the prompt. Adjust the parameters if needed and save the promotion.

Efficiency and scale

One of the major benefits of using AI for promotions is the increased efficiency. Configuring promotions manually can be time-consuming, tedious, and error-prone. With Einstein Copilot, this process is streamlined, allowing a single e-commerce specialist to set up a complex and multi-tiered promotion strategy across different customer segments with ease.

For a company such as LH&D Manufacturing, which has a diverse range of industrial products, this is particularly beneficial. By using Copilot to create targeted promotions, they can ensure that each promotion is relevant to the specific needs and preferences of their customers. This not only enhances the effectiveness of the promotions but also improves customer satisfaction and loyalty.

Hypothetical promotion review exercise

LH&D Manufacturing has decided to conduct a review of their promotional strategies. They find that many of their current promotions are generic and not tailored to specific customer segments. A recent marketing data initiative has resulted in the creation of a category affinity attribute, by which each customer is given a classification based on the top categories they tend to view online and purchase. The category affinity is then used to generate 24 different segments. Furthermore, they already have access to segments that provide a recency classification of customers into New, Active, At Risk, and Lost segments. Their plan involves crafting a different promotional campaign for the product of these two segmentation strategies, requiring a total of 96 distinct promotions. Using Einstein Copilot, they initiate a project to create targeted promotions for different segments. Before using Copilot, they first write a prompt for each different promotion they want to configure, describing the customer segment and the intended offer.

Example detailed prompt: Buy a total of $100 worth of any products from the "Wheels and Bearings" category and get 10% off the entire transaction. Valid during Q4 2024:

- **Recency segment**: At Risk
- **Category affinity**: Wheels and Bearings

When a prompt like this is entered into the **Draft With Einstein** configuration interface, Copilot proceeds to fill out the configuration form. After a quick review, the e-commerce specialist proceeds to generate each of the 96 promotions in record time.

Whether these promotions are displayed on the B2B storefront or received in an email message, customers are likely to appreciate the improved level of personalization shown in the messaging and discount availability. In the next section, we'll consider how generative AI can play another role in giving customers a great experience when they're browsing the e-commerce storefront.

Enabling conversational commerce for shoppers with Copilot

Providing a seamless and personalized shopping experience is essential for modern e-commerce businesses. The human connection is very important when the customer is getting frustrated, but the realities of staffing or outsourcing a call center mean that e-commerce businesses are always interested in automating the responses to simple customer questions. To that purpose, Salesforce Service Cloud comes with an Einstein Bots feature, offering a way to script a conversational interface on the website that's capable of answering some of the customer's questions before transferring them to a service agent upon request. Einstein Copilot has now arrived as a sharp new tool in this toolbox, making use of generative AI to create a more natural form of conversation without losing any of the imposed structure from the Einstein Bot configuration. As a result, businesses can set up AI-driven conversational commerce, allowing shoppers to interact with a digital concierge for personalized product recommendations and support.

Defining the use case

Using a template for use case documentation helps to fully understand business expectations and rules before implementation begins.

Requirement

Implement a conversational AI bot to provide personalized product recommendations and support through natural language interactions.

User story

As a shopper, I want to have a natural language conversation with a digital concierge so that I receive personalized product recommendations and support, enhancing my shopping experience.

Acceptance criteria

- Given a shopper initiates a conversation with the digital concierge, when the shopper asks for product recommendations, the bot should provide personalized recommendations based on the shopper's preferences and behavior

- Given a shopper interacts with the bot, when the bot provides product recommendations, the recommendations should be relevant and accurate

Business value

This use case will enhance customer engagement and satisfaction by providing personalized and efficient support. It will also increase sales by guiding shoppers to products that match their preferences and needs.

Technical considerations

- Ensure the bot is integrated with the store's product and customer data. Use of the Product2 and PricebookEntry objects is mandatory.

- The bot is compatible with B2B and D2C commerce, and also with B2C Commerce. The B2C Commerce setup instructions, while not shown here, involve providing API access to the bot so it can retrieve product and pricing data.

Dependencies

- Availability of product, price book, and customer data within Salesforce

- Deployment to the existing e-commerce platform

Testing notes

- Test the bot's ability to understand and respond to various customer inquiries

- Include edge cases where customer preferences might be ambiguous or complex

- Perform regression testing to ensure existing functionalities are not disrupted

Preparation

To set up the Commerce Concierge for B2B or D2C storefronts using Einstein Bots and Shopper Copilot, ensure the following prerequisites are met:

- **Enable Commerce Concierge settings**: In Salesforce, navigate to **Setup** and enable **Einstein Generative AI for B2B and D2C**.

- **Enable Einstein Bots**: There is another toggle switch on a **Setup** page named **Einstein Bots**.

- **Create a Bot Integration user**: Create a new Standard User profile to be used as the Bot Integration user. Add the AI Commerce Agent permission set assignment to the user.

Step-by-step activities

Follow these steps:

1. **Create the bot**: Navigate to **Setup** in Salesforce and search for `Einstein Bots`. Enable **Einstein Bots** and follow the wizard to create a new bot. Make sure you select the **Commerce Concierge** template, as shown in the following screenshot:

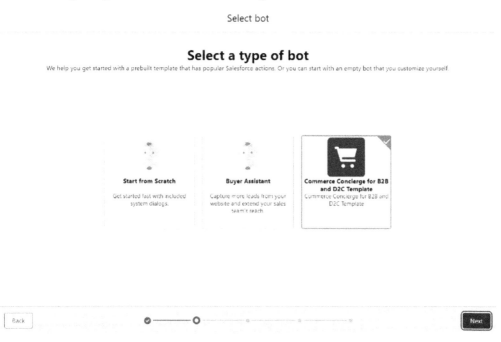

Figure 11.8 – Choosing the right template for your Einstein Bot

2. **Connect the bot to a user**: In **Setup**, on the **Einstein Bots** page, select your bot and then choose **Overview** from the **Bot Builder** menu. Under **Settings**, for the Bot User, select the integration user you created previously.

3. **Configure Omni-Channel flows**: Customize the inbound and outbound Omni-Channel flows so that the bot can hand off support conversations to a customer service queue appropriately. Define how incoming customer queries are handled and assign agents or automated processes to respond.

4. **Connect the bot to your store**: Link the bot to your online store by adding the store's web store ID, login page URL, and cart page URL in the bot settings. Consult the B2B Commerce product documentation for information about how to identify these values for your store.

After the initial setup is complete, you'll be looking at the Bot Builder **Dialogs** workspace, where you can define the bot's behavior and how it interfaces with Salesforce Flow to take automated actions:

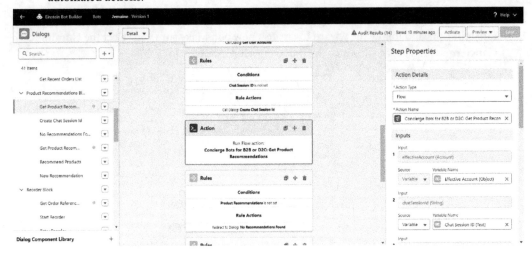

Figure 11.9 – The Dialogs screen – the main interface for bot scripting

5. **Train the intent recognition model**: Use the Bot Builder to define intents and provide example phrases. Within the Bot Builder, navigate to **Model Management**, and train the model so that it can accurately recognize and respond to customer queries. As shown in the following screenshot, an extensive set of conversational phrases is provided as a default starting point, but it's fully customizable to suit your business:

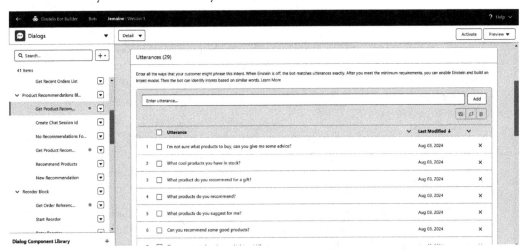

Figure 11.10 – Sample customer utterances that can begin a dialog

6. **Customize the bot's responses**: Within the **Model** tab, use the Input Tester to provide an "intent" message to the bot. Continue to provide the kinds of questions you'd expect from your customers. To improve your responses, you can go to the **Product Recommendations Block** area on the **Dialogues** screen and add utterances to the **Get Product Recommendations** intent to assist the bot in recognizing the product mix sold in your store. If it's necessary to customize further, a Salesforce admin can enhance and extend the Flow that runs when a product recommendation is requested by the customer. Here's what the default Flow implementation looks like:

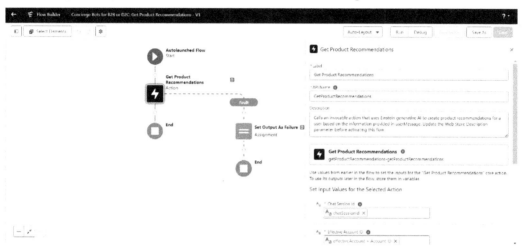

Figure 11.11 – Extensible logic for requesting product recommendations

How LH&D Manufacturing benefits from deploying Commerce Concierge

For LH&D Manufacturing, deploying Commerce Concierge on their B2B website is expected to bring substantial benefits:

- **Enhanced customer engagement**: The AI-powered digital concierge provides personalized interactions with professional buyers, answering their inquiries and making tailored product recommendations. This level of engagement helps to build stronger customer relationships and loyalty as buyers feel their specific needs are understood and met.

- **Increased efficiency**: By automating routine tasks such as answering common questions and suggesting relevant products, Commerce Concierge allows LH&D's sales and support teams to focus on more complex and strategic activities. This not only improves overall productivity but also ensures that high-value tasks receive the attention they deserve.

- **Improved sales and conversion rates**: Personalized product recommendations based on detailed customer data can lead to higher conversion rates. This digital concierge can suggest complementary products, upsell opportunities, and relevant promotions, driving increased sales and average order values.

- **Scalability and consistency**: Implementing an AI-driven solution ensures that all customers receive a consistent level of service, regardless of the time of day or the volume of inquiries. This scalability is particularly beneficial for handling peak times or when launching new products and promotions.

- **Data-driven insights**: The interactions between the digital concierge and customers provide valuable data that can be analyzed to gain insights into customer preferences, common queries, and potential areas for improvement. These insights help LH&D Manufacturing to refine their product offerings, marketing strategies, and customer service processes.

- **Cost savings**: Automating parts of the customer interaction process reduces the need for extensive human support, leading to significant cost savings. This is especially important for managing a large and diverse product catalog efficiently.

The deployment of AI in Conversational Commerce represents a major upgrade over the previous generation of more scripted bot interactions that presented a limited number of choices. Truly a strategic advancement for e-commerce, it empowers businesses to offer high-quality, personalized customer interactions at scale, drives engagement, and supports long-term business objectives with an automated interaction channel. The Einstein Bot architecture provides all the necessary tools to continue enhancing the types of interactions the customer can accomplish through this channel, including additional commerce-focused activities such as viewing order data or placing a reorder.

Next, we'll see how AI is applied to one of the most troublesome aspects of an e-commerce business: how to analyze and influence customer behavior when it comes to returning products.

Improving customer satisfaction with Return Insights

Managing returns effectively is a crucial aspect of e-commerce operations that significantly impacts profit margins. Returns are often considered the "forgotten" part of e-commerce, yet they can disrupt a merchandiser's operations and erode profits. With rising shipping costs and increasing consumer expectations, reducing return rates is more important than ever. Salesforce's Return Insights, part of the Commerce Cloud **order management system** (**OMS**), provides a solution by pinpointing the reasons behind returns, enabling businesses to address these issues proactively and improve customer satisfaction. This is an example of a Salesforce feature that could never have been built before the arrival of Einstein Copilot as a building block for natural language processing and automated summarization of text, as well as Data Cloud for the advanced analytical processing of complex order outcomes data.

Defining the use case

Using a template for use case documentation helps with fully understanding business expectations and rules before implementation begins.

Requirement

Utilize Returnÿ« Insights to analyze and reduce product return rates by identifying and addressing the root causes of returns.

User story

As a merchandiser, I want to use AI-driven Return Insights to understand why products are being returned so that I can make informed decisions to reduce return rates and improve customer satisfaction.

Acceptance criteria

- Given a set of up to 20 products, when the merchandiser uses Return Insights, the system should provide a detailed analysis and reasons why these products were returned

- Given the insights provided, when the merchandiser reviews the data, they should be able to identify actionable steps to reduce future returns

Business value

This use case will help reduce return rates, save on shipping and restocking costs, and improve profit margins. It will also enhance customer satisfaction by ensuring that the products they receive meet their expectations and needs.

Technical considerations

- Ensure that Return Insights is integrated with the Salesforce OMS

- Project the likely amount of usage and the corresponding consumption of Data Cloud and Einstein credits

Dependencies

The availability of detailed return data, including reasons or return codes within Salesforce OMS.

Preparation

To set up Return Insights, your Salesforce admin must follow the setup guide to build out some Data Cloud objects and install a custom package from AppExchange. The result of this is that a **Return Insights** tab becomes available within the Order Management application. In brief, the setup steps are as follows:

1. **Configure permissions**: The data that's collected in Order Management needs to flow into Data Cloud using the Salesforce CRM connector. In **Setup**, navigate to **Permission Sets**, and find **Data Cloud Salesforce Connector**. Select **Object Settings**. Enable **Read** and **View All** permissions for the **Order Summaries** object and read permission for every field. Repeat the process for the additional objects: **Order Delivery Methods**, **Orders**, and **Products**.

2. **Set up a data stream for the Order Product Summary object**: In Data Cloud, navigate to the **Data Streams** tab and click **New**. Choose **Salesforce CRM** as the data source. Select **Order Product Summary** as the object that will be ingested. Configure this data stream by choosing the **Engagement** type and then choosing **Created Date** as the event time field.

3. **Data mapping**: Start the mapping from the data stream display. Select **Sales Order Product** as the target object from the Customer 360 Data Model. Create mappings for five fields. Ensure that **Order Product Summary ID** is mapped to **Sales Order Product**, **Product ID** is mapped to **Product**, **Quantity Returned** is mapped to **ProductReturnQuantity**, **Quantity Net Ordered** is mapped to **AvailableQuantity**, and **TypeCode** is mapped to **SalesOrderProductSubType**. When the field mapping is complete, save your work.

4. **Calculated Insights:** The Salesforce Order Management setup guide for Return Insights provides a SQL query to be used as the definition of a calculated insight named **Om Return Rate By Product**. The query is as follows:

```
SELECT ssot__SalesOrderProduct__dlm.ssot__ProductId__c
as product__c, SUM(ssot__SalesOrderProduct__dlm.ssot__
ProductReturnQuantity__c)/SUM(ssot__SalesOrderProduct__dlm.
ssot__AvailableQuantity__c) as return_rate__c FROM ssot__
SalesOrderProduct__dlm WHERE ssot__SalesOrderProduct__dlm.
ssot__SalesOrderProductSubType__c = 'Product' GROUP BY ssot__
SalesOrderProduct__dlm.ssot__ProductId__c
```

5. This calculated insight will contain a record for every product, with a **Return Rate** metric as a percentage of the total quantity ordered that has been returned.

6. **Install the package**: Go to http://sfdc.co/ReturnInsights to install the OM Return Insights package. This package includes a tab that displays the Return Insights application, as well as the Apex code and Flows that implement the components on the page.

7. **Enable the Return Insights tab**: Open **Order Management** from the App Launcher. From the **Order Summary** tab, click the arrow menu and choose **Edit**. Enter Return Insights in the search field, click **Add**, and then **Save**.

8. **Add classifiers to the Flow**: Customize the **Analyze Returns** Flow, which was added by the package installation. There is a step called **Add Classifiers** where you can see the default set of classifications installed with Return Insights, and you can customize this list to ensure that the reporting is relevant for your company. Example starter classifiers include strings such as "Runs Small," "Defective," and "Arrived Late." The classifiers listed here determine what categories returns will be sorted into in the final analysis.

Step-by-step activities

The setup activities took a lot of effort, but now that the app has been configured, here's the new workflow it enables for the e-commerce team:

1. **Request Return Insights**: Navigate to the **Order Management** application using App Launcher, and then open the **Return Insights** tab. Select up to 20 products for which returns will be analyzed. Use the **Return Insights** dashboard to analyze return data and identify common reasons for returns.

2. **Analyze product return reasons**: Generate reports and visualizations to understand trends and patterns in return behavior. By default, the model uses the **Return Reason** text field on **Return Order** to determine the reason why the customer returned the product. The values that were entered in that field do not need to be standardized; Einstein Copilot is responsible for determining how to map them into the standard categories displayed in the analysis. If you have online product reviews, customers will often use them to provide feedback about why a product didn't work for them. You can also include other data streams, such as product reviews, in the model's analysis of return reasons. However, this will require a Salesforce Apex developer to extend Return Insights with the additional product data.

3. **Implement corrective actions**: Based on the insights gained, implement corrective actions such as updating product descriptions, improving quality control processes, or providing better customer support. Monitor the impact of these actions on return rates and customer satisfaction.

Efficiency and scale

Again, we can see that one of the major benefits of applying the natural language model to the problem of analyzing return reasons is the ability to scale the analysis, extract statistics from a large number of returns, and monitor those KPIs regularly to see whether they are changing. In combination with using generative AI to accelerate the rewriting of product descriptions, this can lead to making steady improvements against the products that generate the most returns. For a company such as LH&D Manufacturing with a very large product catalog, this capability is particularly valuable as a way to reduce the impact of excessive returns.

LH&D Manufacturing's benefits from deploying Return Insights

For LH&D Manufacturing, deploying Return Insights offers several key benefits:

- **Enhanced customer satisfaction**: By identifying and addressing the root causes of returns, LH&D Manufacturing can ensure that products meet customer expectations, leading to higher satisfaction and loyalty

- **Reduced return rates**: Implementing corrective actions based on AI-driven insights helps reduce return rates, saving on shipping and restocking costs, and improving profit margins

- **Improved operational efficiency**: Automating the analysis of return data allows the merchandising team to focus on implementing solutions rather than manually sifting through data

- **Data-driven decision-making**: Return Insights provides actionable data that supports informed decision-making, enabling the team to proactively address issues and improve product offerings

Example scenario: Using Return Insights, LH&D Manufacturing identifies that a significant number of returns for their industrial valves are due to unclear installation instructions. They take action by updating the instructions and adding a downloadable installation guide to the product detail pages and also send a communication to customers who purchased the affected products over the last year. Over the next few months, they observe a reduction in return rates and improvements in customer satisfaction.

Using AI to analyze and reduce product returns not only increases customer satisfaction but also significantly improves operational efficiency and profit margins. For companies such as LH&D Manufacturing, this practice leads to better product information, fewer returns, and increased customer loyalty. By integrating Return Insights into their merchandising workflow, they can ensure that their products meet customer expectations and that operational processes are continually optimized for success.

Summary

In this chapter, we explored how Einstein Copilot enhances e-commerce operations, from generating product descriptions and creating targeted promotions to enabling conversational commerce. We also examined how Return Insights can improve customer satisfaction by identifying and addressing the root causes of returns. As we move forward, the next chapter will focus on integrating Copilot with Flows and Apex, unlocking even greater potential for automation and customization in your Salesforce environment. Stay tuned to discover how these powerful tools can further optimize your business processes and drive success.

12

What's Next with Einstein Copilot

As we approach the end of our book on Salesforce Einstein Copilot, it is important to reflect on our journey through the preceding chapters. We began by setting a foundation by providing information about Einstein Copilot, its capabilities, and its potential impact on the Salesforce ecosystem. This served as a crucial primer, ensuring you, regardless of your prior knowledge, could grasp the essentials of Einstein Copilot and why it matters.

We unpacked the core functionalities and features of this powerful **artificial intelligence** (**AI**)-driven tool. We explored its intuitive interface, ability to streamline complex workflows, and potential to revolutionize how Salesforce professionals approach their daily tasks. We looked at how Einstein Copilot can be integrated into existing Salesforce environments, emphasizing its versatility and user-friendly nature.

We provided a step-by-step guide to configuring Einstein Copilot within the Salesforce platform, which is particularly valuable for developers and administrators, offering practical insights into the setup process, key configurations, and best practices to ensure a smooth deployment. We highlighted the importance of proper setup to leverage the full potential of Einstein Copilot.

We looked at Prompt Builder and Copilot Builder and explored how to create and manage configurations that guide Einstein Copilot's actions. The integration of Einstein Copilot with various Salesforce components was a key theme. We examined Data Cloud and Model Builder, where we uncovered advanced features and customization options available to users.

Then, we focused on practical applications of Einstein Copilot across different Salesforce clouds, spanning Sales Cloud, Service Cloud, Marketing Cloud, and Commerce Cloud.

As we now venture into this chapter, we stand on the shoulders of our explorations and practical implementations. This chapter looks forward at the evolving role of AI in the Salesforce ecosystem. We will consider how Salesforce professionals can continue to innovate and leverage Einstein Copilot to stay ahead in a rapidly changing technological landscape.

The future of fully conversational AI interfaces for Salesforce

This future represents a significant shift from traditional application navigation paradigms to more intuitive and efficient ways of interacting with information. Historically, Salesforce users have been accustomed to navigating through multiple pages, sections, and fields requiring numerous clicks to accomplish tasks. However, conversational AI promises to transform this experience by enabling users to interact with the platform using **natural language (NL)** conversations – written and spoken. This trend signifies a move away from the rigid structures of visual form-based interfaces toward a more fluid and user-centric approach.

Conversational AI interfaces are controlled to enhance user productivity and satisfaction by allowing users to perform complex tasks through simple dialogues. Imagine a sales representative querying the system for a customer's purchase history, generating a forecast report, or even updating records—all through a conversational interface without switching between different modules or manually entering data in multiple fields. This saves time and reduces cognitive load on users, making the entire experience more seamless and enjoyable.

The shift to conversational AI is supported by advancements in **natural language processing (NLP)** and **machine learning (ML)**, making it possible for systems to understand and respond to user queries accurately. These technologies enable Salesforce's Einstein Copilot to interpret user intent, fetch relevant information, and execute commands contextually. As these AI systems continue to learn and evolve, they will become even more adept at handling complex queries, anticipating user needs, and providing proactive assistance.

The move toward conversational interfaces aligns with broader technology and **user experience (UX)** trends. As consumers become more accustomed to interacting with AI through smart speakers, chatbots, and virtual assistants in their personal lives, they will expect the same level of convenience and responsiveness in their professional tools. By integrating conversational AI into Salesforce, organizations can meet these expectations, ensuring their workforce remains engaged and empowered to achieve their goals efficiently.

The integration of fully conversational AI interfaces in Salesforce will likely lead to innovations and capabilities. We can anticipate more personalized and context-aware interactions, where the AI responds to queries and provides insights and recommendations based on historical data and user behavior. This evolution will drive a fundamental change in how users perceive and interact with enterprise software, moving from a tool-centric view to a more holistic, conversation-driven experience that bridges the gap between technology and human interaction. As Salesforce continues to pioneer these advancements, it will redefine the standard for **customer relationship management (CRM)** and set the stage for the future of work.

Evolution of conversational AI in Salesforce

The evolution of Salesforce interfaces from traditional, form-based designs to advanced conversational AI represents a remarkable transformation in how users interact with the platform. Today, Salesforce interfaces rely heavily on structured pages, sections, and fields, necessitating numerous clicks and navigation through multiple screens to accomplish tasks. While effective, these traditional interfaces could be cumbersome and time-consuming, often requiring extensive training for new users to become proficient.

With the advent of conversational AI, Salesforce is moving toward a more intuitive and user-friendly approach. Conversational interfaces allow users to interact with the system through NL dialogues, reducing and eliminating the need to navigate complex menus and forms. This shift is driven by the need to enhance user efficiency, reduce cognitive load, and improve overall user satisfaction. By enabling users to ask questions and perform tasks using everyday language, Salesforce has democratized access to its powerful features, making it easier for users of all skill levels to leverage the platform effectively.

The transition to conversational AI is a technological upgrade and a substantial shift in UX design. It reflects a broader trend in the software industry toward more natural and human-centered interactions. This change has profound implications for how organizations train their workforce, design workflows, and engage with customers. As conversational AI continues to evolve, it promises to redefine the standards for usability and accessibility in enterprise software.

Key advancements in AI and ML

The journey from traditional interfaces to conversational AI in Salesforce has been made possible by significant advancements in AI and ML. One of the critical enablers of this evolution is the development of sophisticated algorithms that can process and analyze vast amounts of data quickly and accurately. These algorithms have improved the ability of AI systems to understand context, recognize patterns, and make informed decisions.

ML, in particular, has played a core role in enhancing the capabilities of conversational AI. Through techniques such as **deep learning (DL)** and **neural networks (NNs)**, AI systems have become more adept at processing complex language inputs and generating meaningful responses. These advancements have allowed Salesforce to develop tools such as Einstein Copilot, which can understand user intent, provide relevant information, and execute commands based on NL inputs. The ability to learn from user interactions and continuously improve over time has made conversational AI increasingly reliable and effective.

A crucial advancement is the integration of AI with cloud computing. By leveraging the scalability and computational power of the cloud, Salesforce can deploy sophisticated AI models that can handle large-scale data processing and real-time interactions. This integration ensures conversational AI systems remain responsive and efficient, even as they process vast amounts of user data and interactions. The convergence of AI, ML, and cloud computing has thus been instrumental in driving the evolution of conversational AI in Salesforce.

The role of NLP in making Einstein Copilot conversational

At the heart of conversational AI in Salesforce lies NLP, a branch of AI focused on enabling computers to understand and generate human language. NLP is crucial for making Einstein Copilot conversational, as it allows the system to interpret user inputs, understand context, and generate appropriate responses. NLP technologies enable Einstein Copilot to process NL queries, extract relevant information, and provide answers or perform tasks seamlessly.

Advancements in NLP have enabled Einstein Copilot to handle a wide range of languages and dialects, further enhancing its accessibility and usability. By incorporating machine translation and multilingual capabilities, Salesforce ensures that users worldwide can interact with Einstein Copilot in their preferred language. This inclusivity is essential for global organizations relying on Salesforce to manage customer relationships and business operations.

The evolution of conversational AI in Salesforce marks a significant milestone in the platform's journey toward more user-friendly and efficient interfaces. Key AI, ML, and NLP advancements have enabled this transformation, making tools such as Einstein Copilot powerful allies for Salesforce users. As these technologies evolve, they will unlock new possibilities for enhancing UX and driving business success.

Integration with Salesforce the ecosystem

Einstein Copilot has been designed to seamlessly integrate with a diverse range of Salesforce clouds, providing a unified AI-driven experience across the entire Salesforce ecosystem. By embedding conversational AI capabilities within various Salesforce products, Einstein Copilot enhances functionality and user productivity, making it a pivotal tool for businesses striving to optimize their operations:

- **Sales Cloud integration**: In the Sales Cloud platform, Einstein Copilot assists sales teams by streamlining lead management, forecasting sales, and automating routine tasks. It can analyze vast amounts of customer data to provide personalized insights and recommendations, helping sales representatives prioritize their efforts and close deals more efficiently. By leveraging NLP, Einstein Copilot allows sales professionals to update records, schedule follow-ups, and generate reports through simple conversational commands, significantly reducing time spent on administrative tasks.

- **Service Cloud integration**: In the Service Cloud platform, Einstein Copilot transforms customer service by offering intelligent case management and real-time assistance. It enables service agents to resolve customer issues faster by providing instant access to relevant knowledge articles and suggesting the next best actions based on historical data and context. Einstein Copilot also supports automated chatbots that handle routine inquiries, allowing human agents to focus on more complex issues. This integration enhances customer satisfaction by ensuring timely and accurate responses.

- **Marketing Cloud integration**: For Marketing Cloud, Einstein Copilot enhances campaign management and audience segmentation through AI-driven insights. Marketers can use conversational interfaces to create, modify, and analyze marketing campaigns without navigating through multiple menus. Einstein Copilot can also predict customer behavior and preferences, enabling marketers to tailor their messaging and offers for maximum impact. This integration helps businesses execute more effective marketing strategies and achieve higher **return on investment (ROI)**.

- **Commerce Cloud integration**: In the Commerce Cloud platform, Einstein Copilot supports e-commerce operations by providing personalized shopping experiences and optimizing inventory management. It can recommend products to customers based on browsing history and preferences, driving higher conversion rates. Additionally, it helps merchants manage orders and inventory through conversational commands, ensuring efficient and accurate fulfillment processes. This integration facilitates a seamless shopping experience, enhancing customer loyalty and satisfaction.

Enhancements in integration capabilities

Salesforce continues to enhance the integration capabilities of Einstein Copilot to ensure it works seamlessly across its ecosystem. One significant enhancement is the ability to connect Einstein Copilot with custom objects and third-party applications, extending its functionality beyond standard Salesforce products. This flexibility allows businesses to tailor Einstein Copilot to their specific needs, integrating it into their unique workflows and processes.

Furthermore, Salesforce has improved data synchronization between Einstein Copilot and other Salesforce clouds. This ensures that the AI model has access to the most up-to-date information, enabling it to provide more accurate and relevant recommendations. Enhancements in API capabilities also facilitate smoother data exchanges and interoperability between different Salesforce modules, ensuring a consistent UX.

Salesforce has also focused on improving the scalability and performance of Einstein Copilot integrations. As businesses grow and their data volumes increase, Einstein Copilot's robust architecture ensures it can handle larger datasets and more complex queries without compromising performance. These enhancements are critical for maintaining high levels of efficiency and responsiveness as organizations scale their operations.

Future prospects of seamless integration across all Salesforce products

The future of Einstein Copilot integration within the Salesforce ecosystem is poised for even greater advancements, driven by ongoing innovation and technological progress. One of the most exciting prospects is the development of a fully integrated, AI-powered Salesforce platform where Einstein Copilot seamlessly interacts with all Salesforce products, providing a unified and cohesive UX.

As AI and ML technologies evolve, expect Einstein Copilot to become even more intuitive and context-aware. Future enhancements will likely include more sophisticated NLP capabilities, enabling Einstein Copilot to understand and respond to user queries with greater accuracy and nuance. This will further reduce the learning curve for users and enhance their productivity.

In the future, we will see more proactive and predictive features in Einstein Copilot. By leveraging advanced analytics and real-time data processing, Einstein Copilot will be able to anticipate user needs and provide insights before they are even requested. This proactive approach will empower users to make informed decisions faster and stay ahead of potential issues.

Another exciting prospect is the deeper integration of Einstein Copilot with emerging technologies such as IoT and blockchain. By incorporating data from IoT devices, Einstein Copilot can offer more comprehensive insights and recommendations, particularly in industries such as manufacturing and logistics. Similarly, integrating with blockchain can enhance data security and transparency, giving users greater confidence in their transactions and interactions.

The integration of Einstein Copilot with the Salesforce ecosystem represents a significant leap forward in how businesses leverage AI to optimize their operations. With ongoing enhancements and future advancements, Einstein Copilot is set to become an indispensable tool that drives efficiency, innovation, and growth across all Salesforce products. The journey toward seamless integration continues, promising a future where AI-powered interactions are at the heart of every business process.

Advanced capabilities of Einstein Copilot

Einstein Copilot's Prompt Builder and Copilot Builder functionalities represent significant advancements in how users can customize and optimize their AI interactions within the Salesforce ecosystem. Prompt Builder allows users to create more sophisticated and tailored prompts that guide Einstein Copilot's responses and actions. Prompt Builder enables users to specify complex conditions and context-specific instructions to ensure that the AI delivers more accurate and relevant outputs.

With the latest updates, users can leverage advanced customization options such as multi-step prompts, conditional logic, and dynamic content inclusion. These enhancements allow building prompts that adapt to various scenarios and user needs, providing a more interactive and engaging experience. For instance, a sales manager can create a prompt that retrieves customer data and suggests personalized follow-up actions based on recent interactions and purchase history.

On the other hand, Copilot Builder has evolved to offer a more intuitive and user-friendly interface for configuring and managing Einstein Copilot. The features include drag-and-drop functionality, pre-built templates, and integration with third-party applications. These features simplify creating and maintaining Copilot configurations, allowing users to quickly deploy and modify their AI-driven workflows without extensive technical knowledge.

Improved Model Builder features and their future iterations

Model Builder is a cornerstone of the platform's advanced capabilities. It features intuitive interfaces and powerful tools for developing, training, and deploying ML models. Users can take advantage of automated model generation, which leverages predefined algorithms and best practices to create high-performing models with minimal manual intervention.

One of the standout features of Model Builder is its ability to handle large datasets and complex data structures. With enhanced data preprocessing and feature engineering tools, users can prepare their data more effectively, ensuring their models are built on clean and relevant information. Including visualization tools also allows users to explore their data and gain insights into patterns and trends that can inform their modeling decisions.

Looking to the future, anticipated iterations of Model Builder will focus on further enhancing its automation and intelligence capabilities. Features such as automated hyperparameter tuning, model explainability, and continuous learning are expected to be integrated into the platform. These advancements will make it easier for users to build robust and interpretable models that adapt to changing data and business conditions.

Anticipated developments in Data Cloud integration and its impact on data-driven decision-making

Data Cloud integration is a critical aspect of Einstein Copilot's advanced capabilities, and its anticipated developments promise to revolutionize data-driven decision-making. Integrating Einstein Copilot with Salesforce Data Cloud allows organizations to harness vast amounts of data from diverse sources, creating a unified and comprehensive view of their business operations.

One of the key developments in Data Cloud integration is real-time data processing and analytics. With these features, Einstein Copilot can access and analyze data as it is generated, providing users with up-to-the-minute insights and recommendations. This capability is particularly valuable in dynamic environments where timely information is crucial for making informed decisions.

Another significant development is the integration of advanced data privacy and security features. As organizations collect and process more data, ensuring security and compliance with regulatory requirements becomes increasingly important. Future iterations of Einstein Copilot will incorporate robust encryption, data masking, and access control mechanisms, ensuring that data is protected throughout its life cycle.

The impact of these developments on data-driven decision-making cannot be overstated. By providing users with real-time, accurate, and secure data, Einstein Copilot will enable organizations to make more informed and strategic decisions. For example, a retail company can use real-time sales data and customer insights to optimize inventory management, tailor marketing campaigns, and improve customer service.

Integrating Data Cloud capabilities with Einstein Copilot will facilitate more sophisticated predictive and prescriptive analytics. Organizations will be able to leverage advanced ML models to forecast future trends, identify potential risks, and recommend proactive measures. This forward-looking approach will empower businesses to stay ahead of the competition and drive continuous improvement.

The advanced capabilities of Einstein Copilot, particularly the Prompt Builder and Copilot Builder functionalities, Model Builder features, and anticipated developments in Data Cloud integration, position it as a powerful tool for transforming how organizations leverage AI and data. As these capabilities continue to evolve, they will unlock new opportunities for innovation, efficiency, and strategic decision-making across the Salesforce ecosystem.

Enhancing productivity and UX

Einstein Copilot fundamentally enhances user productivity by streamlining workflows and automating routine tasks. By integrating advanced AI capabilities into the Salesforce ecosystem, Einstein Copilot enables users to accomplish more with less effort. One of the primary ways it achieves this is through its conversational interface, which allows users to interact with Salesforce using NL. This reduces time spent navigating complex menus and forms, enabling users to focus on more strategic activities.

For sales professionals, Einstein Copilot can automate tasks such as lead qualification, follow-up scheduling, and report generation. Instead of manually entering data and switching between different modules, sales reps can ask Einstein Copilot to perform these tasks, saving valuable time and reducing the likelihood of errors. Similarly, agents can quickly resolve cases in customer service by accessing relevant knowledge articles and suggested solutions through conversational queries, improving response times and customer satisfaction.

Einstein Copilot also enhances productivity by providing intelligent insights and recommendations. Analyzing vast amounts of data in real time can identify patterns and trends that might not be immediately apparent to users. For example, it can highlight opportunities for cross-selling or upselling based on customer behavior and purchase history, helping sales teams maximize revenue. In marketing, it can suggest optimal times to launch campaigns and target specific customer segments, ensuring more effective and impactful marketing efforts.

Moreover, Einstein Copilot's integration with other Salesforce cloud platforms ensures a seamless flow of information across departments. This interconnectedness eliminates data silos and enables a more holistic approach to decision-making. Users can access comprehensive views of customer interactions, sales performance, and marketing effectiveness, allowing for more coordinated and informed strategies. By reducing manual effort and providing actionable insights, Einstein Copilot significantly boosts user productivity across various roles and functions.

Future UI and UX enhancements

Looking ahead, Salesforce is committed to continuously improving Einstein Copilot's **user interface** (**UI**) and UX to ensure it remains intuitive and user-friendly. One of the key areas of focus is enhancing the conversational interface to make interactions even more natural and efficient. Future updates will likely incorporate more advanced NLP capabilities, enabling Einstein Copilot to understand and respond to a broader range of queries and contexts.

Another anticipated enhancement is the integration of more visual elements into the conversational interface. For instance, users might soon be able to view dynamic charts, graphs, and dashboards directly within their conversations with Einstein Copilot. This will provide a richer and more interactive experience, allowing users to visualize data trends and insights without switching to different screens or applications. Such visual aids will make interpreting complex information easier and make data-driven decisions.

Personalization is also a key focus for future UI and UX enhancements. Einstein Copilot will leverage user behavior and preferences to offer a more tailored experience. This could include personalized dashboards, customized prompts, and context-aware recommendations. By understanding individual user needs and workflows, Einstein Copilot can provide more relevant and timely assistance, further boosting productivity and user satisfaction.

Salesforce is likely to explore integration with emerging technologies such as **augmented reality** (**AR**) and **virtual reality** (**VR**). Imagine a sales manager using AR glasses to interact with Einstein Copilot, viewing real-time sales data and customer information overlaid in their physical environment. Such innovations have the potential to revolutionize how users interact with Salesforce, making it even more immersive and engaging.

Predictive and prescriptive analytics for proactive decision-making

Einstein Copilot's ability to leverage predictive and prescriptive analytics represents a significant advancement in proactive decision-making. Predictive analytics uses historical data and ML algorithms to forecast future trends and outcomes. Einstein Copilot can analyze patterns in sales data, customer behavior, and market trends to predict future opportunities and challenges. This allows users to anticipate changes and make informed decisions to capitalize on potential growth or mitigate risks.

For instance, a sales team can use predictive analytics to identify which leads will most likely convert, enabling them to prioritize their efforts and allocate resources more effectively. Similarly, marketing teams can predict the success of upcoming campaigns and adjust their strategies accordingly. Predictive analytics also plays a crucial role in inventory management, helping businesses forecast demand and optimize stock levels to prevent shortages or overstock situations.

Prescriptive analytics goes a step further by predicting future outcomes and recommending specific actions to achieve desired results. Einstein Copilot can provide prescriptive insights by analyzing various scenarios and suggesting the best action based on historical data and current conditions. For example, it can recommend optimal pricing strategies, suggest personalized offers for customers, or identify the most effective channels for marketing campaigns.

Integrating predictive and prescriptive analytics into Einstein Copilot transforms it from a reactive tool to a proactive partner. Users can rely on its recommendations to make data-driven decisions that enhance efficiency and drive business growth. By continuously learning from new data and refining its models, Einstein Copilot ensures that its predictions and recommendations remain accurate and relevant over time.

The advanced capabilities of Einstein Copilot in enhancing productivity and UX are transforming how users interact with Salesforce and make decisions. Through intelligent automation, personalized interfaces, and sophisticated analytics, Einstein Copilot empowers users to achieve more with less effort. As Salesforce continues to innovate and enhance these capabilities, the future holds even greater potential for improving productivity and user satisfaction, driving organizations toward greater success.

AI ethics and responsible use

As AI becomes increasingly integrated into CRM applications, the importance of ethical AI and responsible use cannot be overstated. AI has the potential to revolutionize how businesses interact with customers, offering unprecedented levels of personalization, efficiency, and insight. However, with this power comes significant responsibility. Ethical considerations are crucial to ensure that AI applications do not inadvertently cause harm, bias, or discrimination.

In CRM applications, AI-driven interactions often involve processing sensitive customer data, making ethical considerations even more critical. Ensuring the privacy and security of customer information is paramount. Moreover, AI systems must be designed to operate transparently and fairly, avoiding biases that could lead to unjust or unequal treatment of customers. Ethical AI practices help build trust with customers, who need to feel confident that their data is being used responsibly and that the AI systems they interact with are fair and reliable.

The responsible use of AI in CRM also involves accountability. Businesses must be able to explain and justify decisions made by their AI systems. This is particularly important in customer service and sales, where AI-driven recommendations and actions can significantly impact customer satisfaction and business outcomes. By prioritizing ethical AI, companies can ensure that their CRM applications contribute positively to customer relationships and business success while mitigating risks associated with AI misuse.

Future use cases and applications

Einstein Copilot's potential extends far beyond the current applications within the Salesforce ecosystem, offering transformative opportunities across many industries. As AI technology continues to evolve, new use cases for Einstein Copilot are emerging that can significantly enhance operational efficiency, customer engagement, and strategic decision-making in various sectors.

In the healthcare industry, Einstein Copilot could revolutionize patient care and administrative processes. By integrating with **electronic health record** (**EHR**) systems, Einstein Copilot could assist healthcare professionals in quickly accessing patient information, suggesting personalized treatment plans based on historical data, and automating routine documentation tasks. Additionally, it could aid in scheduling and managing appointments, optimizing resource allocation, and providing real-time updates to patients and their families.

In the financial services sector, Einstein Copilot could enhance customer service and fraud detection. Financial advisors could use it to provide clients with personalized investment advice, generate detailed financial reports, and track market trends. Moreover, it could analyze transaction data to detect unusual patterns indicative of fraud, alerting security teams to take timely action. By automating compliance checks and regulatory reporting, Einstein Copilot could help financial institutions meet their legal obligations more efficiently.

The retail industry stands to benefit significantly from Einstein Copilot's capabilities. Retailers could use it to provide personalized shopping experiences, manage inventory, and optimize supply chain operations. For example, Einstein Copilot could assist in analyzing customer preferences and purchasing behaviors to recommend products and offers tailored to individual shoppers. In logistics, it could predict demand, streamline inventory management, and reduce stockouts or overstock situations by optimizing supply chain processes.

In the manufacturing sector, Einstein Copilot could drive significant improvements in production efficiency and quality control. Integrating with **manufacturing execution systems** (**MESs**) could monitor production processes, predict equipment failures, and suggest preventive maintenance schedules. This would minimize downtime and enhance the longevity of machinery. Additionally, it could analyze production data to identify defects and optimize quality control measures, ensuring higher product standards and customer satisfaction.

The education sector could also leverage Einstein Copilot to enhance learning experiences and administrative efficiency. Educators could use it to personalize learning plans based on student performance and preferences, automate grading and feedback, and provide real-time assistance to students. It could streamline enrollment processes, manage student records, and optimize resource allocation, allowing educational institutions to operate more efficiently.

A day in the life of Einstein Copilot

Imagine Bill, a sales professional, waking up 5 years from now in a world where Einstein Copilot has evolved into a highly proactive personal assistant, seamlessly integrated into his daily routine. As a Salesforce user, Bill starts his day by glancing at his smart device, where Copilot has already organized his tasks and prioritized his schedule based on the latest data and upcoming deadlines.

Starting the day – reviewing sales pipeline and tasks

At 8:00 A.M., Bill sits down with his morning coffee and engages with Einstein Copilot to review his sales pipeline. "*Good morning, Copilot. What does my day look like?*" he asks. Copilot responds with a comprehensive overview of his schedule, highlighting critical tasks and meetings. "*You have a meeting with Acme Corp at 10:00 A.M. and a follow-up call with Beta Industries at 2:00 P.M. Based on recent interactions, I suggest focusing on Acme Corp as they show high potential for closing this quarter.*"

Copilot's analysis is based on AI-driven insights and real-time data, providing Bill with prioritized tasks. It also offers opinions on where to focus his efforts. "*Given the recent activity and engagement from Acme Corp, dedicating more time to this account could significantly boost your sales pipeline for the quarter,*" Copilot advises.

Engaging with customers – scheduling meetings, sending personalized communications

As Bill prepares for his day, Copilot helps him schedule meetings and send personalized communications. "*Copilot, please schedule a follow-up meeting with John at Acme Corp for next week,*" Bill says. Within seconds, Copilot finds an available slot in both calendars and sends a meeting invite. "*Meeting scheduled for next Tuesday at 10:00 A.M.,*" Copilot confirms.

Bill then asks Copilot to draft a personalized email to another key client. "*Copilot, draft an email to Jane at Beta Industries, thanking her for the recent meeting and outlining the next steps.*" Copilot quickly generates a tailored email incorporating details from his last interaction. Bill reviews and approves the email, and Copilot sends it on his behalf. This seamless interaction saves Bill valuable time and ensures that his communications are timely and relevant.

Analyzing performance – generating reports, getting insights

At noon, Bill needs to analyze his sales performance to prepare for an upcoming team meeting. "*Copilot, generate a report on my sales performance for the past month,*" he requests. In an instant, Copilot compiles a detailed report with visual graphs and key metrics. "*Here's your performance report, highlighting a 15% increase in closed deals and a 10% improvement in lead conversion rates,*" Copilot reports.

Bill digs deeper into the data, asking Copilot for insights. "*What factors contributed to the increase in closed deals?*" Copilot responds, "*The key contributors were increased engagement with high-priority leads and effective follow-up strategies. Additionally, the new promotional campaign had a significant impact.*"

Closing deals – automating follow-ups, predictive sales guidance

As the day progresses, Copilot continues to support Bill in closing deals. After his meeting with Acme Corp, Copilot analyzes the conversation and suggests the next steps. "*Based on the meeting notes, I recommend sending a detailed proposal and scheduling a follow-up call within 2 days,*" Copilot advises.

Bill follows Copilot's guidance, and it automatically drafts the proposal, incorporating relevant data and insights. "*Proposal ready. Shall I send it to the client?*" Copilot asks. Bill reviews and approves it, and Copilot sends it out. Copilot automates follow-ups for other leads, ensuring no potential opportunity is missed. "*I've scheduled follow-up emails for all leads that have not responded in the last week,*" Copilot informs Bill.

Continuous learning – receiving training and updates through Copilot

Copilot helps Bill stay ahead of the curve by providing continuous learning and updates. "*Copilot, any new training modules or updates I should be aware of?*" he inquires. Copilot responds, "*Yes, there are new training modules on advanced sales techniques and updates on the latest Salesforce features. Would you like to review them now?*"

Bill spends some time going through the training materials, which Copilot has tailored to his specific needs and interests. This proactive approach ensures Bill is always equipped with the latest knowledge and skills to excel in his role.

The impact of fully conversational AI on productivity and user satisfaction

The integration of a fully conversational AI such as Einstein Copilot has a profound impact on Bill's productivity and user satisfaction. By automating routine tasks, providing intelligent insights, and facilitating seamless interactions, Copilot enables Bill to focus on high-value activities and strategic decision-making. The AI's ability to personalize and predict enhances his efficiency and effectiveness, leading to higher sales and better customer relationships.

Copilot's intuitive and proactive nature transforms Bill's UX, making it more engaging and enjoyable. He feels supported and empowered, knowing that Copilot is always there to assist him, anticipate his needs, and help him achieve his goals. This continuous collaboration boosts his productivity and enhances his overall job satisfaction and professional growth.

> **Final thoughts**
>
> As a proactive personal assistant, Einstein Copilot represents the future of AI-driven interactions in the workplace. By embracing its evolving capabilities, users such as Bill will unlock new productivity, efficiency, and success levels in their Salesforce journey.

Summary

This chapter has looked at the growing role of AI in Salesforce and how professionals can continue to innovate with these tools. With the shift toward fully conversational AI, we are all part of a transformation in how users interact with Salesforce—from navigating structured forms and fields to engaging in natural, fluid conversations that intuitively help manage tasks. This shift is not just a technological evolution but a profound change in UX, promising greater efficiency, personalization, and satisfaction. As AI continues to evolve, Salesforce and Einstein Copilot will pioneer new standards in enterprise software, driving a more holistic and human-centric approach to CRM.

As we conclude this journey through Salesforce Einstein Copilot, we are thrilled to be a part of your continued exploration and innovation, and we can't wait to see how you'll connect the power of AI to transform your Salesforce experience and achieve even greater success.

Further Reading and Resources

Salesforce provides a wealth of information in its help resources, knowledge bases, Trailblazer Community and Trailhead, among other places like Salesforce+ and YouTube. Because of the ever-changing rapid pace of AI revolution, we encourage you to check these resources for further learning.

You can find these resources by clicking the link in the ebook version of our book or using your favorite browser to search for these key terms in the print version.

General Items

- Salesforce+ "Einstein Copilot" Recordings: `https://www.salesforce.com/plus/search#q=Einstein%20Copilot`
- Salesforce Einstein1 Studio AI Developer Guide: `https://developer.salesforce.com/developer-centers/einstein-1-studio?_ga=2.208051089.2018128890.1724615931-80668540.1724166273`
- Salesforce Developers "Einstein Generative AI" Setup Guide: `https://developer.salesforce.com/docs/einstein/genai/guide?_ga=2.208051089.2018128890.1724615931-80668540.1724166273`
- Salesforce Devs YouTube Channel: `https://www.youtube.com/@SalesforceDevs`

Chapter Specific

Chapter 2 – Setting Up Einstein Studio

- Readiness Assessment and ROI Estimation for your organization: `https://einsteinreadiness.salesforce.com/`
- Salesforce Help Docs | Einstein Gen AI: `https://help.salesforce.com/s/articleView?id=sf.generative_ai.htm&type=5`
- Salesforce Help Docs | About Einstein Generative AI: `https://help.salesforce.com/s/articleView?id=sf.generative_ai_about.htm&type=5`

- Salesforce Help Docs | Set Up Einstein Generative AI: `https://help.salesforce.com/s/articleView?id=sf.generative_ai_enable.htm&type=5`

- Salesforce Help Docs | Set Up Einstein Copilot: `https://help.salesforce.com/s/articleView?id=sf.copilot_setup.htm&type=5`

Chapter 3 – Utilizing Prompt Builder

- Salesforce Help Docs | About Prompt Builder: `https://help.salesforce.com/s/articleView?id=sf.prompt_builder_about.htm&type=5`

- Salesforce Help Docs | Get to Know Prompt Builder: `https://help.salesforce.com/s/articleView?id=sf.prompt_builder_get_to_know.htm&type=5`

- Salesforce Developers - Get Started with Prompt Builder: `https://developer.salesforce.com/docs/einstein/genai/guide/get-started-prompt-builder.html`

Chapter 4 – Working with Copilot Builder

- Einstein Copilot In-Depth: What It Is, How It Works, and What It Can Do: `https://www.salesforce.com/news/stories/about-einstein-copilot/`

- Salesforce Help Docs | Copilot Overview: `https://help.salesforce.com/s/articleView?id=sf.copilot_overview.htm&type=5`

- Salesforce Help Docs | Copilot Setup: `https://help.salesforce.com/s/articleView?id=sf.copilot_setup.htm&type=5`

- Salesforce Developers - Copilot Get Started: `https://developer.salesforce.com/docs/einstein/genai/guide/get-started-copilot.html`

Chapter 5 – How Data Cloud Works with Einstein Studio

- Salesforce Help Docs | About Data Cloud: `https://help.salesforce.com/s/articleView?id=sf.c360_a_data_cloud.htm&type=5`

- Salesforce Developers - C360 Data Model: `https://developer.salesforce.com/docs/atlas.en-us.c360a_api.meta/c360a_api/c360dm_model_data.htm`

Chapter 6 – Exploring Functionalities of Model Builder

- Salesforce Help Docs | Gen AI LLM's: `https://help.salesforce.com/s/articleView?id=sf.generative_ai_large_language_model_support.htm&type=5`

- Salesforce Help Docs | Using AI Models: `https://help.salesforce.com/s/articleView?id=sf.c360_a_ai_use_ai_models.htm&type=5`

Chapter 7 – Leveraging Copilot Actions with Flows and More

- Salesforce Help Docs | Einstein Copilot Actions: `https://help.salesforce.com/s/articleView?id=sf.copilot_actions.htm&type=5`

- Salesforce Help Docs | Let Einstein Help You Build Flows: `https://help.salesforce.com/s/articleView?id=sf.flow_build_let_einstein_help_you_build_flows.htm&type=5`

Index

E

packtpub.com

Subscribe to our online digital library for full access to over 7,000 books and videos, as well as industry leading tools to help you plan your personal development and advance your career. For more information, please visit our website.

Why subscribe?

- Spend less time learning and more time coding with practical eBooks and Videos from over 4,000 industry professionals

- Improve your learning with Skill Plans built especially for you

- Get a free eBook or video every month

- Fully searchable for easy access to vital information

- Copy and paste, print, and bookmark content

Did you know that Packt offers eBook versions of every book published, with PDF and ePub files available? You can upgrade to the eBook version at packtpub.com and as a print book customer, you are entitled to a discount on the eBook copy. Get in touch with us at customercare@packtpub.com for more details.

At www.packtpub.com, you can also read a collection of free technical articles, sign up for a range of free newsletters, and receive exclusive discounts and offers on Packt books and eBooks.

Other Books You May Enjoy

If you enjoyed this book, you may be interested in these other books by Packt:

ChatGPT for Accelerating Salesforce Development

Andy Forbes, Philip Safir, Joseph Kubon, Francisco Fálder

ISBN: 978-1-83508-407-6

- Masterfully craft detailed and engaging user stories tailored for Salesforce projects
- Leverage ChatGPT to design cutting-edge features within the Salesforce ecosystem, transforming ideas into functional and intuitive solutions
- Explore the integration of ChatGPT for configuring Salesforce environments
- Write Salesforce flows with ChatGPT, enhancing workflow automation and efficiency
- Develop custom LWCs with ChatGPT's assistance
- Discover effective testing techniques using ChatGPT for optimized performance and reliability

Salesforce CRM Administration Handbook

Krzysztof Nowacki, Mateusz Twarożek

ISBN: 978-1-83508-569-1

- Discover strategies to stay up-to-date with Salesforce releases
- Integrate Salesforce products seamlessly to meet diverse business needs
- Explore Sales and Service Cloud and its transformative impact on sales and customer support operations
- Master opportunity management for successful deal closures and pipeline forecasting
- Understand Salesforce Orgs, managing users, settings, and customization
- Explore data import and export methods and data mapping
- Discover best practices, mock tests, and valuable tips and tricks to prepare for Salesforce certification

Packt is searching for authors like you

If you're interested in becoming an author for Packt, please visit `authors.packtpub.com` and apply today. We have worked with thousands of developers and tech professionals, just like you, to help them share their insight with the global tech community. You can make a general application, apply for a specific hot topic that we are recruiting an author for, or submit your own idea.

Share Your Thoughts

Now you've finished *Hands-On Salesforce Einstein Studio and GPT Intelligence*, we'd love to hear your thoughts! Scan the QR code below to go straight to the Amazon review page for this book and share your feedback or leave a review on the site that you purchased it from.

https://packt.link/r/1836203772

Your review is important to us and the tech community and will help us make sure we're delivering excellent quality content.

Download a free PDF copy of this book

Thanks for purchasing this book!

Do you like to read on the go but are unable to carry your print books everywhere?

Is your eBook purchase not compatible with the device of your choice?

Don't worry, now with every Packt book you get a DRM-free PDF version of that book at no cost.

Read anywhere, any place, on any device. Search, copy, and paste code from your favorite technical books directly into your application.

The perks don't stop there, you can get exclusive access to discounts, newsletters, and great free content in your inbox daily

Follow these simple steps to get the benefits:

1. Scan the QR code or visit the link below

https://packt.link/free-ebook/978-1-83620-377-3

2. Submit your proof of purchase
3. That's it! We'll send your free PDF and other benefits to your email directly